ENGLISH COUNTRY HOUSES

MID GEORGIAN

1760-1800

OSTERLEY PARK, MIDDLESEX. THE GREAT PORTICO.
Adapted by Robert Adam c. 1761 from the Temple of the Sun at Palmyra.

ENGLISH COUNTRY HOUSES

MID
GEORGIAN
1760–1800

CHRISTOPHER HUSSEY

COUNTRY LIFE LIMITED LONDON

First published in 1956
by Country Life Limited
Tavistock Street London WC2
Printed in Great Britain by
Robert MacLehose & Co Ltd
University Press Glasgow

PREFACE

This volume of *English Country Houses* continues *Early Georgian* 1715–1760 and is to be followed by *Late Georgian* 1800–1840. The term 'Georgian' in the titles of all three volumes is used to emphasize the continuity of the epoch as a whole, and for concision in distinguishing the three component 'periods'. The termination of the present one at 1800 corresponds closely to a recognisable division between the earlier phase of 'neo-classicism', and its later phase which not only included the 'Regency' style but continued through the reign of George III's sovereign sons into the earliest years of Victoria. Division at 1800 has the additional advantage of giving two equal periods for the Mid and Late Georgian volumes, approximating to the 45 years covered by *Early Georgian*. The decisive factor, however, in determining this volume's limit was the quantity and quality of the material requiring to be included in it.

Any attempt to treat comprehensively the 18th century's latter half is confronted with the problem of integrating the work of Robert Adam with that of his contemporaries and successors, or *vice versa*. Books of similar scope to this are inclined to evade this difficulty by concentrating upon one or the other aspect. That was the solution adopted in *English Homes, Period VI*, published in 1926, in which H. Avray Tipping covered the years 1760–1820. But he dealt fully with only three Adam houses, because A. T. Bolton's two volumes, *The Architecture of Robert and James Adam* (1922), were available to supplement his presentation of the first part of the period. In the latter part of it Regency architecture, not then fully appreciated, was far from adequately represented. Concentration on Adam, or on 'the rest', has much to commend it, but has the great disadvantage of giving an incomplete picture of the period, the most significant aspect of which, the interaction of Adam and his competitors, cannot be adequately represented by that method. Publication of this volume provided an opportunity to illustrate this relationship more fully, so far as it is displayed in country houses. I have therefore tried to integrate the work of Adam with a balanced view of the period as a whole. A section in the *Introduction* is devoted specifically to the Adam phenomenon, and six representative Adam houses are described in detail. Of these, two were given by both Tipping and Bolton, and one by Tipping alone with any fullness. Of 'the rest', seventeen of the houses described have not previously been republished. Of the twelve that appeared in *English Homes, Period VI*, facts have since come to light regarding several of them, which, with the view of the period expressed in the *Introduction*, rendered a reconsideration desirable. But some traversing of familiar ground is scarcely to be avoided in seeking a comprehensive view of the period. A new feature in this volume, introduced for the same reason, is the Appendix listing architects of country houses with their principal works during this period in England and Wales.

In other respects this volume's general purpose, and the principles applied in the selection, arrangement and treatment of its contents, are the same as in the case of *Early Georgian*: to trace the development of domestic architecture by concise accounts of the most notable country houses of the period that are at present in occupation as such. The latter limitation has born rather severely on Adam's representation, since Osterley is now an unlived in 'show place', Bowood in course of partial demolition, and others of his houses that would have qualified for inclusion are in no condition for suitable photographs to be obtained replacing the ancient ones available. Nevertheless the majority of them are represented in the *Introduction*, together with James Wyatt's Heaton Hall, an uninhabited house of such architectural importance that its representation is essential. In cases where the interval between the design and completion of a house overlapped the end of the period, its predominant affinities have been taken as the criterion for inclusion or otherwise. Whilst several that were finished after 1800 are included, three important houses then already in hand (Dodington Park, Southill and Luscombe) are reserved to *Late Georgian*, to which the style of their finishing eminently belongs. Several houses begun before 1760 but completed subsequently are, for the same reason, included at the beginning of this volume. A usage in the text, intended to be helpful and to which attention may be drawn, is that references to a room that is illustrated are indicated by a capital initial being accorded to it.

Acknowledgement is made in the text to the principal authorities consulted, but I would like to pay special tribute to Mr Lees Milne's *The Age of Adam*, and to the relevant chapters in Mr John Summerson's *Architecture in Britain 1530–1830*. I should perhaps state that where I have based accounts of houses on articles in *Country Life* by my colleagues Mr Arthur Oswald and Mr Gordon Nares, I have myself examined the houses in the first instance.

1956   CHRISTOPHER HUSSEY

CONTENTS

Preface   5

INTRODUCTION

(i) Neo-Classicism   9
(ii) The Adam Synthesis   11
(iii) The Sublime and Beautiful, 1770–80   15
(iv) The Picturesque   22
(v) Prefabricated Materials   26

Houses illustrated in the Introduction

Cranbury Park: The Ball Room   8
Compton Verney, from Adam's Bridge   9
Bowood: West front and 'Diocletian Wing'   11
Shardeloes: The Library   13
Osterley: The Eating Room   13
Osterley: The Tapestry Room   14
Worksop: Section   16
Tusmore, Oxfordshire   16
Gorhambury, Hertfordshire   16
Denton Hall, Yorkshire: Staircase   17
Gorhambury: Chimneypiece after Piranesi   17
Heaton Hall, Lancashire: The South Front   19
Heaton Hall: Plan of Ground Floor   19
Heaton Hall: The Cupola Room   19
Heaton Hall: The Staircase Hall   20
Heaton Hall: The Billiard Room   20
Heaton Hall: The Saloon   21
Broadlands, Hampshire   21
Woburn Abbey, Bedfordshire: The Greenhouse   21

HOUSES DESCRIBED

Uppark, Sussex   29
Arbury Hall, Warwickshire   41
Hatchlands, Surrey   49
Tabley House, Cheshire   55
Harewood House, Yorkshire   61
Kedleston, Derbyshire   70
Shugborough, Staffordshire   79
Syon House, Middlesex   86
Mersham le Hatch, Kent   98
Brocket Hall, Hertfordshire   105
Peper Harow, Surrey   111
Trafalgar House, Wiltshire   115
Wardour Castle, Wiltshire   119
Saltram, Devon   125
Claremont, Surrey   135
Newby Hall, Yorkshire   141
Downton Castle, Herefordshire   148
Crichel, Dorset   153
Doddington Hall, Cheshire   160
Heveningham Hall, Suffolk   165
Woodhall Park, Hertfordshire   177
Berrington Hall, Herefordshire   184
Attingham Park, Shropshire   195
Althorp, Northamptonshire   203
Farnley Hall, Yorkshire   214
Chillington Hall, Staffordshire   222
Courteenhall, Northamptonshire   228
Stourhead, Wiltshire   234
Ickworth, Suffolk   239

APPENDIX

Architects of Country Houses in England and Wales
1760–1800   247

Index   251

CORRIGENDA

Page 17. For *Tabulated List of Architecture*, read *Tabulated List of Architects*.

Page 18. For Penrryn, read Penrhyn.

Page 19. For North front above, read North point above.

Page 123. For entrance (west), read entrance (east).

Page 239. For Owner The Marquess of Bristol, read Owner The National Trust. Since this volume went to press, Ickworth has been given by the Marchioness of Bristol, widow of the late Marquess, to the National Trust.

Pages 241, 243, 245. In the headline, for Sussex read Suffolk.

Page 248. Under Carr, John: for Burton Constable (E.R.), read Constable Burton (N.R.) and add: Burton Constable (E.R.), D.†

ion of the following, for which acknowledgements are due:
5, 146, 150; *National Buildings Record*, 263, 264, 267, 272,
J. Roland Bainbridge, 492; *National Portrait Gallery*, 505.

1. *Cranbury Park, Hampshire. The Ball Room. George Dance* c. 1780.

INTRODUCTION

I. NEO-CLASSICISM

In the months before and after the accession of George III in 1760 Britain's destiny as the first great industrial power began to take shape. Victories in three continents and their seas extended the foundations of an empire while coal was first being brought to Manchester by Brindley's canal, the Carron Ironworks and the Soho factory at Birmingham came into production, and Watt experimented in steam pressure. In the country, real wages stood as high as ever they had been for three centuries, and agriculture was finally abandoning subsistence methods. The cost of Pitt's war shocked the conservative, disturbed further by such manifestations of rococo 'modernism' as Gainsborough's painting, *Ossian* and *Tristram Shandy*, while from France came Rousseau's romantic doctrines and the shocking rationalism of the Encyclopedists. In this context of experiment and apprehension the young king prepared to lead reactionaries back to political traditions; and Robert Adam, just returned from four years abroad, gauged the appetite of the aristocracy, as he toured their country houses, for accepting a new synthesis of architecture combining these revolutionary elements with a restatement of classical values.

In the previous volume the view was expressed that the English creative genius is essentially unsystematic and empirical; moved by sentiment, but inventively practical; 'romantic' as contrasted with 'classical': traits originating in race, climate and geography. But that, the arts requiring observance of certain absolute values, aesthetic expression of the national romanticism needs the discipline of 'classical' form in order to be permanently satisfying. A synthesis, or fusing, of these impulses to design does, in fact, continually take place. But the results vary, depending on how prevailing conditions affect the relative strength of the conforming and nonconforming currents, and on the presence or absence of an artist gifted to effect their fusion. For example, it was claimed that in architecture the Wren School achieved a 'Baroque synthesis', but that in the Early Georgian period no such fusion quite took place between its strong bias to classical qualities and its growing concern with 'natural' values —which latter underlay the aesthetic ferment of its later years (1745–60). Rococo, the derogatory term applied to this phase, was explained to be inadequate, as was the style it denotes, to express the simmering movements taking place beneath the surface at the time when, as it proved, a new age was being born.

There was at least a possibility in 1760 that history might have developed very differently but for the fusion of the

2. *Compton Verney, Warwickshire, from Adam's Bridge. Showing the wings and portico added by him to the Vanbrugh house,* c. 1760–65.

national energies in Chatham's crucible. And, equally, that had not the 'electric power' of Robert Adam produced a similar result in architecture, something like the 19th century 'battle of the styles' would have ensued, with Chambers's gallic classicism, Stuart and Revett's Grecian, and the rococo Goths at issue over the exhausted body of Palladio.

Instead, with startling suddenness, these potentially antagonistic forces were for a time synthesized into a romantic classicism. The process that took place about 1760 is in no way more clearly to be seen today than in the great country houses then under construction. The fundamental difference in the new approach lay in the age's consciousness of separation from the past and hence of modernity. Hitherto civilization and its arts had been generally conceived as synonymous with and continuous from those of 'antiquity' (but for the unfortunate interruption of 'barbarism'); therefore bound by the superior precedents of 'the ancients', and capable of asserting rule only by subjecting the uncertainties of nature to the framework of humanist reason.

Now 'natural philosophy' had begun to establish an alternative, scientific, basis of perspective from which both the world of nature and the past could be examined with critical detachment, moreover with freedom to select and combine such elements from them as appeared valuable for strictly contemporary needs. Thus there emerged in the arts, replacing traditional humanist values, an archaeological and eclectic approach, leading to the possibility of a consciously modern style; and this, it was discovered, could be enriched from the natural world not only by new materials but by new standards of beauty. The neo-classical movement in architecture, the Romantic Revival and the cult of the Picturesque, are thus seen, with the revolutionary trends in industry and political thought, as complementary facets of the new age crystallizing in 1760. In Britain, and more especially in country houses, these ideas coloured the use of the new wealth derived from conquest and colonization, industrial and agricultural development. And to some extent they moulded the first fruits of industrialism itself which, by facilitating techniques and transport of 'applied' art, came to replace the traditional craftsman by the centralized factory.

The men now in a position to build or enlarge country mansions, although still for the most part coming of territorial families or the old aristocracy, were in the majority of instances connected closely with the nation's expansion. Where the wealth applied to buildings described in this volume can be traced, it derived from these typical sources: promotion of agriculture, industries, minerals, etc. 9; Government contracts, 4; armed services, including the East India Company, 4; West Indies, 1; Borough-mongering, 1. On the other hand the actual impulse was due to aesthetic interests in five instances (including several of the foregoing). These sources, in this ratio, would probably be found to be representative on a wider basis of selection.

In the architecture of Europe the Neo-classical movement had been gathering momentum for a generation. It is possible to regard both the Rococo and English Palladianism itself as early manifestations of it. Yet in England the discovery of Greek architecture in successive publications after 1752 (Wood's *Palmyra*, 1753, *Baalbec*, 1757, Stuart and Revett's

Athens, 1762) had little immediate effect beyond widening eclectic knowledge and stimulating the taste for a grander simplicity. In Italy, however, it inspired in reaction, the passionate championship of Roman grandeur by G. B. Piranesi, the influence of whose sublime representations and reconstructions, combined with the fresh treasures yielded by archaeology, appealed much more strongly to romantic Englishmen and was indeed, for a generation, to be 'one of the most vital elements in English architectural development'.[1]

It is characteristic of the movement's parallel side that Piranesi's plates, like Stuart's and Wood's, brought out the scenery and texture of its ruins as picturesquely as Gibbon was soon to describe those of the ancient world's decline. Both these aspects of the dawn of neo-classicism are concisely represented in this volume at Shugborough (p. 79), whilst Arbury (p. 41) and Downton Castle (p. 148) illustrate its gothic phase, and display the movement's equal attention to classical and medieval antiquity as sources for a modern idiom.

The latter quest led, in the realm of theory, to the French Abbé Laugier's *Essai sur L'Architecture* (English edition, 1755) that was to influence profoundly many architects of the century's later decades. Laugier sought to revalue classical architecture on the same principles of rationalism that the Encyclopedists applied to ethics and institutions. Tracing the elementary forms of architecture back to the imagined 'rustic cabin' of primitive man, he insisted that the same principles of structural logic should govern the most magnificent architecture. This archaeological puritanism demanded that the orders and other structural members should be used only functionally, and also denied the authenticity of 'harmonic ratios' for the controlling of formal relationships: these would follow naturally from the use that Laugier advocated of pure geometrical shapes in plan, and from the architect's intuitive sense of proportion.

In the same way, intuitive feeling was substituted for intellect as the source of aesthetic appreciation both by Hume's *Essay on Taste* (1757) and in Burke's *Enquiry on the Sublime and Beautiful* (1757)—the works which most influenced English taste thereafter. According to Burke, proportion, calculation, geometry, being operations of the understanding, had nothing to do with Beauty, to which reaction was instantaneous, and of which the attributes were delicacy and sinuous line. For 'Sublimity', buildings must possess greatness of dimension, succession and uniformity, or that 'rotund form' which simulates infinity. 'Nothing is more prejudicial to greatness than for a building to abound in angles' from an inordinate thirst for variety.

The almost bare simplicity of many of the Adams' and Wyatts' façades, and the delight in 'rotund' forms exemplified by the curious structures of Belle Isle (Fig. 25) and Ickworth (p. 239), reflect this 'intuitive geometry'. Inspired by the new natural philosophy, the classical aesthetic system was being dismembered. That its elements were reassembled into a new 'scientific and romantic' classicism was chiefly due, in Britain, to the genius for synthesis of the Adam family.

---

[1] John Summerson, *Architecture in Britain, 1530–1830*, Part V gives an admirable summary of the neo-classical movement.

II. THE ADAM SYNTHESIS

3. *Bowood, Wiltshire. The 'Diocletian Wing'. Adam, 1769. On the right, the West front designed by Keene.* c. 1755.

John, Robert and James, the sons of William Adam, had been carrying on their father's large Scottish practice for at least a decade before Robert Adam arrived in London from Italy in the winter of 1758. It will not be attempted to narrate his meteoric career.[1] But since the course of architecture in Britain for a generation was so largely determined during the next few months, the factors that appear to have influenced him must be reviewed in the light of what has been said.

Robert was then aged thirty and it is believed that he spent the winter and spring acquainting himself with the state of architecture in England and with the tastes and requirements of potential clients. This was the next step according to the great design that seems to have been arranged between the partner-brothers towards establishing the Adam firm as 'the undisputed primate' of English architecture.

He found that title in abeyance and the character of its realm uncertain. In London Robert Taylor, an architect of accomplishment and authority, held sway, and in its environs was producing a type of villa developing Burlington's model for Kirby Hall, Yorks., which combined rococo 'variety' with classical forms (Harleyford, Bucks., *E.C.H., Early Georgian;* Asgill House, Richmond). In the north and midlands James Paine was at work on a dozen mansions in which he was adapting Palladian tradition to rococo taste by what has been termed 'staccato' breaking down of the main

masses of a design (cf. Brocket, p. 105). The most active exponent of Palladian convention was perhaps Capability Brown, whose practical bent imparted notably convenient plans to rather undistinguished houses. Yet where his visual and historical sense suggested it, Brown would restore, even copy, gothic and Elizabethan work, as at Corsham (*E.C.H., Early Georgian*) and Burghley. A remarkable instance of rococo-Elizabethan is the rearranged and enlarged staircase to fill the great hall at Blickling, Norfolk, by Thomas and William Ivory, 1767. Even Stephen Wright (the Duke of Newcastle's Palladian architect) was to show that, as a pupil of Kent, he could decorate in 'rococo gothick' when required, witness the Library and Chapel added to Milton Manor House, Berks. (1764–72, Fig. 506).

Henry Keene was the leading professional exponent of medieval idiom, as is shown by his work for Sir Roger Newdigate at Arbury (1762, p. 41), though he was also in request for classical rococo, notably at Bowood (Fig. 3) and Uppark (p. 29). But this field was, and largely remained, the preserve of amateurs and antiquaries. Horace Walpole, the foremost of them, put together the greater part of Strawberry Hill between 1760–70; this was excelled by Newdigate in quality and would soon be in originality by Payne Knight at Downton.

Of the archaeologists, James Stuart, the fruits of his explorations not yet published and still practising as a mural painter, was finding most scope for his Greek learning in landscape architecture—apart from his remodelling of Shugborough and building of 15 St James's Square. Personal failings disqualified him from the leadership that he

[1] See the condensed list of his principal country houses, p. 247. Also J. Lees-Milne, *The Age of Adam* (1947); J. Summerson, *Architecture in Britain, 1530–1830,* Part V (1954); H. Colvin, *Dictionary of British Architects, 1600–1840* (1954); A. T. Bolton, *The Work of Robert and James Adam,* 2 vols., 1922.

might have exerted; but neither he nor his former companion Revett (see Trafalgar House, p. 115) were endowed with the faculties demanded by that position. Robert Wood, who led the expeditions to Palmyra and Baalbec, was not an architect. But his draughtsman Giambattista Borra, 'architect to the King of Sardinia', was established as architect at Stowe, where his Hellenising hand can be distinguished (among the many concerned) at least in the remodelled interiors of some of the Temples.[1]

There remained William Chambers, creator of the garden architecture at Kew for the late Prince of Wales and tutor in the art to the future King. Having thrice visited China he was the only first-hand authority on *chinoiserie*. But, of far greater significance, he had also studied with Sufflot under Blondel in Paris, then spent five years in Italy with eyes sharpened by French precision. His *Designs for Chinese Buildings* (1757) had been in the nature of self-advertisement; but his important *Treatise on Civil Architecture* (1759, 1768, 1791) offered in its eclectic scholarship the regimen of which English architecture stood in need. He drew for his examples on a wider range than hitherto of the Italian renaissance architects, and with classical French fastidiousness. The book consisted only of details, with nothing about plans or construction, nor of course of Chinese or rococo. With utmost distaste would the King's architect revert under compulsion to applying gothick to Milton Abbey, Dorset (1770); nor were Stuart's 'Attic deformities' more to his taste. Even Somerset House (1775–80), which afforded his ideals scope and freedom beyond any private commission such as Peper Harrow (p. 111), has been aptly described as neo-classical merely as the result of 'French influence ironing out the bolder terms of English Palladianism'.[2]

It is difficult, in fact, to deny, even before so noble a building as his stables at Goodwood (Fig. 23), or what is now Manresa College, Roehampton, that Sir William Chambers was a fastidious but visually dull designer, notwithstanding that his writing and teaching were, in the end, to have a more lasting influence on English architecture than the achievements of his life-long rival. But in 1760, though people of taste recognized the necessity for chaste discipline and elegant simplicity—virtues exemplified by the young King—to curb 'inordinate variety', yet dullness they would not have. The times were too exciting, and their eyes too eager for the new quality which they called 'the picturesque'.

So, there are many reasons for believing, Robert Adam concluded from reviewing English architecture. Taste and time were ripe for a reassertion of classical values; there lay 'the high game',[3] the only highway to unquestionable greatness in architecture. But the verities, though eternal, he now saw were not absolutely but relatively so, and could be presented so that they appealed to men's awakened sight and sense of romantic modernity. The innumerable sketches that he made for his own pleasure reveal the young Scot himself to have had a vividly romantic imagination. Whether drawn from nature or more often out of his head, the salient quality of these landscape fantasies or improbable Piranesian, even romanesque and gothick, buildings is their rococo picturesqueness. Of measured studies of classical models, such as we would expect, there are none; nor of the 'Etruscan' excavations, Renaissance *grottesche*, nor yet of current French practice in planning and furnishing, all of which he had seen and which were to enter so largely into his style. For these he could rely on visual memory or published books. On the other hand, of course, there were his survey drawings of Spalato (by Clerisseau and other draughtsmen) to be published in 1764: a notable first-hand contribution to archaeology to set against Stuart's and Wood's.

The nature of these diverse preoccupations—all of which were on the fringe of rococo taste but which no single mind had hitherto focused together—accounts for the instantaneous triumph and, no less, for the character of Adam's new style or, as it can be best described, synthesis. Moreover they warrant the conclusion that Adam's was not a fundamentally intellectual and classical mind which carefully acquired picturesque empiricism, but that he had a naturally empirical genius which mastered every aspect of 'the classics' in order to achieve his ambition. Throughout his early performance it is the picturesque (in the broadest sense), not the classical, even the neo-classical, qualities in it that are the more constant and remarkable. Similarly, if his work is viewed from the technical aspect, the variety of novel materials and processes which he applied to architecture from industry is significant.[1]

After 1770, when cynicism seems to have replaced enthusiasm in him, and the American war bedevilled costs and ideals, it is precisely the emotional quality that is missing from the firm's increasingly automatic output. Synthesis had become system. But the Adam achievement is to be judged by the amazing creativeness of the decade 1760–70 and especially of the two or three years immediately following 1760 when he had in hand at different stages of completion or inception: Harewood (p. 61), Croome, Compton Verney (Fig. 2), Kedleston (p. 70), Bowood (Fig. 3), Osterley (Frontispiece, and Figs. 5, 6), Syon (p. 86), Mersham (p. 98), and Lansdowne House.

The first thing to notice in this list is that all were existing buildings, either ancient or begun by other architects, which Adam was required to remodel or complete—except the last two, neither of which is among his most notable creations. Indeed, among his great houses of which Fate permitted Adam to devise the outward aspect unrestricted, one alone, the south front of Kedleston and that only in part, fulfils his declared aims.

These aims are stated, with no false modesty, in the firm's

---

[1] Possibly also at Stratfield Saye House, in the Dining Room for Lord Rivers.

[2] Summerson, *op. cit.* 270.

[3] The phrase is Sir Edwin Lutyens's, coined at a very similar juncture 150 years later (see the author's *Life of Sir Edwin Lutyens*, 1951). The similarity of Adam's and Lutyens's way of approach to a classical-romantic synthesis is apparent from other traits of the former, mentioned in this paragraph.

[1] E.g. 'Liardet's Composition' stucco, cast iron, Coade stone, Soho ormolu, papier-mâché, pre-painted decorative panels, purpose-woven silk and carpets (see §5). It was, according to Sir J. Soane, 'manufacturers of every kind (who) felt the electric power of the (Adam) Revolution in art'. Mrs Montagu comments on his 'regiment of artificers'.

4. *Shardeloes, Buckinghamshire. The Library. Adam, 1761.*   5. *Osterley, Middlesex. The Eating Room (detail). Adam c. 1765.*

manifesto, *The Works of Robert and James Adam.*[1] So long as the Adam style is thought of as refined classical embroidery, the manifesto's stress on the quality of 'movement' seems far fetched. But once the Adam objective is recognized as the synthesis of neo-classical forms with the forces of romanticism, it is explicit and consistent.

'Movement' in architecture is defined as identical with the picturesque quality in landscape: 'the rise and fall, advance and recess, with other diversity of form, in the different parts of a building, so as to add greatly to the picturesque of the composition: that is . . . agreeable and diversified contour that groups and contrasts like a picture and creates variety of light and shade (giving) great spirit, beauty, and effect.' The outstanding example of movement cited is the composition formed by the west front, piazza and dome of St Peter's (by Bramante, Rainaldi and Bernini)—also Kedleston as proposed by Adam. And its great English exponent is acknowledged to have been Vanbrugh, 'whose works, in point of movement, novelty and ingenuity have not been exceeded in modern times', although 'his taste kept no pace with his genius, and none but the discerning can separate their merits from their defects'. Reynolds later paid equal tribute 'to an architect who composed like a painter' (in his 13th Discourse, 1786), as subsequently did Uvedale Price, Payne Knight and James Wyatt. But Adam, who had recently 'polished Vanbrugh's rough jewels' in his additions to Compton Verney (Fig. 2), was the first to recognise the value of the pictorial

[1] The first volume was issued in 1773 to assert the Brothers' origination of the manner that, by then, had been adopted by most other architects, notably James Wyatt.

element in his work. The chapter on Kedleston (p. 70) analyses his great external embodiment of movement. But he achieved it again and, in another way, that of dramatic surprise, at Osterley, breaking into the Elizabethan quadrangle —its pavement raised to first floor level—with his Palmyrene portico approached by monumental steps (Frontispiece). We can detect the same pictorial approach to his completion of Keene's unsatisfactory essay at Bowood, in the juxtaposition of the 'Diocletian Wing' (Fig. 3) itself screening subsidiary buildings, and particularly in the Vanbrughesque mausoleum there. And it enters decisively into the manner of his additions to Newby (p. 141).

But 'movement', fused with the 'antique style', permeates Adam's planning and decoration. He achieved this synthesis most completely at Syon, of which his own description explains both its components and his theory of 'the form, arrangement, and relief of apartments'. This 'movement in plan' or space-modelling, he observed, 'has hitherto been extremely little understood or attended to, even in the greatest houses of this country'. The claim is sweeping but justified. Wren had proportioned churches empirically; Vanbrugh juggled with volume; and the designers of Holkham caught the idea. But, for a generation, planning had been tied to the half-understood creed of 'harmonic proportions'; and interior design to Lord Burlington's rules when not given over to rococo licence.

Now, Adam said, there must first be 'variety and gracefulness of form'. 'The ancients' demanded it. He does not specify which, or where, but probably he had in mind Piranesi's reconstructions. All the Renaissance architects ('those great

6. *Osterley. The Tapestry Room. Adam. 1775. 'Rose du Barry' Gobelins Tapestries, after Boucher's 'Les Amours des Dieux',*
by Neilson 1765–75.

restorers of the arts'), from Bramante to Palladio and Jones, had neglected this conception of space-modelling; 'only of late has it again been introduced into Great Britain with some rays of its ancient splendour' (by, of course, himself).

Next, 'a proper arrangement and relief of apartments'. This is explained as the synthesis of 'magnificence and utility', the varied but related expression of the uses of a suite of rooms, in which the French were the exemplars. Indeed 'to understand thoroughly the art of living', Adam asserted, 'it is necessary perhaps to have spent some time among the French'. (The complete reversal of this view during the ensuing century is an interesting result of the English new classical synthesis which is not often acknowledged.) The main difference in English planning, he continued, must be in the relative importance of the dining room, usually a plain apartment in France where 'the display of the table' is its chief ornament. But 'with us, where the nature of our climate induces more indulgence in enjoyment of the bottle' and our democratic constitution encourages every gentleman to 'enter with ardour into discussion of political arrangement', the eating room is the main apartment of conversation, 'in which we are to pass a great part of our time, detached from the society of the ladies'. Therefore it needs to be fitted up with elegance and splendour, but with stucco, statues and paintings (e.g. the Eating Room at Osterley, Fig. 5) instead of with damask and tapestries 'that they may not retain the smell of the victuals'.[1]

His treatment of the other rooms at Syon, with the analysis of them given (p. 86), makes clear Adam's synthesizing procedure, in which, just as clearly, his empirical invention was stimulated by the structural problems. Which really came first, the theory or the solution, we can never know. As so often in creative architecture, it may be guessed that each prompted and confirmed the other, and that the apparent integrity of his neo-classical solution expresses what was originally an empirical one.

His wholly personal style of decoration evolved similarly from synthesis: of a wide variety of eclectic sources with that which he was convinced represented the ancient Roman style of *internal* decoration, and with his conception of the 'proper arrangement and relief of apartments'. The sources

have been penetratingly distinguished by Mr Summerson as (1) Palladianism, more particularly in its 'staccato' phase; (2) France, notably in planning, and in details of furniture and design and such adjuncts as ironwork; (3) archaeological, especially Palmyra which his ceilings of the 1760s constantly echo, and what was then regarded as Etruscan art; and (4) the Italian Renaissance masters, from Raphael's *grottesche* to Piero Ligorio, which Adam believed to be directly derived from then-existing Roman originals. In fusing these with English requirements, he was aided by archaeology's and Piranesi's revelation that the Romans had not in fact been bound by Vitruvian rules but enjoyed almost unlimited freedom in designing; and hence by the conviction that 'the "rules" of architectural grammar were not rules at all but a matter of style, feeling, taste'.[1]

Thus in his hands a Corinthian entablature, for example, hitherto inflexible, became 'a thing whose qualities could be abstracted and then rendered back with an infinity of variation, the whole reduced or expanded to fit the occasion . . . but the total effect still that of an entablature and in its new form possessed of an intensified character'.[2] In his own words, 'the proportions of columns depend on their situation.'

In Adam's great period, and in the hands of his successors, Dance and Soane, this process of abstracting and re-rendering was conducted with a scholarship, refinement of perception, a pervading sense of 'movement', and moreover in a range of materials, which endow the outcome with inimitable vitality. In his own later manner, the germ of which can be detected in one of his most empirical solutions of a decorative problem—the Long Gallery at Syon (Fig. 162)— the process became a formula, as capable of application by others as by the team of draughtsmen, plasterers, painters and manufacturers originally assembled in the Brothers' office.[3]

---

[1] Summerson, op. cit., p. 263.   [2] ibid.

[3] One of the greatest of these was Joseph Rose, 1746–99 (cf. Syon, Kedleston: also *E.C.H.*, *Early Georgian*). Both his grandfather and father (of the same name, living 1776) were well-known plasterers, the latter being Paine's decorator at Nostell Priory; also his brother Jonathan. He himself was architect, with Sir Christopher Sykes, of Sledmere, Yorks., 1788–92. He was a witness for Adam in the case of Adam's patented stucco (1778). His will directed his stock in trade to be sold (Information communicated by Mr C. W. Beard).

---

[1] Cf., for this home truth, 'A Plan of a Bristol merchant's house', quoted in *E.C.H.*, *Early Georgian*, p. 12.

III. THE SUBLIME AND BEAUTIFUL, 1770–80

The founding of the Royal Academy of Arts in 1768, facilitated by Chambers's influence with the King, fulfilled the Whig Ideal envisaged as early as 1711 (cf. *E.C.H.*, *Early Georgian*). From the first it stood for consolidation and ignored the Adams, who were connected rather with the rival academy for applied science, the Society of Arts, formed in 1758 during the 'Rococo impetus'. Adam's waning prestige and the Academy's rise was to coincide with a marked change not only in taste but in the social and political atmosphere. Grandeur and Simplicity, in other words the Sublime and Beautiful, became the fashionable qualities, reflecting at least a truer appreciation of neo-classicism's meaning than

was to be found in the late Adam style's exquisite but emasculated parody of its earlier self. Moreover the decade was that of George III's personal government through Lord North and the Tories. Its accompanying misfortunes of personal cynicism and public disasters certainly contrasted with the triumphant optimism of the reign's dawn, and seem reflected in the prevalent debility of the decade's architecture compared with the vitality of that preceding.

Toryism's recrudescence produced a recognizable line-up in architectural politics. The old Palladian academism, represented by Paine and Taylor, grouped itself with Chambers and his outstanding recruit James Wyatt, forming the official

7. *Worksop, Nottinghamshire, 1763. Section on central axis (the front on the left). By James Paine, from 'Plans . . . of Houses',*
1767

body of architects patronized by supporters of the King and Government. On the other hand the Whig opposition found a non-academic architect, sympathetic to their French liberalism, in Henry Holland; whilst its radical element, represented by such individualists as Payne Knight (cf. Downton Castle, p. 148) and the 5th Earl of Bristol (cf. Ickworth, p. 239), turned to an extremer neo-classicism, of which the most notable exponents in architecture were to be George Dance and Soane.

Thus, after the spectacular 'Adam decade', Paine was still building Palladian palaces, but now for Tories, at Worksop (Fig. 7), Thorndon, Wardour (p. 119) and Sandbeck—all but the last for ancient Roman Catholic families. In Paine's opinion, archaeology threw 'no new light on the grand part of architecture, though valuable for ornaments'. Certainly his

elevations remain wholly Palladian. But his interiors show the new influence; and his later plans splendidly developed the neo-classical conception of moulded and contrasting spaces from the point where Burlington and Kent had carried it (Fig. 7).

Taylor was principally engaged, after 1766, on the Bank of England and more or less official buildings, in which his accomplished refinements of the Palladian canon admitted many neo-classical and Adam innovations. Gorhambury, Hertfordshire, for Lord Verulam (built 1777–84 near the remains of Francis Bacon's Elizabethan mansion) was wholly Palladian till insensitively altered in the 19th century; redeemed from dullness, however, by the grand portico (Fig. 9) and proportioned rooms—which incidentally contain two marble and porphyry chimneypieces inspired if not supplied

8. *(left) Tusmore, Oxfordshire. The garden front. R. Mylne,*
1766. 9. *(above) Gorhambury, Hertfordshire. The Portico.*
Sir R. Taylor, 1777.

by Piranesi (Fig. 11). At Hevingham (1778, p. 165), where J. Wyatt soon replaced him, Taylor carried his 'neo-Palladian' compound to its last expression.

The working career of John Carr of York, begun under Burlington, extended well into the Regency. A first-rate builder, he rarely omitted from his plans the half-octagon bows characteristic of rococo, but was always open to the latest London fashions. At Harewood (p. 61) he had the advantage of close and early contact with Adam, thereafter adopting his idiom so far as he could—and one of his office draftsmen, it seems likely. Denton Hall, 1778, near Otley (Fig. 10), is externally in the style of an Early Palladian mansion but full of Adamesque ornament. Yet whilst he was building Farnley (p. 214) to much the same formula as Tabley (p. 55) he made a late contribution to rococo gothick with his triangular castellated design of Grimston Garth (1786) on the bleak coast of Holderness. Towards the end of his life Peter Atkinson took over Carr's practice and designed Hackness Hall, near Scarborough, 1796, looking almost as though Talman had been its author.

But around 1770 there also entered the field a new generation of architects, all bred to the business—and for the most part trained in Italy where several had gained academic honours in international competition. The least known of them, Matthew Brettingham II (1725–1803), son of the builder of Holkham, had been in Athens with Stuart and

11. *Gorhambury. Chimneypiece in Carrara marble and porphyry. From a design by G. B. Piranesi.*

Revett. He became Lord North's protégé and was favoured by him for Surveyor General but for the King's attachment to Chambers. His chief identified work is the N. and E. fronts added in its Jacobean style to Charlton Park, Wilts. (1772–74), with a neo-classical hall in the courtyard.

Charles Cameron (c. 1740–1812) courted his fellow Scot Lord Bute with an impressive folio *The Baths of the Romans Explained* (1772), but, apparently failing in competition with Wyatt and Holland, became architect to Catherine the Great at Tsarskoe Seloe, exporting Adam neo-classicism to St Petersburg.

Robert Mylne, descended from a long line of Scottish master masons, gained a premium during his studies in Italy, and immediately on his return won the competition for Blackfriars Bridge, London (1759). Thenceforth he combined engineering with particularly sensitive neo-classical country houses.[1] At Kings Weston, Glos., which he redecorated, the garden houses and steps to the portico (1763–72) refine beautifully on the Vanbrugh manner; Tusmore, Oxon. (1766–69), is a great neo-classical house à la française with unusually good ceilings in the manner, and The Wick, Richmond Hill, a miniature. As a decorator Mylne is seen best at Inveraray Castle, Argyll (1772–82).

George Dance, son of the architect of the London Mansion House, also distinguished himself in Italy before homing in time to design, at the age of twenty-four, the remarkable little church of All Hallows, London Wall (1765) and four years later the magnificently gloomy Newgate Prison. The originality that he displayed in buildings is referred to in connection with the most notable example of his earlier domestic work, at Cranbury Park, Hants., c. 1780 (Fig. 1),

10. *Denton Hall, Yorkshire. The upper Staircase Hall. Carr of York, 1778.*

[1] A series of commissions between 1764–79 in Shropshire, to which Mylne was introduced by the sporting squire Jack Mytton of Halston Park, has recently been traced by Mr C. G. Gotch (see *Tabulated List of Architecture*, p. 247).

for to do so at this point would anticipate Dance's actual impact on country house design.

Joseph Bonomi (1739–1808), though not known to have practised on his own before 1784, should be mentioned at this point, since he was born and educated in Italy, and came to England in 1767 at the invitation of the Adams. He worked in their office for some years, then *c.* 1772 for Leverton (see below). His drawings for the ballroom of Montagu House, Portman Square, which he completed *c.* 1790 after Stuart's death, show him a neo-classical decorator of great refinement, and it is probable that his services to Adam and Leverton were in this capacity (cf. Woodhall, p. 177 and (?) Crichel p. 153). Till after 1800 his chief independent works were distinguished rooms for persons of taste, in the treatment of some of which Mr Summerson has detected that 'elision' of conventional parts which is the hall-mark of neo-classical design.

This occurs in the extremely elegant little hall of No. 1 Bedford Square, London, built by Leverton in 1780, who can be suspected not himself to have been given to such modernism. Thomas Leverton (1743–1824) was an Essex builder's son who began exhibiting at the R.A. in 1771 and engaged largely in speculative building in London. Woodhall Park (1777, p. 177), when Bonomi was presumably working with him, is by much his most distinguished country house.

James Wyatt[1] was the sixth son of Benjamin Wyatt, a Staffordshire yeoman with a local business as timber merchant and builder. His third son, Samuel, developed this after 1770 into a large architectural practice in the north midlands with a branch in London; another, Benjamin, managed the Penrryn slate-quarries (see *E.C.H., Late Georgian*). The eldest brother John was a London doctor with theatrical interests. James, the most brilliant of an evidently talented family, is said to have shown equal facility for music and painting (in which admirers thought he rivalled Pannini). In 1762, aged sixteen, he accompanied Richard Bagot, brother of the dilettante Sir W. (later Lord) Bagot of Blithfield, Staffs., on an embassy to Venice led by the Earl of Northampton. He remained in Italy for six years, so that presumably his father was supporting the venture—the aim of which, it may be inferred, was to develop the family practice of architecture on the lines of the Adams', perhaps with James as the specialist in decoration. Antonio Viscentini, under whom he worked for two years in Venice, was similarly versatile as painter and architect. In view of James Wyatt's chameleon aptitudes, it is significant that his approach to architecture was, at one stage at least, through painting. At Venice he made two useful contacts—Consul Smith, the great connoisseur, and Richard Dalton, George III's librarian. At Rome his architectural studies of the Pantheon and St Peter's aroused astonishment by the intrepidity with which he caused himself to be slung horizontally on a ladder in order to measure the details of their domes.

On his return in 1768 it is likely that he rejoined the family firm (the plans of Stafford General Infirmary, 1769, are signed 'Benj. Wyatt and *Sons* Archt'). In 1770, partly through the influence of his doctor brother and Dalton, James won the competition for rebuilding the Pantheon,

Oxford Street, as a 'winter Ranelagh for assemblies and masquerades'. His studies of the Roman prototype were presumably useful for the dome of the great central space; but it has been shown that he derived the plan of this from Sancta Sophia, Constantinople—a degree of eclecticism remarkable at this date.[1] The dome, constructed of timber (recalling the family concern with that material), could consequently be carried on the flattened segmental arches that the Wyatts were so frequently to employ; and much decorative use was made of scagliola and painted arabesque. The Pantheon, rendering in more durable materials a conception similar to Adam's temporary rotunda at Syon (see p. 150) and pavilion at The Oaks, was hailed as an architectural portent, 'the wonder of the British Empire'; though the rococo of Ranelagh was considered gayer.

The qualities that contemporaries admired in the Pantheon were the greater simplicity and judgment of his version of the antique, compared to Adam's ornate refinement. Subsequently, Wyatt deplored that 'there had been no regular architecture since Sir William Chambers', so that 'when he came from Italy he found public taste corrupted by the Adams, and he was obliged to comply with it'.[2] There are later buildings such as his mausolea at Cobham and Brocklesby, and Dodington Park, Glos. (1797–1813, see *E.C.H., Late Georgian*) which confirm his potentialities as a classicist, had he had greater opportunities for monumental design and more concentration of purpose. And up and down the country there are restrained and elegant neo-classical country houses due directly or indirectly to the Wyatts. For the most part of two storeys, the use of the semi-circular bow is their distinctive feature. With a proportioned simplicity, lightness and restraint of decoration, yet often an element of 'movement' imparted to the elevations, their designs distil Adam's effervescence to a calm sense and sensibility corresponding closely to the English view of gentlemanly virtue. They illustrate well that balance or synthesis of classical and native qualities in which the most satisfying English architecture is held to consist, and do so, it must be owned, more consistently than Adam's relatively few executed elevations.

The extent to which James was responsible for the external 'Wyatt style', however, is questionable. Collegiate and public commissions formed the more important part of his practice, in which he succeeded Keene at Westminster Abbey (1776), and made himself the leading exponent of gothic. The large majority of his more notable country house designs were in this still essentially rococo gothic, whereas a great deal of his classical domestic work was in decoration or additions. Even in the aggregate these are of less note than the country houses for which his brother Samuel was responsible during the same period.

The notable exception to this generalization is Heaton Hall, Manchester. Yet although the designs exhibited at the R.A. (1772) bore James's signature, and the decoration is wholly typical of his style, the design was also attributed (Neale, *Seats*, 1824) to Samuel, whose subsequent buildings developed Heaton's characteristic innovations. This uncertainty in attribution may point, if not to a partnership, to a

---

[1] For the sparse biographical materials that exist, see Antony Dale, *James Wyatt*, 1936, and a valuable article in Colvin, op. cit.

[1] Summerson, op. cit., p. 281. But its dismissal as a 'lucky choice of a recondite theme' is something less than generous.

[2] Farington Diary, 1801.

12–14. *Heaton Hall, Lancashire. James Wyatt, 1772. (above) The south front.*

(right) Plan of Ground Floor. North front above.

(below) The Cupola Room, on the first floor. Painted by Biagio Rebecca.

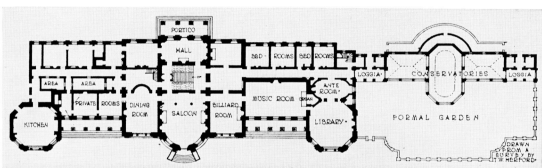

15, 16. *Heaton Hall. Upper part of the Staircase Hall and (right) a doorway therein.*

close collaboration between the brothers. If James originated at Heaton the 'Wyatt style' and carried it on at Bowden, Wilts. (1796), he certainly left it largely for Samuel to exploit—at Baron Hill, Anglesey (1776), Doddington, Salop., p. 160, Herstmonceux Place, Sussex *c.* 1777, Winnington Hall, Cheshire, *c.* 1780, Shugborough, p. 79, and Belmont, Figs. 28–31. Hence it is that Heaton is so important a land-

mark in the evolution of country house design; but also that houses by Samuel figure as prominently in this volume as work by James Wyatt.

Heaton, commissioned in 1772 by Sir Thomas Egerton, 1st Earl of Wilton, is actually a big extension of a small slightly earlier house, retained as the centre of its N. front. This having been of only two storeys without basement de-

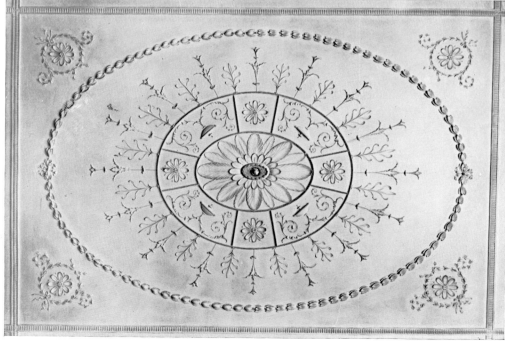

17, 18. *Heaton Hall. In the Billiard Room: a doorway, and the ceiling.*

19, 20. *Heaton Hall, Saloon: details of the screen and of the chimneypiece.*

termined the character of the additions, which were to provide a suite of reception rooms at ground level facing S., with an upper storey only in the centre, the bedrooms and offices being disposed in the prolongations of the N. front. The kitchen, however, was not concealed as was customary, but placed in the W. pavilion of the new front, quite near to the dining room. In his design for the new front Wyatt took advantage of having to provide all the principal accommodation at ground level by abandoning completely the Palladian tradition of a *piano nobile*, whilst retaining flanking pavilions

linked by colonnades (as at Castle Coole, 1790). By giving unusual height to the colonnades, and facetted fronts to the pavilions, however, he set up a rhythm of 'movement', which the arched Venetian windows in the main block carry through to the columned semicircular bow in its centre. Moreover, to strengthen and dramatize the skyline he placed behind each colonnade a remarkable turret of concentrated chimneys reminiscent of Vanbrugh's 'towers'. The bow, as a central feature, had been accepted rather tentatively by Adam at Mersham le Hatch (p. 98), where it contains an entrance;

21. *Broadlands, Hampshire. The west Portico.*
Brown, 1766.

22. *Woburn, Bedfordshire. The Greenhouse (Sculpture Gallery).*
Holland, 1787–88.

but the Wyatts, in their many variations of the theme, never used the bow functionally, only schematically. Thus analysed, the Heaton elevation is found to combine Palladian, 'baroque' and Adam elements in a new classical composition at once integrated and original. Further, owing to the intractable sandstone employed, the enrichments had to be of new synthetic materials: cast iron for the capitals, artificial (probably Coade) stone for the reliefs.

The house has for half a century been owned by the Manchester Corporation and used for public purposes. The illustrations (Figs. 12–20) show the characteristics of Wyatt's new 'grandeur and simplicity', notably in the handling and decoration of the staircase (Fig. 16), and in the more elegantly 'Grecian' style of ornament which is restricted to ceilings, doorcases, and chimneypieces—except in the elaborately 'Roman' Cupola Room. This, in the first floor of the bow (Fig. 14), was painted by Biagio Rebecca who was to work much for the Wyatts (Doddington Hall, Salop., p. 160, Heveningham, p. 165, also Crichel, p. 153.

There are many stories of James Wyatt's conceit and dilatoriness which, though due in part to the pressure of his very large and varied practice, may help to explain why no immediate successor on the scale of Heaton was required of him. Between 1773–90 his most important works were collegiate and ecclesiastical: he built only six medium-sized country houses, of which Ammerdown, Somerset (classical), and Lee Priory, Kent (gothic, demolished), were the most notable. But he made extensive alterations to many, the outstanding example of which is his complete internal treatment of Heveningham (p. 165). The rise of Holland as the fashionable architect, and the American war, probably contributed to this absence of important private commissions. But during the '90s, when he succeeded Chambers as Surveyor General (1796), they increased considerably. Notable examples both in his neo-classic and gothic styles will be found in the next volume.

Holland (1745–1806) alone of the 'young entry of 1770' was trained at home and scarcely ever left England. The son of a well-known master builder, and from 1771 the architectural partner of 'Capability' Brown, whose daughter he married, he inherited not only good connections but technical ability and Brown's reputation for sound construction and planning. He made up for his lack of first-hand Continental experience by close study of the publications of French neo-classical architects, and after 1785 by employing French craftsmen. Both Soane and C. H. Tatham were his assistants in their early days, the latter of whom he sent to Italy in 1794 partly to collect motifs of Graeco-Roman decoration.

His innate *flaire* for elegantly 'sweet' design was thus enlarged by a fashionable, mainly French, vocabulary, but he remained the most English of late Georgian architects, completely synthesizing neo-classicism with the gentleman's ideals of commonsense and modesty—typified in his later decoration by ornament reduced to its essence, if also by a certain smallness of scale.

Launched in 1771 by his father on speculative building (Sloane St., London), his adroit manners and sympathies commended him to the Whig circle, for which he designed Brooks's Clubhouse (1776), and so to the Prince of Wales. The succession of country house commissions to which this led is well represented in this volume by Claremont, in collaboration with Brown (1771, p. 135), Berrington Hall (p. 184), which immediately preceded his first designs for Carlton House, and remodelling of Althorpe (p. 203). In his reconstruction of Carlton House (1784–86) it was 'the august simplicity . . . all delicate and new, with more variety than Greek ornaments' that pleased Walpole, and because it was 'full of perspectives'. In its plan contrasting succession of rotund and rectangular spaces recalls Paine's later plans but without their subservience to a Palladian frame. The decoration, illustrated in Pyne's *Royal Residences*, is most nearly approached at Berrington. In the informality of the Royal Pavilion, Brighton (1786–88), Holland had greater freedom for manipulating his sweet curves in its bows, verandahs and rotunda which were to set a persistent fashion in marine terraces and villas. The Pavilion's facing with 'Mathematical Tiles' also popularized a new manufactured 'material' (see §5). For rural buildings Holland was an early advocate for reviving the old use of rammed earth (*pisé de terre*).

Elsewhere, Holland continued his father-in-law's preference for white brick. Brown had used this for Broadlands, Hants., in 1768–69, a house on which Holland may possibly have worked as a young man designing the Adam-style decoration of the drawing room. He returned to it in 1788 to provide a new east entrance with recessed Ionic portico and a dining room typical of his mature (but not final) style. This, well seen at Althorpe (p. 203), is best illustrated by the great Franco-classical orangery, now sculpture gallery, at Woburn (Fig. 22), the library and W. front there, and the now demolished tennis court and riding school. His final manner, synthesizing the essences of these sub-styles, developed during his long transformation of Southill (1796–1806) into perhaps the most sophisticated neo-classical country house, description of which, owing to its predominant date, is reserved for the succeeding volume.

IV. THE PICTURESQUE

Those 'golden hours', when the younger Pitt had retrieved the situations lost or imperilled by his predecessors, when the fall of the Bastille presaged a liberal millennium with taxes and armaments reduced, and young poets found it 'bliss to be alive', still linger in the country houses designed by Holland and his contemporaries about 1785. Nature and reason seemed to speak alike. Burke beheld liberty indissolubly linked with order. Yet the buildings of the century's last

decade rose against a background of war and panic, famine prices and rapid industrialization. The old small scale of England was disrupted as surely as the course of events withered the idealism that had seen France as the neo-classical Utopia.

The debacle had the same repercussions on the aesthetic plane. The old idealistic synthesis of mansion and landscape park began to look as stilted and bigotted as the Court at St

23. *Goodwood, Sussex. Remodelled by James Wyatt, 1800. The Stables (left) by Sir W. Chambers, c. 1760.*

James's; yet the new classicism was also tainted, in as far as it emanated from Paris. In their places, the eyes of sentiment and sensibility turned to the visual and historic heritage of the homeland, with an ardour quickened by sudden apprehension of its imminent danger. The English romantic spirit, implicit in Wren and Vanbrugh, had entered into the rococo and coloured Adam's synthesis. Now it was to produce an aesthetic philosophy defining the visual qualities, not only of natural landscape but of architecture, as 'the Picturesque'—a category to be accepted as no less important artistically than the Sublime and Beautiful. The new aesthetic was launched in 1794 by three books: the *Essay on the Picturesque* by Uvedale Price, a Herefordshire squire; *The Landscape*, a poem by his neighbour Payne Knight of Downton (p. 148), primarily an attack on 'systems' of behaviour and on that of Brown's landscapes in particular; and *Sketches and Hints on Landscape Gardening* by Humphry Repton, Brown's principal successor.[1]

The agreed tenets of the philosophy (its differences were fiercely argued by the protoganists for a decade) were that landscape painting as developed from Titian by Claude, Poussin and Salvator Rosa, and by their followers up to Gainsborough, revealed all the qualities in nature that mattered to the artistic eye (as distinct from the intellect and the heart), and which therefore must be preserved or incorporated in any alterations to scenery—including the addition of buildings to landscape. The principal qualities were the contrast of light and shade, variety of form and richness of texture. In architecture great importance was attached to the visual unity of a building with its setting, which might justify assymetrical planning and, through a

[1] Cf. *The Picturesque* by C. Hussey, 1927.

24. *Wimpole, Cambridgeshire. The Drawing Room. Sir J. Soane, 1791–93.*

25. *Belle Isle, Westmorland. John Plaw, 1774–75.*

26. *Moor Place, Hertfordshire. Robert Mitchell, 1777.*

27. *Clare House, Kent. Michael Searles, 1797.*

link as yet tentative with empiricism, a greater subordination of design to the requirements of use than was enabled by classical principles.

Thus a much extended meaning, at once more precise and more complex, was given to the word that Adam had used as complement to 'movement'. By their concentration on the superficial and scenic aspects of the conception, the amateur theorists left its application to architecture extremely vague, though agreeing that Vanbrugh's, and 'mixed' old buildings, illustrated their thesis. The Picturesque was to be the principal architectural sanction of Late Georgian architecture, inspiring Barry and Pugin's Palace of Westminster.

Before 1800 'the principles of the Picturesque' in their expanded form had little time to affect architecture fundamentally (Price's additional essay 'On Architecture' appeared only in 1798). In Payne Knight's youthful creation of Downton Castle (p. 148) we have a crude expression of his still unformulated creed. At Farnley (p. 214) Carr of York squared an essentially picturesque problem in bluff Palladian way. Repton's recommendations for Attingham (p. 202) and Courteenhall (p. 203), though employing the Picturesque approach to the problems, illustrate rather what true picturesquers criticized in his compromises. About 1795—that is just after his association at Courteenhall with Chambers's pupil Saxon—he entered into a partnership with John Nash which was to result, but not before the beginning of the next century, in a number of houses intended to be picturesque in themselves.

But many of the ideas and compulsions underlying the Picturesque were already influencing neo-classical architects independently. The most original mind among 'the young men of the '70s' was that of George Dance who, in his later years, was to produce a curious picturesque amalgam of his own, part gothic, part classical, which he used in refacing the Guildhall, London (1788). He had little practice in country houses before 1800, but his alterations to Cranbury Park, Hants., *c.* 1780 (Fig. 1), afford a very remarkable instance of his earlier style and of those innovations which were so to affect the outstanding architect of this phase, John Soane.

At Cranbury, Dance was required to provide a majestic entrance hall and ballroom for an existing house.[1] The hall is barrel-vaulted with a columnar screen at its inner end behind which is a sky-lit apse. Opening to the left from this, a lobby leads at right angles into the ballroom parallel to the hall. This superb room is in plan a Greek cross, having semi-domed apses in its N. and S. sides, a barrel-vaulted 'nave' (by which we have entered) and a Venetian window in the outer end. The central square is covered with an eight-pointed star vault springing from fan-like pendentives at the four corners. The whole is geometrically coffered and enriched, the colouring being in the original pastel shades, in a technique reminiscent of Adam but probably derived from

[1] The owner was Thomas Dummer, whose widow in 1790 married (Sir) Nathaniel Dance-Holland, R.A., the architect's brother. This connection strongly supports the attribution to George Dance. But the only documentation forthcoming relates to chimneypieces supplied 1781–84 by Soane, Dance's former pupil. This date is more consistent with the style of the ballroom, etc. than 1790 and implies earlier contact of the Dances with Mr and Mrs Dummer.

28. Belmont, Kent. Samuel Wyatt, c. 1792. The entrance and south fronts.

Piranesi's reconstructions and evidencing in its working out an original mind. That it is due to Dance is rendered virtually certain by the elimination of the entablature to the Order and its replacement by an enriched frieze, a simplification that Dance had introduced at All Hallows Church, London Wall (1765–67). The vaulting system also is an elaboration of that of his Guildhall Hall Council Room, and prophetic of Soane's.

John Soane (1753–1837), the son of a Berkshire bricklayer, was trained at the R.A. Schools where in 1776 he won the Gold Medal with a design for a triumphal bridge. Meanwhile, he worked first with Dance and then in Holland's office (see Claremont, p. 135). Through Chambers he received the King's Travelling Scholarship in 1778, at Rome encountering the Bishop of Derry (see Ickworth, p. 239). After his consequent return in 1780, the evidence of his working at Cranbury suggests that he temporarily rejoined Dance, prior to building up a modest practice with country houses. These show traces of Holland's influence and of his Roman studies, but become increasingly idiosyncratic. Marden Hill, Herts., and Shottesham, Norfolk, are typical. He published these and other designs in 1788, the year when Pitt obtained his appointment as Architect to the Bank of England in succession to Taylor.

In at least two of his alterations of country houses, Soane had encountered the problem of top-lighting a large enclosed space, which was so largely to evoke his characteristic designs: at Chillington 1786–89 (p. 222); and Wimpole, Cambs., 1791–93, where a Drawing-Room (Fig. 24) was inserted in an internal court of the house enlarged by Gibbs for the 2nd Earl of Oxford. In the peculiar surface-modelling with varieties of flute and fret (discounting the 19th-century paintings), in the near-elimination of the Order, and in the *chiaroscuro* produced by the top-lighting from the dome-lantern, we can see his debt to Dance but also the beginnings of his synthesis of neo-classicism and the picturesque. In this, as developed after 1800 more especially at the Bank, Soane distilled and fused much of the essences of both Gothic and Greek architecture in what can best be described as a synthesis. In his recourse to pure, 'primitive' forms, especially in dome and vault and curiously abstracted ornament, his reading of Laugier and admiration for Dance are evident. But annotated copies of Price, Knight and Repton's

books show too the attention he gave to picturesque theory, as, fantastically, do also the watercolours he later commissioned to depict his principal buildings as ruins.

The domed rotunda—to Burke sublime, fundamentally pure to Laugier—was the neo-classical form *par excellence* for aspirants to those high qualities. Only Soane essayed the picturesque sublime. Others relied on the setting, whether in nature or their perspectives, to contribute the picturesque element, if that was to be included. In the numerous books of designs that were published (actual building having diminished owing to the war), *fermes ornées*, gentlemen's

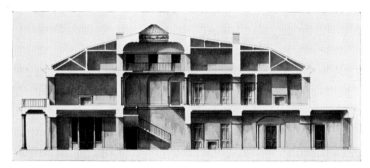

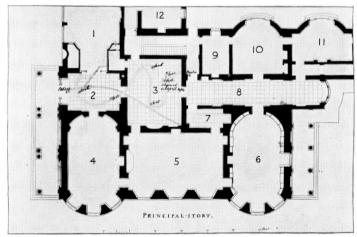

29, 30. Belmont. Section from east to west, and (below) Plan of principal rooms. 1. Greenhouse. 2. Entry Hall. 3. Staircase. 4. Drawing Room. 5. Dining Room. 6. Library. 7. Servery. 8. Corridor. 9. Childrens' Dining Room. 10. Breakfast Room. 11. Study. 12. Butler's Pantry.

31. *Belmont. Coade stone tablet on south front.*

villas and rustic cottages were depicted against scenic backgrounds. The first and most popular of these was the *Rural Architecture* (six editions, 1785–1804) of John Plaw (*c.* 1745–1820), who described himself 'architect and master builder in Westminster'. These were largely Laugier's rustic cabins anglicized to be built in cob, thatch and tree-trunks. But as early as 1774 Plaw had essayed sublimity itself and in the highly romantic setting of Windermere, by designing Belle Isle (Fig. 25) on an island in that lake for a Mr English —according to Wordsworth the first stranger to settle in the District for the sake of the scenery. For this focal site he chose a small version of the Pantheon. The cylindrical house rises from a square area surrounded by a low wall and containing the half-basement offices. As at Mereworth the chimney-flues are carried to the crown of the dome, in which they alternate with lights to the main staircase; the parapet hides from below the sky-lights of attics in the dome. The main floor provides two large rooms 18 ft by 24 ft with one segmental side, an oval library, and square vestibule. The rooms are decorated with simple Adamesque ornament. Notable as Belle Isle is as an early attempt to combine the picturesque and sublime, it is the more so as having been chosen by that sublime eccentric, the Bishop of Derry, as the prototype for Ballyscullion and Ickworth (p. 239), the two pre-eminent great neo-classical country houses.

The latter stands in isolated oddity as the product of neo-classical logic unchecked by synthesis with visual and empirical sense, i.e. the picturesque. Other neo-classical architects of country houses designed circular and domed buildings, but not as country houses. George Steuart pro-

duced St Chad's Church, Shrewsbury, with its circular nave, but Attingham (p. 195) is distinguished for its squareness (howbeit intended to contain a great domed space). The Rotunda that stood in Leicester Square was designed by Robert Mitchell (1793), little known, but shown to be an admirable architect by Moor Place, Much Hadham (Fig. 26; 1777), distinguished by its arched fenestration and delicate internal detail; and by Cottesbrooke, Northants., where he added tall semi-circular bows (*c.* 1795) to a Queen Anne mansion. Plaw's and Soane's rustic, and Holland's marine, neo-classicism begot many suburban villas for city gentry. Clare House, E. Malling, Kent, for John Larking (1797), with its combination in plan of circles, octagon and squares, and of tiered verandahs in elevation, is delightfully typical (Fig. 27). Michael Searles, its architect (1750–1813), was son of a Greenwich surveyor and showed the same skill for planning with basic forms both in his Circus there and in his picturesque ordering of the Paragon, Blackheath.

Not least remarkable is the Wyatts' reaction to picturesque neo-classicism. Fonthill Abbey (1796, collapsed 1807) was the gothic counterpart to Ickworth in that both were the unsynthesized fantasies of over-rich romantics. But in Belmont, Kent (*c.* 1792), for General, later Lord, Harris of Seringapatam, Samuel Wyatt showed how adaptable the domed bow and colonnade themes, first used at Heaton, were to picturesque deployment. He had used a pair of domed bows as angle-features in his reconstruction of Hurstmonceux Place, Sussex, *c.* 1777. At Belmont he virtually repeated that façade, like it adorned with Coade stone plaques, and similarly intended to be approached obliquely to an entrance elsewhere. The front, faced with yellow 'mathematical tiles' is in the nature of a decorative screen linking two colonnaded sides, both of which contain an entrance, the bows serving as hinges, and their domes helping the balance of these assymetrical but nicely integrated flanks. The verandah-colonnades, so effective in the composition, are here associated with a greenhouse, another adjunct demanded by neo-classical naturalists (cf. Shugborough, Fig. 146), which here is part of the house-plan no less than of the entrance elevation. Tiered colonnades, and the device of angle bows used as hinges, were repeated by James Wyatt (1800) in his extension of Goodwood House, Sussex, originally a plain rectangular house by Chambers, to a hexagon plan (Fig. 23): a picturesque and ingenious if scarcely the most successful application of neo-classical geometry to a country house.

V. PREFABRICATED MATERIALS

The progress of the 'industrial revolution' from 1760 onwards virtually introduced a new element to architecture—prefabricated or purpose-made components. This element entered largely into the neo-classical synthesis and eventually contributed to its discredit, replacing hand-craft by mechanical precision and making its refinements available to the middle class. It began to have both effects on the quality of the Adams' work after 1770, and after 1800 increasingly dominated the character of design, particularly internal decoration. During our period as a whole, however, architects

frequently inspired and controlled technics, in which the quality of design attained a high level. The contemporary development of ceramics and woven textiles are not included in the following notes.

Cast Iron

After 1750 the Darbys' methods of smelting by mineral fuel began to extend the production of cast iron from its traditional uses to engineering, building and decoration. From then till 1820 constant innovations were being made. T. F.

Pritchard's famous iron bridge over the Severn at Coalbrookdale was erected 1777–79; Boulton and Watt's engines, produced at the Soho Works, Birmingham, from 1774, facilitated development of various industrial processes (cf. below, Ormolu). The first and principal factory for secondary iron products was a branch of the Carron Ironworks at Falkirk, opened in 1759 by Roebuck and Garbett, of which John Adam became a partner in 1764. R. Adam's delicate ornamental detail was well adapted to cast iron (cf. Kedleston, Newby); and where previously railings, gates, verandahs, fireplaces, vases and urns had been wrought, architects could now obtain standard cast designs, or combine cast with wrought iron, lead, or steel[1]—notably in grate-furniture. The Carron designers 1779–1837 were the brothers William and Henry Haworth, sons of a London carver and R.A. students, to whom are due the neo-classical patterns of many hob grates and their panels. By the end of the century several firms supplied the elegant cast iron balustrading, later derived from L. N. Cottingham's designs, used for verandahs and balconies. The structural use of cast iron was greatly developed by Nash (see Attingham, p. 201) and Smirke in the early 19th century; but the Wyatts introduced cast iron capitals for columns at Heaton *c.* 1772 (p. 19).

Coade Stone

A factory was established (near the S. end of Waterloo Bridge) by Richard Holt who, with Thomas Ripley the architect, in 1722 patented 'a compound liquid metall by which artificial stone and marble is made by casting . . . as statues, columns, capitalls, etc.' This functioned for some thirty years. The same patent appears to have been used by Daniel Pincot at his works at Goldstone Square, Whitechapel, from whom emanated a stock of 'busts, figures, vases, tables, friezes, medallions and chimneypieces' sold by Christie in 1767 and 1771. At the latter date Pincot was tenant of the site (on Belvedere Road, Lambeth) identified since 1769 with Coade's. Their grinding-pan, various moulds and fragments, came to light during excavation of the Festival of Britain site.

After George Coade died in 1770, the business was carried on by his widow Eleanor, then aged sixty-one, with their daughter (1733–1821) of the same name, herself a capable modeller, and possibly the directing mind throughout. After Mrs Coade senior's death in 1796, her nephew John Sealy was taken into partnership. The family came from Lyme Regis, where Mrs Coade afterwards owned an existing house ('Belmont') in which the material is used.

Both Holt (1730) and Pincot (1770) issued treatises on their material, the latter stating that its discovery was a bi-product of experiments for perfecting porcelain. Coade's 'Lithodipyra, Terra-Cotta or Artificial Stone' was evidently an improvement (see Syon, where it was used to replace almost immediately a rival brand that had crazed in frost). Its exact composition and production method was the Coades' secret and died with them, but the results of modern analysis are given by S. B. Hamilton (see below).

From the first, John Bacon (1740–99) was retained as principal modeller at Coades, but subsequently other sculptors supplied designs and James Paine was one of several designers of architectural components. The firm's first catalogue (produced for private circulation) contains 36 pages of designs ranging from the 'River God' statue (engraved by Blake) after Bacon's bronze at Somerset House. A catalogue of 1784 lists 778 patterns, an Ionic capital costing 13s., the 'River God' £105, 'frizes' and fascia from 7s. 6d. to 5 guineas per foot. The prospectus issued in 1799 refers to the new exhibition gallery (at the corner of Westminster Bridge Road) as containing 135 objects including a statuary group 12 ft high, numerous chimneypieces, and replicas of the figures erected round the dome of Holland's Brighton Pavilion. A list is also given of places where the products had been used (they have been found from Poland to Boston, U.S.A.). In 1813 on Sealy's death the foreman William Croggon entered the partnership. His son Thomas succeeded in 1836 but production ended the next year.

In a large proportion of the houses depicted in this volume Coade stone was used for external or internal ornament. Its qualities of fine texture, ductility, sharpness of profile and indestructibility perfectly suited it for repetitive enrichment and decorative sculpture, in which the artist's direct touch is not required, e.g. Fig. 31.

(Cf. R. Gunnis, *Dictionary of British Sculptors* ('Coade'); H. S. Kessels, in *Country Life Annual*, 1955; S. B. Hamilton, in *Architectural Review*, Dec., 1954.)

Facing Materials and Stucco Compositions

J. Gwynne's *London and Westminster Improved*, 1766, stated that 'no publick edifice ought to be built of brick unless it is afterwards stucco'd, for a mere brick face . . . makes a mean appearance'. The same opinion was generally held respecting country houses, particularly of red brick, Brown objecting to its clash with the green of nature. There was, however, no serviceable material available till David Wark of Haddington invented a stucco-duro in 1765, and in 1773 Liardet, a Swiss pastor, a much improved composition. The patents of both were bought by the Adams who obtained an Act of Parliament vesting in themselves the making and sale of 'Adam's new invented patent stucco'. In fact a number of such compositions were now on the market. J. Wyatt used Higgins's cement in 1779, in 1796 Parker's 'Roman Cement' was introduced which Nash was to use extensively until he changed, *c*, 1820, to Hamelin's or Dehl's Mastic. (See Ickworth, p. 239. for the Earl of Bristol's advocacy of 'dear old impeccable Palladio's stucco' on practical and historical grounds). The use internally of a quick-setting and therefore economical substitute for gesso-plaster undoubtedly had a deleterious effect on the character of the Adams' later designs, and of their imitators', by encouraging the use of slight and facile mouldings in ceilings, inset frames, etc. (see also *Papier Maché*).

'Mathematical or Rebate Tiles'

A flanged tile so made as to present when hung a vertical face which in appearance is scarcely distinguishable from brickwork, in place of which it was much used for weather-

---

[1] J. Gloag and D. Bridgwater, *A History of Cast Iron in Architecture*, 1948. J. Summerson, in *The Official Architect*, vol. VIII, No. 5.

facing. Prior to *c.* 1780 it is termed 'weather tile'—from which it was no doubt a specialized development—so that it is difficult to be certain whether references are to the flush setting which distinguishes the true 'mathematical tile'. There are examples in the south-eastern counties of *c.* 1720–50, which simulate red brickwork and suggest that weatherproofing was the primary purpose. The first use of white mathematical tiles is associated with Brown and Holland. For Sloane Place, his London house built *c.* 1775, the latter used 'weather tyles made in the New Forest, the price delivered in London £4 per thousand (which) will go as far as 1200 Bricks and (they) will resist weather longer' (quoted in D. Stroud, *Henry Holland*). Brown used white tiles (with Coade stone) at Cuffnells in the New Forest, *c.* 1775, and Soane at Sidney Lodge, Hamble, 1786, but significantly on S. and W. exposures only in both these instances. For Althorp in 1787 (p. 203) 100,000 white 'Rebate tiles' costing £315 were delivered at Lynn by William Gooding of Ipswich, who was also the principal maker of white bricks in East Anglia. Mathematical tiles were used by S. Wyatt at Belmont, Kent, 1792 (Fig. 28), for facing solid brickwork, presumably therefore for weather-tightness; at Attingham by Steuart, *c.* 1785 (p. 195), for lightness; and by Holland for the Brighton Pavilion (1786–88). They were much employed for 'modernizing' the fronts of old timber-framed houses in the south-eastern counties (*e.g.* at Canterbury), and in 'marine architecture'—*e.g.* the black glazed tiles of Royal Crescent, Brighton, *c.* 1800. Putty was sometimes used instead of mortar for the very fine bonding which usually distinguishes façades of Mathematical tiles and which encouraged their use.

Ormolu

Matthew Boulton (1728–1802) founded the Soho Works, Birmingham, in 1762, there combining heavy iron castings with his father's 'toy makers' business. This developed into the leading manufactory of ormolu. He was connected with and assisted by Mrs Montague, 'Queen of the Blues', and was employed by Adam, and by J. Stuart. Boulton is especially associated with candelabra and cassolets of blue john mounted in ormolu to Adam's designs, fashionable as chimney garniture, of which there are fine examples at Saltram. Ormolu was applied to the enrichment of chimney-pieces and doors, notably at Syon.

Papier Maché

This process, long practised in the East, was introduced in connection with japanning for picture frames, etc., *c.* 1670. In 1763 P. Babel, 'designer and modeller' in Long Acre, advertised 'Papier Maché Ornaments for Ceilings, Chimney-pieces, etc.'—of which examples in rococo taste are found at about that date, and thereafter as applied decoration in the Adam style. This was also developed by Henry Clay of Birmingham, who in 1772 perfected a type of board for japanning or painting in connection with furniture. An early decorative example of this is some door-panels at Kedleston (p. 70). The Earl of Bristol is stated (1791) to have had side-tables 'painted with designs brought from Rome' made by Clay.

Carpets

The first factory to be established in England, by French refugees, was that at Wilton in 1701 and appears to have originally specialized in strips of Turkey pattern till *c.* 1740, when the method of weaving pile carpets was introduced there and at Kidderminster. A short-lived carpet factory was established, also by French refugees, at Fulham 1750–55, after which it is said to been moved to Exeter *c.* 1758. The most successful factory, however, was that of Thomas Moore, at Chiswell St., Moorfields, to whom the Society of Arts awarded a premium in 1757. R. Adam provided many designs, surviving specimens of which are dated 1775 and 1778. Actual carpets are here illustrated at Syon (1769), and Saltram (cf. also Mersham le Hatch, Downton Castle, and Woodhall).

Wall-paper

Small sheets of paper printed from wood blocks for applying to walls were almost co-eval with printing itself. The French method invented about 1620 of producing flock papers in imitation of damasks, etc. was being practised in England in 1702, and about 1750 this English product became very fashionable in France.

In 1753 Edward Deighton patented a method of printing papers from engraved metal plates by a rolling mill, the impression then being coloured by hand. In the following year Jean Baptiste Jackson, an engraver who had established works in Battersea, issued a pamphlet on his 'Venetian prints and *chiaroscuro* papers', which Horace Walpole shortly afterwards used extensively at Strawberry Hill. A fine example of Jackson's *chiaroscuro* paper, which survives at Harrington House, Bourton on the Water, Glos., is in design a blend of rococo and landscape elements. The use of wallpaper increased during the period of rococo taste after 1745, but the greater part appears to have come from France, until 1779 when import from the Continent was prohibited. The effect of this protective measure was that the annual output of English wallpaper, given in 1770 as being 255,730 pieces, had risen thirty years later to twelve million. In 1786 A. and F. Eckhart in Chelsea, and Sheringham in Great Marlborough St., established factories of partly printed and partly hand-coloured papers. By 1795 Harwood, J. G. Hancock, and Robson, Hale and Co. were leading manufacturers. A development from J. B. Jackson's 'Venetian prints' was the rooms mounted with engravings for which both Chippendale and R. Parker supplied the materials (see Woodhall Park, Mersham le Hatch, Uppark; cf. also Heveningham, Stratfield Saye, Ston Easton).

Chinese wallpapers, often called 'Indian papers' from having been imported by the East India Company, were known and used before 1700. But the large, brightly coloured and populated sheets were a novelty in 1772, and few existing sets are prior to 1780, when they ranged in price from 7s. to 4s. per sheet. A notable group is illustrated at Saltram, Figs. 249–251.

(*Historic Wall-papers*, by Nancy McClelland, 1924; *English Interior Decoration*, 1550–1830, by M. Jourdain, 1950; *Chinese Export Art in the Eighteenth Century*, by M. Jourdain and R. S. Jenyns, 1950.)

32. *On the crest of the Sussex Downs: the William and Mary house from the south west.*

UPPARK, SUSSEX

Built for **The Earl of Tankerville**, *c.* 1690

Altered by **Sir Matthew and Sir Harry Fetherstonhaugh, 1747–75**

Architects **William Talman 1690; Paine** (?) *c.* 1750;
Keene *c.* 1770; **Repton 1805–13**

Owner **The National Trust (Admiral the Hon. Sir H.
Meade-Fetherstonhaugh)**

The bloom of intact continuity suffusing Uppark has caused it to be called 'the Sleeping Beauty house'. This effect, actually due to extraordinary chances of inheritance, is emphasized by the unusual site: on the top of the West Sussex Downs. The brick walls that rise from the short turf have been scoured by the gales of four centuries, but their summers seem to linger in the faded rooms. The art and air that fill them are of the 18th century, meticulously maintained through the 19th and lovingly revived in the 20th. But the site, defying convention and one would say hydraulics, is due to 17th-century science. The story of how that was brought to bear on the choice of site forms the first of the sequence of coincidences that gives Uppark's history the character of a fairy tale. It was also the first process in the synthesis of 'romance' with classical art which has produced the most typical English country houses and in this case perhaps the most appealing of any.

The manor of East Harting was already owned under Henry VIII by the Ford family of whom Sir Edward became not only the Royalist leader in West Sussex but a noted engineer. Mastering the principles of the water-ram, he in 1656, according to Anthony Wood, 'raised the Thames water into all the highest streets of London, 93 ft high in pipes with a rare engine of his own invention'. Esteemed 'a great virtuoso' for his various 'experimented proposals', he was buried at Harting in 1670, when his estate went to his daughter, wife of Lord Grey of Wark. Their son Ford Grey

inherited the Northumbrian title and Sussex estates in 1674, together with his father's extreme Whiggism. A prime mover in the Oates and Rye House plots, and a partisan of Monmouth at Sedgemoor, his nonconformity at length triumphed with William of Orange who created him Earl of Tankerville. As speculative in planning as in politics he then, after 1689, was enabled by knowledge of his grandfather's 'rare engine' to make the 'up park', already planted with avenues, the site for a new house. Indeed this mechanism, contained in a building still standing at the foot of the approach from the village, long continued responsible for its water supply.

On the uncorroborated authority of Dallaway (*History of West Sussex*, 1815) his architect was William Talman (1650–1720) who, if it was he, was content to give elevations in the William and Mary idiom to a U plan suggestive of an earlier period, leaving the re-entrant north side rather plain 'Mary Ann'. The brick elevations of the three fronts, with stone dressings, wood cornice and pitched roof, bear no analogy to Talman's generally baroque work and drawings, but resemble Swallowfield (Berks.), Herriard and formerly Stansted (Hants.) attributed to him. Close counterparts are Webb's Ramsbury (1669), and Stoke Edith (1699). In this case Talman, like Wren sometimes, may have given or approved a straightforward design for a local builder to carry out. In the sculptured pediment the white-painted Portland stone shield bears the arms of Fetherstonhaugh replacing those of Tankerville now on a cottage at Rake.

The original entry was in the E. side where a forecourt was flanked by detached stable pavilions linked by a *claire-voie*. Their position is shown both by Kip's engraving and a landscape by Wootton in the house (Figs. 37 and 38); they were removed probably *c.* 1770, when similar blocks were erected N.E. and N.W. of the house, to which they are joined by long subterranean passages. In 1698 Celia Fiennes 'rode through a very ffine Park, stately woods and fine trees', which must therefore have ante-dated the new house. She confirms that this stood 'in the midst of fine gardens, gravell and grass

33. *The Dairy, and the west wing.*

and when lawns, as here, extend twenty miles in each direction over hill and dale, with the chequer-pattern of farms and woodlands instead of flower beds, the grand simplicity is felt to be appropriate. About 1805 Repton scarcely presumed to 'suggest any improvement or alteration to a place possessing so many natural advantages.' His proposals of a great terrace ending in a sheer drop, and the linking of house to wings with colonnades as part of his replanning of the approach, were not adopted. But he designed the existing N. entrance where his Doric portico screens a labyrinth of office quarters and partly conceals the original rear elevation.

On Lord Tankerville's death in 1747, Chillingham and the title passed to his daughter, Lady Ossulston, but the Sussex estate was sold. By the second of the strange chances that have shaped Upark's character, there had recently died a rich citizen of London named Sir Henry Fetherston, without children as were also his nine brothers and sisters. For his heir he had selected a young and remote kinsman, Matthew Fetherstonhaugh, son of a Mayor of Newcastle, and be-

walks with breast walls. At ye Entrance a large Court with Iron Gates open to a less'. But 'ascending some steps (freestone in the round) thence up more steps to a terrass so to the house,' she evidently strayed to the S. front where Kip shows the terrace. The positions of this and the 'breast walls' are still traceable in the turf, but they are not shown in Wootton's view, *c.* 1740. One suspects that Dutch gardening on this exposed site was soon abandoned in favour of landscape;

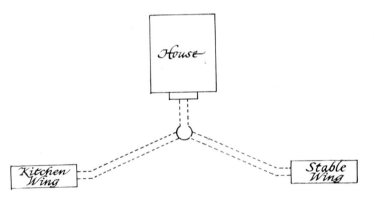

35. *Diagram showing the subterranean passages to the kitchen and stable wings.*

queathed to him £400,000 conditionally on his acquiring a country seat and a baronetcy. Sir Matthew, as he promptly became, bought Upark and had the fortune to be ideally married to Sarah, only daughter of Christopher Lethieullier, of Belmont, Middlesex. This well-to-do family, portrayed in eight small portraits by A. Devis which hang up the stairs (Figs. 54–56), was of Huguenot stock and cultivated tastes; these and some fine furniture she brought to Upark, together with her doll's house (Fig. 59) completely furnished in the Palladian taste of her childhood. Sir Matthew's and his lady's meticulous accounts record exemplary lives. When they had first came to Upark the bell-ringers of Harting welcomed them (1 guinea); in 1749–51 they went abroad; by 1759 they estimated that £16,615 had been spent at Upark on buildings, pictures, furniture, etc.—but no reference is made to any architect.

About the same time (1755–58) Sir Matthew built a London residence since known as Dover or Melbourne House in Whitehall, now the Scottish Office, from designs by James Paine. In the rooms redecorated at Upark there are features characteristic of his style *c.* 1760, but though all have classical cornices and notable chimneypieces of Paine patterns, their treatment is so varied that the impression given is not that of a professional hand but of the owners'

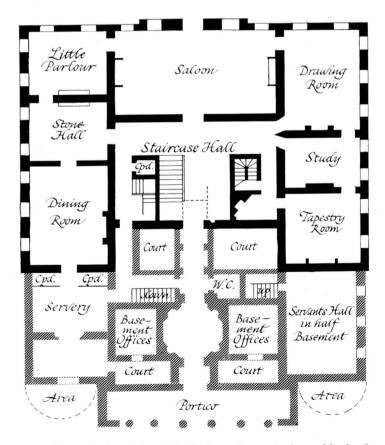

34. *Ground Floor Plan. The Talman house is shown black, the additions by Repton hatched. The top is South.*

36. *Part of the downland view from the south front.*

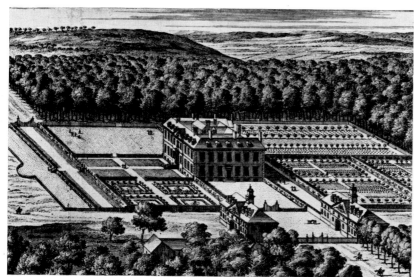

37. *Kip's view of Lord Tankerville's garden and forecourt from the east.*

38. *The house, east pavilions and pool, c. 1740. Detail from a painting by J. Wootton.*

39. *The centre of the south front, 1690.*

41. *The staircase. On the pink painted walls, Lethieullier family portraits by A. Devis.*

40. *The Stone Hall, originally the Entrance Hall, in the east front.*

42. *The Drawing Room, c. 1760. The rococo ceiling pale blue and white; faded crimson flock-paper; a rose and brick red Axminster carpet.* 43. *The south east door of the Saloon, c. 1770. In the entablature writhing snakes take the place of brackets; the return of the window on the right has markedly neo-classical ornament.*

44. *The Saloon in the south front, c. 1770. The original gilding and ivory white walls: indigo blue ground Wilton carpet.*

personal tastes over a decade. Little altered since, they provide a rare index to domestic fashion between 1750 and 1770.

From the Stone Hall, the original entrance in the E. front, coloured duck-egg green, a corridor leads to the opposite front, broadening in the middle into the staircase hall (Fig. 41). This has a rococo ceiling and palest pink walls as painted *c.* 1759. The original eight-panelled doors were retained, instead of the six-panelled pattern inserted elsewhere; also the original oak staircase with spiral balusters, of which the white and gold paint was found beneath Regency graining, with the name of young Harry Fetherstonhaugh scratched on the handrail. His portrait, aged four, by Reynolds hangs over the chimneypiece in the little parlour adjoining the Stone Hall to the S.E., which has its original red brocade curtains and a ceiling of neo-classical pattern *en suite* with the adjoining saloon.

45. One of the Saloon chimneypieces.

46. The Prince Regent's Bedroom. The bed hung with the original crimson damask (1754).

47. *The dressing room above the Saloon. Engravings mounted in printed borders, and, in the dado, flower-pots cut from Chinese paper, decorate the walls. A fixed mirror in stucco frame is provided in several of the bedrooms, as here.*

48. *The Dining Room. The woodwork c. 1690. The relief above the door by Garrard, and the Wedgwood basalt busts, added c. 1810.*

The long Drawing Room, filling the S. half of the West front, preserves most completely the taste of Sir Matthew and his lady at their coming to Uppark (Fig. 42). The rococo-classic ceiling has baskets and wreaths of flowers, modelled *in situ* a little crudely, the ground coloured pale blue. The curtains are of brilliant light crimson dating from 1754; and the flock wallpaper of damask pattern, now faded to burnt sienna, is deep crimson where a picture has covered it. On the oak floor, unstained as throughout the house, is an early Axminster carpet of pink and brick red with a green pattern.

Above the doors are portraits of the children, painted at Rome by Pompeo Battoni in 1751, and above the fireplace that of Harry, the eldest, by the same master twenty-five years later. Between the windows a pair of magnificent rococo mirrors, dating from Sir Matthew's marriage, hang above black and gold japanned commodes probably bought in the '70s. The mahogany furniture, bleached by two centuries of South Down sunshine, is of various dates. Periodical payments are recorded by Sir Matthew to 'Mr Hallet' for furniture. Two square rooms adjoin northwards, also with contemporary wallpapers. The 'tapestry room' was originally the master's bedroom with convenient access to a back stairs; it has a paper of mulberry and buff with black lines, largely covered by a Brussels Teniers tapestry (Leyniers).

The Saloon (Fig. 44), occupying the five centre bays of the S. front, is difficult to assign or date precisely. The spatial treatment is neo-classical. But there is Palladian influence in the compartmented ceiling, and in the two great chimneypieces (Fig. 45) with busts of Homer and Virgil, red granite imposts and Siena entablatures, and plaques of Androcles and Romulus respectively. The simulated dome is even a baroque memory. But the 'flowing *rinceau*' ornament in the ceiling cove and panels resembles early Adam work and indeed Paine's principal ceiling in Dover House. The entablatures of the doors lack Palladian pediments, and are supported by writhing snakes in place of brackets (Fig. 43), or by columns; that of the middle windows has markedly neo-classical ornament. The wall-treatment is dictated by the great pictures by Luca Giordano of the Prodigal Son, brought from Italy by Sir Matthew; over the chimneypieces George III and Queen Charlotte when nearing middle age, by Dance, and over the N. door Harry Fetherstonhaugh *c*. 1770, also by Dance. Except for Regency bookcases, most of these features suggest that the room was completed about 1770, the date to which the indigo-ground Wilton carpet probably belongs.

As the ceiling was raised when the Saloon was formed, the character of the truncated rooms above bears on the problem of date. One is a 'print room' (Fig. 47) analogous to that decorated by Chippendale at Mersham le Hatch, 1770 (cf. also Woodhall Park, dated 1782). The dado is similarly decorated with pots of flowers, probably cut from Chinese wallpaper and pasted on. The fixed mirror in rococo plaster frame is one of several instances in the bedrooms.

If the Saloon's decoration was applied about 1770, it shows suggestive similarities to Henry Keene's rococo-classicism, as at Bowood and Hartwell (*E.C.H.*, *Early*

49. *A carved and painted chimneypiece c.* 1760 *against turquoise blue flock paper.*

Georgian); indeed a bill refers to 'packing cases, etc. ordered by Mr Keene' but left unpaid after Sir Matthew's death in 1774. A drawing by Keene is preserved for a triangular Gothick structure known as the Vandalian Tower erected *c*. 1770 in the park, the ruins of which remain. It is so called from a scheme in which Sir Matthew interested himself for founding a new colony called Vandalia on the R. Ohio. The American War of Independence put an end to the project, this sole surviving relic of which may, however, give the clue to the authorship of the Saloon.

Whatever the secret, the great room has a haunting beauty, with its five tall windows looking to the vast view. The original white paint has that opaque bluish tinge due to the high proportion of white lead that has ensured its permanence. The gilding is equally fresh and applied with notable delicacy, giving an effect of extreme refinement; it is more tarnished in the French chairs upholstered in *petit point* of La Fontaine's fables, but glows in the ormolu chandelier. The curtains, of the original ivory silk brocade, are of the draw-up pattern usual at this period, which has the advantage of not concealing the architraves. It is found in all these rooms, also in the dolls' house (see below).

Sir Harry, aged twenty when his father died, inherited

50. *The entrance vestibule,* c. 1810, *within the north portico (Fig. 53).*   51. *Coloured glass window,* 1813, *in the dining-room lobby.*   52. *One of the subterranean passages, connecting with the wings.*

his parents' culture and affection for Uppark, besides wealth and tastes that soon made him one of the Prince of Wales's circle. In a London 'night club' he discovered Emma Hart in 1780 and brought her to live with him at Uppark. In the Dining Room there is still the table on which she is said to have posed. A year later she was adopted by Charles Greville, who was to introduce her to his uncle Sir William Hamilton. Sir Harry's attachment to her appears to have been genuinely

53. *The north entrance portico: H. and J. A. Repton,* c. 1810.

romantic, so that he was the more disillusioned by the liaison's failure and long remained a hospitably social bachelor. A guest, describing preparations for a vist by the Prince and the Duc de Chartres in 1785, wrote: 'The entertainment is to last 3 days, with races of all sorts to be upon the most beautiful spot of ground I believe that England can produce, and three hot dishes of meat a regular part of each morning's break-fast.' At other times the regime was informal, the same guest, Miss Iremonger, telling how she 'frequently drove in the harvest fields by moonlight and supped on our return by the same light without candles.'

The Prince's bed is preserved (Fig. 46), a noble Chippen-dale four-poster surmounted by gilt cupids and hung with the crimson damask which Sarah, Lady Fetherstonhaugh, brought to Uppark in 1754. Beneath the white paint of the rooms' panelling traces are visible of the original black, green and gilt *chinoiserie* of Lord Tankerville's decoration. The course of the three hot breakfast dishes can still be followed, through the subterranean tunnel leading to the kitchen in the N.E. wing; a good hundred yards under the forecourt, where a similar tunnel branches off to the stables in the N.W. wing.

It was Repton, in 1805, who recommended that a new entrance should be made on the N. side, by building a portico joined to the Staircase Hall by a domed octagon Vestibule and arched corridor (Fig. 50). It would 'give great apparent depth and magnificence to the entrance'; and it enabled the addition of a labyrinth of servants' rooms in the basement, or screened by the portico (see plan, Fig. 34). The correspondence preserved also shows that Repton and his son J. A. Repton in 1810–13 assisted with the remodelling of the Dining Room (Fig. 48). Painted white and gilt, it adjoins the Stone Hall to the N., retaining at either end Talman's baroque woodwork, in which the recessed alcoves have con-

54, 55, 56. *Three members of the Lethieullier family from the series by Arthur Devis hanging on the staircase.*

temporary carved drops. The mirrors were now added; with animal reliefs by Garrard placed above the doors (like those introduced by Holland at Woburn and Southill); and Wedgwood basalt busts over the alcoves—of Napoleon, Fox, 'Wm. Battine Esq.', a Sussex poet of the period, and Francis, Duke of Bedford testifying to Sir Harry's Whiggism. A service lobby was added opening to the N. end of the dining room and given a window of stained glass to be illumined from behind (Fig. 51). 'The principal object', Repton wrote, 'will be figures in clear obscure from a pure classical source, as my son has made sketches from the marbles imported from Athens by Lord Elgin. . . . By candlelight the effect will be magic, as all the light may proceed from this window from Argand lamps adjusted from behind' (in a kind of passage behind the portico). The window is signed W. Doyle, 1813.

Three years later Uppark was among the properties considered for purchase by the Duke of Wellington. Sir Harry, being unmarried and no doubt poorer than he was, apparently considered selling Uppark. But instead, at the age of seventy, he married (in the Saloon) Mary Ann Bullock, said to have

been at one time the dairy maid, whom he had educated in France for her new station. Perhaps she reminded him of Emma. Lady Fetherstonhaugh made him an admirable wife, till he died in 1847 aged ninety-three, and herself lived another thirty years, then bequeathing Uppark to her unmarried sister, Miss Bullock-Fetherstonhaugh. Meticulous in maintaining everything 'as Sir 'Arry 'ad it', so she would say, she lived till 1895, with her housekeeper Mrs Wells. The latter's son was H. G. Wells. He has described how, in this household thus essentially unchanged since the mid-18th century, he would as a boy chase the maids along the tunnels.

To perpetuate this singular continuity, Miss Fetherstonhaugh left Uppark and her name, subsequent to the life interest of Major Keith Turnour-Fetherstonhaugh, to the third surviving son of a neighbour, Admiral the Earl of Clanwilliam. In 1930, therefore, the property and name passed to Admiral the Hon. Sir Herbert Meade, G.C.V.O. Conservative repairs were made to the structure and Lady Meade-Fetherstonhaugh began the prodigious task of salvaging the contents. After two centuries the faded, brittle

57, 58. *The hall and (right) the kitchen in Sarah Lethieullier's dolls' house.*

59, 60. The front and (right) the drawing room of the dolls' house.

curtains of windows and beds were hanging in tatters; the papers, tapestries and chair-covers falling apart. The most remarkable operation, which is still going on, has been the repairing from head to foot of the sun-rotted curtains. Each in turn is put on a special frame, restitched to its backing, then the original brilliant colour restored by washing with a lotion of *saponaria*. The final stage in safeguarding the continuity of Uppark was effected in 1954 by its gift by Sir Herbert and his son to the National Trust, which received grants for maintenance from the Pilgrim and Dulverton Trusts. Finally an anonymous benefactor has contributed the cost of roof repairs and the overhauling of Repton's

somewhat shoddy northern additions. The unique contents are on loan to the Trust by the family, who it is intended will continue to live in Uppark.

It is particularly fitting that this uniquely preserved Georgian home should contain the very matrix of the domestic arts that created and have maintained it: the dolls' house in which Sarah Lethieullier as a child practised her technique. The house (Figs. 57–62), presumably dating from *c.* 1730, has a Palladian façade of three storeys, seven bays wide, surmounted by gilt statues and rests on a stand which contained the stable. The front opens in nine sections, each revealing a room furnished and peopled in the style of her youth.

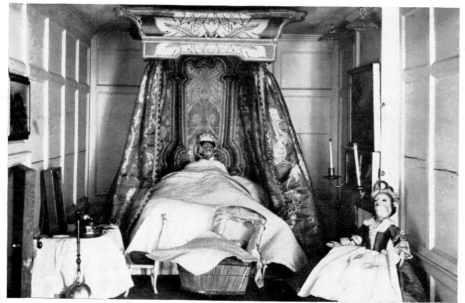

61. *The principal bedroom.*   62. *The Palladian entrance to the dolls' house.*

ARBURY HALL, WARWICKSHIRE

Gothicized by **Sir Roger Newdigate, 1750–1800**

Architects **(Wren, 1674); Hiorn and S. Miller, 1748; Keene, 1762–76; H. Couchman, 1776–90**

Craftsmen **(E. Martin, 1678); W. Hitchcox; R. Moor; B. King; W. Wise; G. Higham; W. Hanwell**

Owner **Mr H. Fitzroy Newdegate**

Sir Roger Newdigate, 5th Baronet (1719–1800), well exemplified the active and versatile trend often found associated with rococo, though in politics he was Tory—'a half converted Jacobite' Horace Walpole called him. As transformed by him during fifty years, Arbury Hall near Nuneaton is indeed the outstanding example of rococo gothick. Mr Gordon Nares, on whose documentary researches this description is based, has commented that when Arbury was illustrated in *Country Life* in 1907 'the author mentioned the Gothic work in passing as a rather unfortunate blemish on a house which nevertheless contained some interesting 17th century decoration'; whereas, he continued, if ideas of structural truth are discarded and it is regarded as a form of rococo decoration, the style of these rooms has 'an undoubted charm, not to say beauty'; offering genuine diversity of shape and vitality of decoration.

The quadrangular house probably preserves the plan of an Augustinian Priory that was acquired from its immediate grantees by Sir Edward Anderson, an ambitious Elizabethan lawyer; but Dugdale states that he 'totally demolished the old fabric and built out of their ruins a very fair structure'.

In 1586, after his appointment to be Chief Justice of Common Pleas, Anderson exchanged this for the more accessible manor of Harefield, Middlesex, with John Newdegate, of a cadet branch of a family established at Newdigate, Surrey, *temp* King John. His son John married Anne Fitton, sister of 'the Dark Lady' of Shakespeare's sonnets (of whom a portrait is preserved). Their second son Richard, who succeeded an elder brother in 1642, continued to build up a lucrative legal practice under both Cromwell, his son and Charles II. Thereby he not only restored the family's declining fortune but added the Astley manor to Arbury and recovered Harefield, besides receiving a baronetcy before his death in 1678. In 1665 he made over Arbury to his son Richard, who undertook important additions before his death in 1710.

A drawing,[1] from a lost original by H. Beighton, 1708, shows the Anderson house still unaltered externally but with the new adjuncts. Of these the stable, N.E. of the quadrangle, survives and is of particular interest owing to its association with Wren. An undated account[2] for this building refers to digging the foundations, making a model, the expenses 'at London with Sir C. Wren and carrying up the Modell', 'meeting Sir C. Wren at Oxford', £11 spent on a pair of silver candlesticks for Sir Christopher, and £2 for 'his men for 2 draughts of ye porch'; also £1 for a drawing by Sir William Wilson. An agreement for the new stables, made with William and Martin Bond, is dated 1675. Wren himself

---

[1] Aylesford Coll. Birmingham Reference Library.
[2] Newdigate Papers, Warwick C.R.O.

63. The south front, as gothicised by Sir Roger Newdigate, 1748–75.

64. The east front, and saloon bow, c. 1785.

65. The entrance, north front, c. 1792.

writes (Aug. 15) sending a design for the porch, and, some-what testily (Nov. 11), submitted an alternative design.[1] The evidence, though inconclusive, warrants assigning the Ionic entablature of the centre porch to Wren (Fig. 67), and sug-gests that Wilson may have provided the design for the whole range which, with its brick walls, stone dressings, mullioned windows and three Dutch gables, is consistent with his other known works in the district.

The Chapel (Fig. 68), in the N. range of the house, was decorated in 1678 when an agreement was made for the

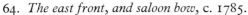

[1] Cf. Wren Society, XII, Pl. XLIX.

highly enriched ceiling with Edward Martin 'of the City of London, Plaisterer'. On the walls the shouldered bolection-framed panels are divided by festoons hanging from putti-heads. Part of an agreement for this was endorsed by Sir Roger (120 years later) 'by Gibbons'. This is stylistically unlikely, but Gibbons executed monuments for Sir Richard at Ashtead and Harefield. The formal garden and pavilions shown by Beighton followed *c.* 1700, when trees were pur-chased from London and Wise's nursery, but these all dis-appeared when Sir Roger naturalized the surroundings. The other chief pre-Georgian feature is the Gallery, running the length of the N. front on the first storey, which is lined with

66. South view, showing the stables, in 1708.
A drawing by H. Beighton.

67. Sir C. Wren's portal to the stables, 1670–75.

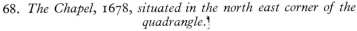

68. *The Chapel,* 1678, *situated in the north east corner of the quadrangle.*

69. *Chimneypiece,* c. 1575, *of the Long Gallery in the north range.*

oak wainscot and retains its original stone chimneypiece of *c.* 1575 (Fig. 69). The painted wood overmantel, containing the arms of Newdegate impaling Fitton, is slightly later and may have been moved from another room.

Sir Roger Newdigate,[1] seventh and youngest son of the 3rd Baronet, succeeded a brother in 1734 at the age of fifteen. His impressionable years were thus the '40s, when thoughtful young men, reacting from Platonism and Walpole, were beginning to view the nature of things empirically, and at Oxford critically. On his Grand Tour he sketched buildings and picturesque views, and for the rest of his life had a dilettante's interest in the antique. But he was also active in managing his estates, developing their mineral resources, and in promotion of canals, and sat for forty years in Parliament, representing Oxford 1750–80. His interest in the University is still commemorated by the Newdigate Prize for poetry, and in his College (University) took the form of assisting the redecoration of its hall in the gothick manner (1766). Significantly it was at the same College that the last traditional gothic work had been carried out, the Radcliffe Gate, in 1719. It is not wholly surprising, therefore, that a man of his temperament, inheriting an old house with monastic connections, set about transforming it as he did during the rest of his long life.

<hr />

[1] He adopted this spelling of his surname.

In 1748, when twenty-nine, he procured Hiorn to make a plan and was perhaps already consulting Sanderson Miller, who shared many of his sympathies; a correspondent of the latter referred in 1750 to meeting him at Arbury and to seeing 'a Bow Window'. Since, in 1752, W. Hitchcox, a mason whom Miller employed, received £50 for the 'Gothick Bow window at ye west end of ye Front', and this window (on the left of Fig. 63) is identical, except for additional cresting, to those built by Miller at Radway, the inference is substantiated. In 1754 the Library that the bow window lights was begun (Fig. 70), and Sir Roger's account book next year is annotated 'Will Hiorn Library fitted up'. The plasterer was R. Moor (who, like Hiorn, worked for Miller at Radway) and the carver B. King (cf. *E.C.H., Early Georgian:* Kyre Park, 1756). Its painted barrel ceiling, rather more Etruscan than Gothick, was painted by W. Wise in 1761, and about the same time Arthur Devis painted Sir Roger sitting in the room with an assured look and a plan of Arbury on his knee (Fig. 72). The Library is closely comparable to that at Strawberry Hill, completed in 1754 and no doubt Newdigate's model; both have painted ceilings, but, whilst Walpole adopted 'Decorated' gothic, here the detail of the panelling sensitively imitates the Late Perpendicular that is so much in evidence at Oxford.

The E. bay of the garden front, the panels of which are cut with deeper conviction, was built in 1760 and the 'Parlour fitted up' within it in 1763. Like the Library it is low and rectangular with a barrel ceiling, but in this case Perpendicular panelling is used throughout confidently (Fig. 74). The chimneypiece, however, is specifically derived from Aymer de Valence's tomb in Westminster Abbey; its carver was Richard Hayward (paid £90 in 1764), who also carved chimneypieces for Sir Roger's London house in Spring Gardens and a monument at Harefield (1776). It is nearly identical to that erected by Sir Roger in University College hall, and both were almost certainly designed by Henry Keene who was Surveyor to the Abbey (see *E.C.H., Early Georgian*.)

The account book for 1762 notes 'H. Keene, Architect, drawings etc. 15 gns', and a number of letters from him dated 1768 are preserved relating mainly to Harefield and none to Arbury. They prove Sir Roger a firm patron, refer to 'our intended building at Balliol', and to a plan for repairing the anti-chapel at Magdalen, 'for all of which I am obliged to you as my kind Introductor'. The Parlour chimneypiece can be regarded as Keene's first work here.

There was a lull at Arbury 1764–70, during which both Sir Roger and Keene were busy at Oxford. In 1770 the staircase, next the Library, was plastered by W. Moor, then in 1771 Keene was paid £24 for 'Front Hall etc.'. This alluded to the kind of enclosed gothick portico projecting in the middle of the S. front (Fig. 63), and to the Dining Room to which this feature provides an 'aisle' (Figs. 73, 77). The external treatment is reminiscent of the Divinity School, Oxford, whilst the fan-vaulting, like Keene's ceiling of Hartwell Church (1753–56), obviously follows such examples as Henry VII's Chapel and Christ Church staircase. The fireplace arch, beneath a noble tomb-like canopy, contains a diapered alcove in which the magnificent steel and brass grate must have been specially designed. The canopied wall-niches contain classical figures, recalling that Sir Roger exerted himself to endow the Radcliffe Library with antique sculpture including the Arundel Marbles. The 'hall' was finished in 1779 (Thomas Morris, mason, Roger Roe, joiner, G. Higham, plasterer), Henry Couchman having taken Keene's place as supervisor after his death in 1776. The room is a wholly pleasing achievement, both in conception and execution, the more so now when hung with a notable assembly of Tudor portraits. Its details can be credited to Keene; but the consistency with which the style is used throughout Arbury, before and after as well as during his association, must indicate Sir Roger as controlling if not also originating the whole. Keene died in debt, for the accounts of the London house contain the entry (1779) 'H. Keene, Builder, who after receiving 500 to pay workmen pd

70. *The Library in the west end of the south front, 1754–61.*

71. The Library chimneypiece.   *72. Sir Roger Newdigate seated in the Library. A. Devis, c. 1761.*

180 and became insolvent'. In 1787 the missing £320 was written off as a bad debt.

Couchman was a Warwick quarry-owner and contractor, besides 'Surveyor' as Sir Roger called him, who could 'take skitches at Westminster Abbey'; payments to him continued till 1790. Chiefly employed on structural work, he completed the battlements of the S. front in 1777, and rebuilt the other fronts and internal cloisters during the 1780s. Their ornamental features are separately credited, the carving of the arcaded *porte cochère* to John Alcott of Coventry in 1796. These elevations, with turrets containing the chimney flues, are as conventionally disposed as is the S. front in fact, but unrelieved by the zest of Keene's or indeed Miller's earlier pastiche. This, by inference, was their contribution. In his later years Sir Roger was evidently satisfied with exteriors that notably lack the 'picturesque' variety of Strawberry Hill and of Payne Knight's contemporary Downton Castle (p. 148). Such was his architectural 'introversion', he might almost have reversed Knight's desiderata; gothick rooms and classical exterior.

The Saloon (Fig. 75), the principal room in the E. front, adjoins the end of the Parlour, and received its plaster decoration by W. Hanwell in 1786. The superlative quality of this remarkable room must be credited to the plasterers. But, since its ceiling so clearly derives from Henry VII's Chapel, Keene not improbably may have at least discussed its treatment before his death, notwithstanding Couchman's 'sundry skitches'. The quality of the stucco tracery, and in particular that of the bow, of which the glazing was supplied in 1795 by James Brooks and Sons, is shown in Fig. 76. Beneath the 'grand Gothic canopy' of fan vaults and pen-

dants, set off by a splendid chandelier, are Romney's portraits of Sir Roger and his second wife, painted in 1791; and the most remarkable piece of furniture at Arbury, the cedar cabinet in the French Renaissance style *c.* 1630, which belonged to Archbishop Laud. In the sitting room adjoining (also with a fan-vaulted ceiling) is a version, probably 17th century, of the panel painting depicting the tournament combats of Sir John Astley with Peter de Masse and Sir Philip Boyle, fought in 1438 and 1441 (Fig. 79), given in 1773 by the Sir John Astley of the time to Sir Roger as lord of the manor of Astley. A set of chairs with needlework copied from the panel formerly belonged to the Astley family at Melton Constable.

For long after Sir Roger's death in 1806, memory of the octogenarian squire and his fifty years' labours on Arbury remained fresh in people's minds, so that 'George Eliot' (Mary Anne Evans, daughter of the agent at Arbury), though born only in 1819, portrayed him in *Mr Gilfil's Love Story*—one of her *Scenes from Clerical Life* (1858). Sir Christopher Cheverel similarly metamorphosed his family mansion, 'thus anticipating, through the prompting of his individual taste, that general reaction from the insipid imitation of the Palladian style towards a restoration of the Gothic, which marked the close of the 18th century'. She perceptively attributed 'that unswerving architectural purpose of his to something of the fervour of genius'. In conclusion, it merits record that in 1954 the Minister of Town and Country Planning (Mr Harold Macmillan) reprieved Arbury from the National Coal Board's decision to mine the 'pillar' on which it stands, on account of the building's outstanding artistic and historic interest.

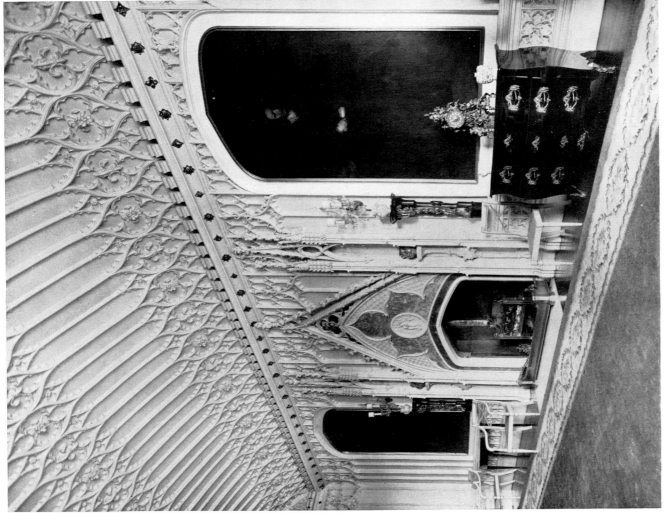

74. *The Drawing Room ('Parlour'), 1761–63. In the east end of the south front. The chimney-piece from the tomb of Aymer de Valence.*

73. *The fan vaulted Dining Room ('Hall'): Henry Keene architect, 1762. It occupies the centre of the south front.*

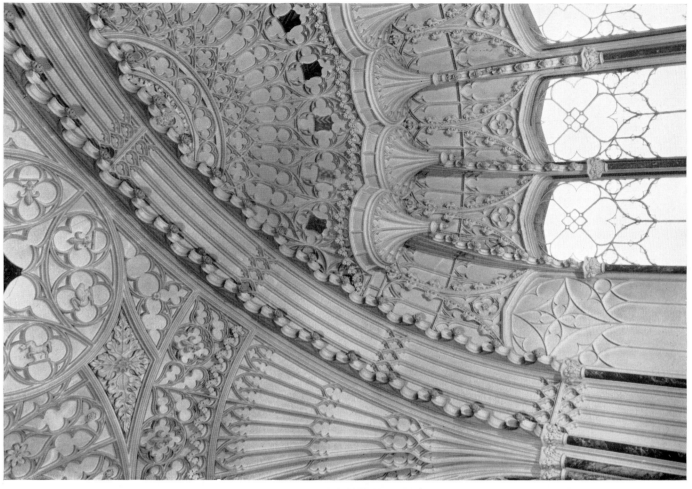

76. *Plasterwork of the bow window of the Saloon. Completed by W. Hanwell, 1786.*

75. *The Saloon, in the east front, 1776–86. Romney's portraits of Sir Roger and his second wife hang on the left.*

78. *Brass box lock by John Wilkes of Birmingham. In the chapel, c. 1678.*

79. *Part of a panel depicting the combat of Sir John de Astley with Peter de Masse at Paris in 1438.*

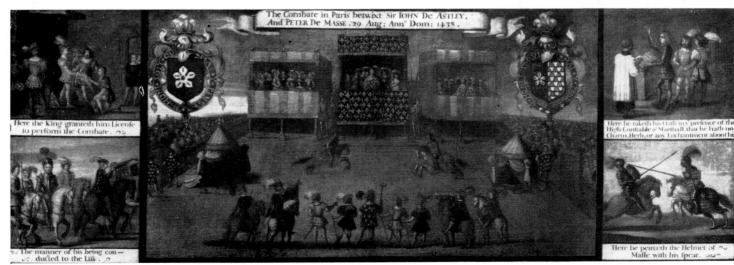

HATCHLANDS, SURREY

Built by **Admiral and Mrs Edward Boscawen, 1756–7**

Decorations by **Adam, 1759–62**

Alterations by **Bonomi, 1797**

Owner **The National Trust (Captain H. S. Goodhart Rendel)**

While Hatchlands was taking shape the British Empire was being established. 1759 was the Year of Victories in which Admiral Edward Boscawen played his part, and Robert Adam here made his debut at Mrs Boscawen's behest. The Boscawens (cf. *Admiral's Wife*, by R. Aspinall Oglander) had bought the property in 1750, but rebuilding of the old house was postponed owing to the Admiral's prolonged absences on service, which suggests his personal concern with its design. Originally a grange of Chertsey Abbey, in East Clandon parish, and recorded to have been moated in 1307, the property had belonged since the Dissolution to Edward Carleton (1502), Lord Aungier (*c.* 1600), Sir Thomas Heath (*c.* 1670), and the house no doubt had been much altered by them. It is believed to have stood a little W. of the present site, and according to Mrs Montague 'it resembles the masters of it, having preserved its native simplicity, though art and care have improved and softened it and made it elegant'. These

qualities, then beginning to be admired, were among those underlying the rococo taste and were to inspire the neo-classical movement, both of which are reflected in the new house. Mrs Boscawen was considering plans ('Lady Essex's house') in 1754, and a start with building was made in 1756–57 when her husband was at the Admiralty. But he was almost at once transferred to N. America.

The probability is that the Boscawens had evolved the design themselves with the help of a competent local builder. The exterior, of warm red brick, is characteristic in its extreme simplicity of the new taste, but also of rococo in its touches of 'variety'. This appears in the typical three-sided bows, one in the S. and two on the E. front; and in the curious change in the fenestration from two to three storeys in the W., originally the entrance, front (Fig. 80), contrived by the end windows of the S. front being dummies. The variation of floor levels was presumably in order to pack in additional rooms, and is more likely to be due to the Admiral's ingenuity than to a professional architect. Since the device, curious when both fronts are seen together, is in fact apt to pass unnoticed, it can be regarded as having succeeded. But rococo's empiricism could scarcely be better illustrated.

The building was 'ready for the roof' in October, 1757, and it is evident that internal decoration proceeded throughout the next year. The W. entrance Vestibule (Fig. 84) retains its

80. *From the south west, showing the difference in floor levels in the fronts.*

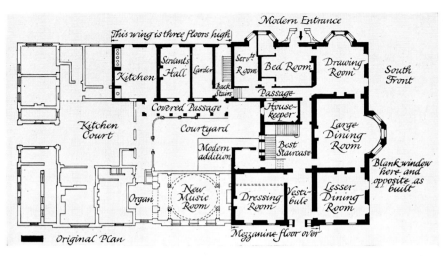

81. *Ground Floor Plan. Drawn by A. T. Bolton from that used by Adam and showing subsequent additions.*

82. *The Admiral's dog 'Becca'. Tablet in the dining room chimneypiece.*

rococo ceiling, several chimneypieces are of types due to James Paine, and the Staircase Hall seems to have been for the most part decorated before Adam arrived (Fig. 85). Its balustrade is *chinoiserie* of the period, unusual for being made of gilt metal, and the architectural compartmenting of the walls is in Palladian tradition. (All the rococo ornament, and the mahogany door-cases, are additions made in 1900.) The ceiling, however, should probably be accepted as Adam's (Fig. 86), perhaps his first in England: the large pendant *paterae* recur in his other early work at Shardeloes: also the

83. *Inscribed board in the servants' hall. Late 18th century.*

scrolling decoration in the corners, which he had used in Scotland *c.* 1755.

The choice by the 'unaffectedly simple' yet fashionable and enlightened Mrs Boscawen, and her distinguished husband, of the brilliant but untried Scotsman to complete the decoration of their house, suggests that he impressed them as offering precisely the novel, yet chaste and simplified, kind of classicisim that they contemplated. Alternative choices could have been 'Athenian' Stuart, or Sir R. Taylor, at one of whose houses, Harleyford, Mrs Boscawen was actually staying the previous summer, or Brown, architect of Sandleford for her friend Mrs Montague (who later also employed Stuart). Presumably during 1758 she had met Adam in London society, since he had been spending that year making contacts and studying fashionable requirements. Decision to engage him can be dated to the winter 1758–59, since the Admiral came home on November 1st, went to sea again in April, 1759, and Hatchlands was fit for occupation by the beginning of 1760. Adam's file at the Soane Museum inscribed *Designs for Admiral Hon. E. Boscawen* is dated 1759 and contains the plan of the house, dated 1757 but unsigned, which evidently was given him, besides the drawings which he prepared.

The rooms to which these refer are those in the S. front, that with the central bow being the dining room (now Drawing Room, Fig. 89); on its E. the former drawing room (now Library, Fig. 87), and to the W. the 'lesser dining room' (now morning room). There are besides two bedrooms with characteristic early Adam ceilings, and there was a large elaborate ceiling, of which drawings exist, in the saloon above the present Drawing Room. This was divided into bedrooms by Bonomi and the ceiling had to be taken down in 1889 as unsafe.

The interest of these very early Adam ceilings is their unlikeness to any of his subsequent designs and affinity to the kind of work which he could have seen in Rome. Yet, although his style was still unformed, they show him determined to break with the Palladian convention of heavy compartmented ceilings; and equally with the Rococo used by his father and by himself (e.g. at Hopetoun *c.* 1755), although his

84. *The original entrance in the west front. Redesigned in 1797 by Bonomi.*

85. *The Staircase Hall from the east.*

86. *Ceiling of the Staircase Hall. Adam, 1759.*

87. *Designed by Adam as the Drawing Room: since 1889 the Library.*

88. *Part of the ceiling of the above, symbolising Admiral Boscawen's naval victories.*

89. *The Drawing Room, designed by Adam as the Dining Room. The wall panels were intended to receive stucco arabesques.*

90. *Part of Adam's ceiling of the above. This and Fig. 88 are among Adam's earliest ceiling designs in England.*

91. *The Drawing Room. Bow in the south front.*

sketches and more ambitious designs show he was intensely alive to the Picturesque of which Rococo was an expression. His work here shows him still feeling his way towards his characteristic synthesis of archaeology, classicism and the romantic.

In the present Drawing Room the drawings establish as Adam's the wall panels and the chimneypiece. The latter, which differs in some details from the drawing, is of the type supported by caryatids which he had used at Hopetoun and strongly favoured at this time introducing again at Croome, Kedleston and Harewood. The sculptor was possibly Rysbrack, who carved that at Hopetoun and, later, the Admiral's monument at St Michael Penkivel, Cornwall. The drawing shows the wall panels decorated with stucco arabesques as at Shardeloes; beneath the silk with which they are now filled, the rough lines have been found for some of this decoration, probably countermanded after the Admiral died in 1762. Although the drawing for the ceiling is missing, its main lines are pencilled in the plan alluded to. The central oval is enclosed in a prolonged octagon frame in which Adam's characteristic honeysuckle motif is introduced. The outer border is formed of another favourite motif, the 'flowing rinceau,' rococo in its freedom, with scallops between seahorses. In the corners, the emphasizing of which was an

Italian memory, are winged boys holding the tails of dolphins. The marine motifs are found closely repeated in the screen to the Admiralty forecourt designed by Adam in the same year —probably through Boscawen's influence—of which the sculptor was Michael Spang. The resemblance prompts the surmise that he may have modelled these reliefs and those in the adjoining room.

The Library (Figs. 87, 88) has a ceiling with eight radiating compartments. Four contain modelled figures—of Neptune, Justice, Fame and Victory; the others twin mermaids perched on martial trophies, the roundels in which may have been intended to frame paintings. The drawing for this exists, as also for the chimneypiece which reflects Piranesi's early influence on Adam. The mahogany bookcases are contemporary. In the other south room, now the morning room, the ceiling is plain, its decoration probably having been countermanded. Its wooden panelling had most likely been put up, and a chimneypiece of the kind that Paine habitually used been procured, before Adam's coming.

Another chimneypiece which the Boscawens had probably already bought is that in the modern dining room. It was previously in the Admiral's gun room; and it is pleasant to think that the spaniel in its tablet (Fig. 82) is his pet 'Becca'. The room was formed in 1889 out of two bedrooms, one the Admiral's and the smaller, adjoining, probably for his personal servant. That they had been rather hastily devised when he got back, a sick man, in 1760 is suggested by the partition between them having halved the bow window which lights the present room. The ceiling is a remaking of that of the smaller room and actually contains some components of its plasterwork re-used.

In 1770 Hatchlands was sold to Mr W. B. Sumner. A plan by Benjamin Armitage for altering the grounds at the time was not executed, and *c.* 1795 Repton recommended coating the exterior with white stucco (his other proposals are now lost). In 1797 J. Bonomi recommended more far reaching Hellenisation, but was confined to internal alterations and designing a new front entrance (Fig. 80). He remodelled and furnished the vestibule (Fig. 84), but its ceiling was retained.

In 1889 Lord Rendel, on acquiring Hatchlands, made extensive and sympathetic alterations with the assistance of his nephew Halsey Ricardo (1854–1928). The entrance was moved to the E. front where a porch was added and three windows in place of two were inserted over it. The new entrance hall, taking the place of the Admiral's bedroom, opens directly into the Staircase Hall, thereby destroying its original enclosed entity that was characteristic of Georgian planning, though contributing to the scenic effect. On Lord Rendel's death in 1913 Hatchlands passed to his nephew Captain H. S. Goodhart Rendel, P.P.R.I.B.A., who in 1945 transferred the property to the National Trust. He has been scrupulous to make no structural alteration other than to correct *gaucheries* by Bonomi. In 1919–20 he formed the parterre lying W. of the house (largely to relieve local unemployment), and has designed most of the excellent modern houses in the village.

92. *The Old Hall and Church as they appeared on the island in Nether Tabley Mere.*

TABLEY HOUSE, CHESHIRE

Built for **Sir Peter (Byrne) Leicester, 1760–70**

Architect **Carr of York**

Craftsmen **T. Oliver (stucco), D. Shillito, M. Bertram (carvers), W. Atkinson (chimneypieces)**

Owner **Mr John Leicester-Warren**

The new house at Over Tabley, near Knutsford, looks at first sight as conservative in design as the family that till then had been content with their island Hall in Nether Tabley Mere. Indeed, when new blood and money initiated the change, it was found that preservation of the Old Hall was stipulated in the late baronet's will. So the symbols of Tory sentiment and Whig principles confront each other, seemingly with no attempt at fusion, although the architect was already in touch at Harewood with the originator of the new synthesis. But in fact, though Carr's design is faithful to the late Palladian standards established in the North by Burlington and Paine, it also made notable innovations in country house planning.

The 17th-century antiquary, Sir Peter Leicester, recorded that his ancestor John de Leycester built *c.* 1380 'the manor hall of Nether Tabley within the pool where it now standeth'. The massive cruck frame of the hall, enlarged and faced in Caroline brick, bore out the tradition; but in 1927 subsidence due to brine extraction necessitated its demolition together with that of the 17th-century chapel adjoining— the latter now re-erected adjoining the Georgian house. Sir Peter, a picturesque figure in the history of a picturesque place, continued to remain on his island for most of the Civil War, annotating his *Historical Antiquities of Cheshire*, although his brother-in-law, Lord Byron, was the Royalist

leader in the district, and his sympathies were with the King.[1]

It was his grandson Sir Francis, last of the male line, who, foreseeing innovations, entailed the preservation of the Old Hall on his son-in-law and successor. He was Sir John Byrne, Baronet, descendant of a rich Irish army clothier, and his mother was prospective heiress of the Cheshire family of Warren. Their son Sir Peter Byrne, 4th Baronet, succeeded

[1] Sir Peter Leicester's and the other family muniments are catalogued in *A Tabley Calendar* (1949).

93. *The Portico on the south, originally entrance front.*

55

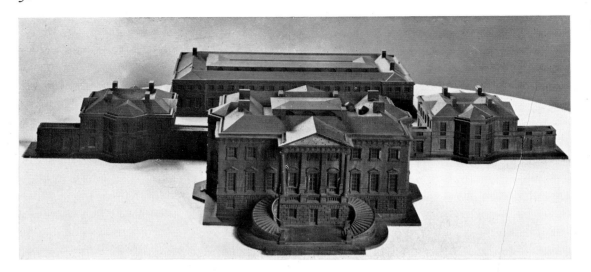

94. *Model of the House and Stables as designed by Carr.*

95. *The north front, converted to the entrance in 1827.*

to Tabley in 1742 and assumed the name of Leicester, proceeding to sell his Irish estate and buy Over Tabley where, overlooking the mere, he intended to build. He then found that Sir Francis's will obstructed the use of Nether Tabley timber on the new property. Trees almost as good were available on the latter, however, since the site was called Oaklands—and Carr's plans are so named by Woolfe and Gandon in *Vitruvius Britannicus*, vol. V. So in 1760 materials began to be assembled, local bricks and Runcorn stone, and James Oates the chief mason arrived from Yorkshire.

In view of the circumstances it is highly likely that the designs had been made and settled some years previously, when Kirby Hall (1749), designed by Burlington and Robert Morris, constituted Carr's chief practical experience, he being Clerk of Works there. The polygonal bows placed as at Kirby in the sides, and in the pavilions, of Tabley might support this hypothesis, although they had then become common features of 'Rococo Palladian'. The portico of the S. front, originally the entrance, has similarly been traced *via* that of Wentworth Woodhouse from Wanstead; yet its four

Doric columns and curved perron have only a generic resemblance to the latter's six Corinthian piers and rectangular stairs. But choice of the Doric order, the frieze of which is continued round the house, might well have been made to give the elevation a note of 'primitive simplicity',

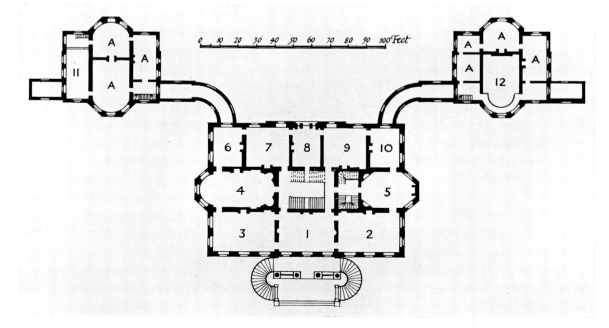

96. *First floor Plan, as in 'Vitruvius Britannicus', vol. IV.*

1. *Hall.* 2. *Dining room.* 3. *Drawing room.* 4. *Library.* 5. *Common Parlour.* 6–10. *Principal Bed and Dressing Rooms.* 11. *Brewhouse.* 12. *Kitchen (Upper halves) A. A. Servants' bedrooms.*

97. (*above*). *The old entrance Hall giving into the Portico.*

98. (*above, right*). *Doorway to the Library from the Staircase Hall.*

99. *The Drawing Room, formerly Dining Room.*

suited to the venerable nature of the view and to the traditional character of the place. And perhaps acknowledgement of the romantic associations of the place may account for the introduction in the new design of 'old fashioned' volutes and shoulders for the upper window architraves.

The 'feudal' element persisting in Cheshire society could also be held accountable for these overtones. The general disposition, well illustrated by the detailed model (Fig. 94), shows the intention to have been that the building should comprise all the traditional services of an ancient mansion. It is the complete realization of this functional aspect in a homogeneous plan that gives Carr's Tabley its chief interest, since it was not often achieved so fully at this time. The three-storeyed central block (roughly 100 ft. by 75 ft.) stands well forward from the square two-storeyed pavilions that partly flanked an office court. On the further side of this (though further away than the space allotted in the model suggests) is a great stable quadrangle, with equally extensive accommodation for retainers on its upper floor (and allowing ample room for a theatre to be contrived later). Further

100. The Staircase. (above) One of the consoles supporting the landing.

101. The 'Common Parlour'.

servants' rooms filled the upper floors of the pavilions which, the eastern containing the kitchen, the western the brewhouse and dairies, are linked by quadrant corridors to the basement of the main block. This, in fact the ground floor, contained mainly further servants' quarters, the servants' hall beneath the portico; but also the gentlemen's billiard room in the S.W. corner and in the E. bow a subsidiary entrance which the family will have habitually used, leading to a broad E.-W. corridor spanned by the stairs to the *piano nobile*.

The Entrance Hall (Fig. 97), ceremoniously entered from the portico, is no higher than the other rooms on the main floor. Intercommunicating, these surround the high top-lit Staircase Hall that occupies the position and (as at Wolterton) fills the visual role of a *cortile*. The secondary staircase E. of it provided service communication, and access to the 'Common Parlour' in the E. bow. The Dining Room was between the latter and the Hall, with the Drawing Room and Library corresponding W. of the Hall. The whole north front consisted of bed and dressing rooms, but there were none of the self-contained 'apartments' required by earlier usage. The plan is thus almost symmetrical, with only four 'sitting' rooms, none of them of much size, those flanking the Hall being 33½ ft. by 22½ ft. The planning of the services relied on, and provided for, the prodigal expenditure of domestic labour forthcoming.

The building accounts give Thomas Oliver as the plasterer (working 1762–67), Daniel Shillito and Matthew Bertram the carvers, probably emanating from York, though possibly from Liverpool whence Mr Rathbone supplied the bulk of the timber other than oak. There is a note of Carr procuring marble chimneypieces and iron grates from Yorkshire. But various unspecific references to 'William Atkinson of Hyde Park Corner' imply that this partner (who died 1766) of Joseph Pickford supplied the principal chimneypieces.

The decoration is of excellent execution if unoriginal in design, enriching Palladian forms (some deriving from Paine) with rococo ornament. This is crisply carved in the handsome doorcases of the principal rooms and no less in the varied wooden chimneypieces of the bedrooms (Figs. 102 and 103). Oliver's stucco in the Dining Room (later converted to the Drawing Room, Fig. 99) resembles Pickford's at Holkham in reproducing 17th century decoration in the Jonesian ceiling. But in the Hall (Fig. 97) his reliefs foreshadow the new classicism; and the ceiling of the Common Parlour has a staid grace. This charming room (Fig. 101), with its canted ends containing china cupboards, is of a form consistently introduced by Carr and the most representative here of his personal style. Spectacular effects were reserved for the Staircase Hall, where the ascent, retaining the old triple-baluster formula, is of almost excessive amplitude and ease.

103. *A typical Carr chimneypiece, with original grate.*

102. *A bedroom chimneypiece.*

104. *'Tabley, a Windy Day', by J. M. W. Turner, 1809.*

Avray Tipping commented on this leisureliness that it 'is accentuated to the eye by the uncompromising plainness and rectangularity of the broad shallow treads, scarcely resting upon each other. The landings, it is true, have the support of far-projecting and beautifully carved consoles (Fig. 100), but these are of such little depth . . . that they give the impression of not being structural supports but ornamental. Stability of course is ensured by the cantilever principle, but the eye remains unconvinced'.

The inventive limitations of Carr's early work were enlarged by his contact with Adam at Harewood but too late to affect Tabley. Subsequently one spacious room was contrived by the builder's son. Sir John Leicester, who succeeded as a boy in 1770 and was created Lord de Tabley in 1820, became one of the Regent's set and, about 1792, an enthusiastic art collector, especially patronizing the English School. To hang the surplus of his acquisitions, beyond what his Hill

105. *The Picture Gallery, formed in* 1792 *(altered* 1827*) out of rooms* 3, 4, 6, 7, *in the plan.*

Street house would hold, Thos. Harrison of Chester (d. 1829) formed a tripartite gallery in the W. side of the main floor previously filled by the Drawing Room, Library and two Chambers. After his death in 1827, the London house and the bulk of the collection were sold, and the Tabley collection reinforced with the remainder. This necessitated altering the gallery to the form shown in Fig. 105—possibly again from Harrison's design. At the same time the portico ceased to be the main entrance, this being moved to the back where the great yard between house and stables was converted to an impressive forecourt entered beneath pedimented arches. A new porch was added beneath Carr's central Venetian window and his quadrants now displayed their convexity (Fig. 95).

Sir John was an early admirer of Turner. In 1809 the artist exhibited two canvasses of Tabley Mere: *A Calm Morning*, bought by Lord Egremont, and *A Windy Day* (Fig. 104), which still hangs at Tabley. This introduces a picturesque tower that had recently been built on the island

and, though the artist drew on his experience of less placid waters, it accurately relates the landscape and mansion. The collection formerly comprised Hoppner's *Sleeping Venus* (of which the model was Sir John Leicester's mistress, Emily St Claire) now at Petworth, and two brilliant Romney sketches of Lady Hamilton, sold in 1927 to pay for the moving of the chapel. The collection is otherwise intact, representing an interesting example of early 19th century connoisseurship. In addition there are old masters and notable earlier family portraits. Of these Dobson's portrait of the Cavalier Lord Byron is seen above the Drawing Room fireplace.

The third and last Lord de Tabley, the Tennysonian poet, died unmarried, leaving Tabley to his sister, wife of Sir Baldwyn Leighton. Her second son assumed the name of Leicester-Warren, and now his son is not only the owner of Tabley but the founder and proprietor of the successful school for boys which fills the great house with a population more plentiful and appreciative than it might otherwise contain.

HAREWOOD HOUSE, YORKSHIRE

Built for **Edwin Lascelles, Lord Harewood, 1759–71**

Architects **Carr of York, 1750; Sir C. Barry, 1843**

Decorators **Adam, 1765; Rose, Rebecca, Zucchi, Chippendale**

Gawthorpe Hall, the ruins of which stand on high ground in the N.W. corner of the park, belonged successively to the Gascoignes, the great Strafford and Sir John Cutler. In 1753 it was bought by Henry Lascelles who, coming of a long line of North Riding squires, had married a Barbados heiress and was a director of the East India Company. His brother, with whom he is sometimes confused and who was father of the 1st Earl of Harewood, became Collector of Customs in that island. Edwin, the former's son, on succeeding in 1754, proceeded to raise Gawthorpe to the style of his political leader's palace of Wentworth Woodhouse a few miles away, by building a new mansion and village—named Harewood. Continuously representing Yorkshire constituencies as a Whig, he (and his successor) supported Pitt after 1790 in

which year he received a barony, taking his title from the renamed property.

Mr Lascelles is depicted in contemporary letters as of fashionably eclectic tastes. Chambers, then a young man fresh from Italy, whom he engaged to build stately new stables, also made a design for the new house. It is not clear why this was rejected; but its splendid character is shown by the design for one of its terminal pavilions having been used later by Chambers for his pavilion at Marino. When the foundation stone of Harewood was laid in March, 1759, only the mason's name is specifically mentioned (J. Muschamp). However, Carr of York stated (*Vitruvius Britannicus*, vol. V) that it was 'erected' in 1760 from his designs. Probably the builder of Chambers's stables, and certainly of the new village, Carr could claim distant kinship (his mother was a Miss Rose Lascelles). As built, Harewood corresponds much more closely to the published plan signed by Carr (Fig. 110) than to those 'for Edwin Lascelles, Esq., at his seat at Gawthorp' by Adam (undated), now in the Soane Museum (Fig. 109). Carr ascribed full credit for the internal decoration to Adam,

106. The south front as remodelled by Sir C. Barry, 1843.

who, after 1765, was clearly in entire charge till completion *c.* 1771. Adam was already being consulted in April, 1759, on the new church at Harewood; and there are elements in Carr's published plan which may have been incorporated from Adam's, suggesting that Lascelles invited proposals from the younger man (as he had earlier from Chambers). But it is significant that the outline and main disposition is the same in both, showing that they were determined by foundations already laid.

Since the exterior was refaced and balustraded by Sir C. Barry in 1843 (though preserving its masses), the evidence for the nature and extent of Adam's influence on the design of this the first of the great houses with which he was associated is obscured and must be derived from comparison of the plans. This suggests that recent writers, following Bolton, have exaggerated Adam's part, and that Carr was materially accurate in his apportionment of the credit.[1]

The site, sloping steeply southwards to a notable prospect but with views to E. and W. also, is approached from the N. and suggested an elongated shape with the wings prolonging the central block but set at right angles to it so as to enjoy the lateral views. The E. half of the plan was to be assigned to private use, the W. wing to be filled by a great gallery, and other reception rooms to be restricted at first to four; the wings to have low links with the centre on both fronts, leaving internal courts. Discussion evidently turned upon the amount of accommodation to be provided for the master and mistress, and the treatment of these courts.

Adam's suggestion was characteristic both of his new approach and of the dynamic quality that he was to restore to English architecture. He proposed semicircular courts between corridors, the quadrant spaces allotted vaguely to 'servants'. Though the owner's suite duly filled the E. wing, a ceremonial Dressing Room for Mr Lascelles (in the Carr plans it was given to the lady) was placed in the main block opening out of the Library. But since a more or less circular room for that position occurs in other Carr plans (cf. Tabley) it cannot be regarded as an Adam innovation. In the Gallery Adam proposed recessing the end windows, using closets (as at Syon) and small staircases to justify what could have been an effective moulding of space. A second plan[2] shows a corridor following the semicircle of the W. court and giving through a domed vestibule into the gallery, the ends of which have apses and columned screens; and the principal staircase with a central flight, as executed. The E. court, however, is square, affording a little more accommodation for the owner, including what may be a lavatory. Turning now to Carr's published plan, which is largely as built, we find the courts smaller and rectangular, enabling three large additional rooms. The owner's suite remains in the E. wing, but a State Bedroom suite has been formed between it and the Saloon, where the former parlour has become a superior dressing room with an alcoved bedroom adjoining, linked

to the circular or octagonal 'lady's Dressing Room'. The parlour has, in effect, been moved W. of the Saloon and become the 'first Drawing Room'; a Music Room has taken the place of the Dining Room, which has shifted next to the Gallery, balanced on the S. front by a 'second Drawing Room'. Corridors have been almost entirely eliminated, the only one being private, leading from the Library to the owner's wing. Whilst the increased accommodation was presumably due to the client's afterthought, the rejection of Adam's various suggestions for visual and physical 'movement' implies that Carr's more practical method of planning prevailed.

The same applies to the elevations. Adam proposed astylar treatment for the N. front (Fig. 108), but it was built (and largely survives) to Carr's scheme (Fig. 107) with a hexastyle engaged portico recalling Paine's at Nostell. Adam's and the adopted design for the S. front of the centre and its portico differ only in detail, Carr's Palladian prevailing over Adam's Grecian Corinthian Order (Figs. 111, 112). In the wings Carr's visible roofs and pillaster scheme was preferred to Adam's balustraded treatment. The pillasters and the pedimented windows in the links were retained when Barry heightened the wings (Fig. 106). Thus, although there are touches, such as the N. end of Carr's wings, that markedly differ from his usual style, suggesting the influence of the new classicism and Adam's specific proposals, structurally Harewood is Carr's.

Adam's designs for the internal decoration are dated from 1765 to 1771, and comprise more alternatives than for any other of his works (implying the extent of his client's interference, as Mr Lees Milne has pointed out). They thus followed after his great schemes for Kedleston and Syon and his engagements at Bowood and Mersham le Hatch. Although in none of these, except Mersham, had Adam designed the building, in all, with the exception of Bowood, he had greater freedom to manipulate the plan than at Harewood where, we have seen, his proposals were rejected. Consequently the rooms do not show his capacity for three-dimensional design and sequence, and he had to rely almost wholly on surface treatment and furnishing. Since his historic collaboration with Chippendale arose from this latter, the result has its particular value.

The Hall (Fig. 113) illustrates these circumstances by the disparity between its 'structural' Doric Order—which he had used with such effect in the hall at Syon—and its flatly ornamented ceiling. Though the plan was not materially changed during evolution from his initial proposal, this had indicated some apsidal figure for the inner end. A deep arch leading to the Saloon did, however, give visual depth until it was walled over and the space thrown into the latter when it became the Library. The date 1767 on one of the mural plaques gives the year of the Hall's completion. The Music Room lying to the right, taking the place of the Dining Room of the first scheme, has 'Roman' arabesque panels alternating with Piranesian ruin pieces by Zucchi (cf. those by Stuart and Dall at Shugborough, Fig. 148), and its original carpet closely repeats the ceiling pattern. The Dining Room, in all the schemes, contained a sideboard recess on its inner side, but as built the alcove contains the chimneypiece. Service needs led to its elimination in the 19th century, when the present

---

[1] 'The worthy owner has spared no expense in decorating the principle apartments from designs made by Mr Adam'. In *Vitruvius Britannicus*, V.

[2] Found in Carr's office by the late Walter Brierley, lineal successor to Carr's York practice; described and reproduced by Bolton, A T., *The Architecture of Robert and James Adam*, I. p. 161.

107, 108. (above) Elevation of the north front. (left) as published by Carr in 'Vitruvius Britannicus', vol. V. (right) As proposed in Adam's original drawing.

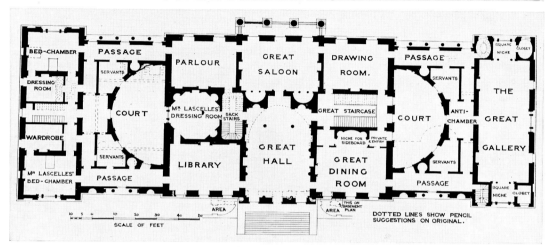

109. Plan of principal floor as first proposed by Adam. Dotted lines show pencilled suggestions in the original.

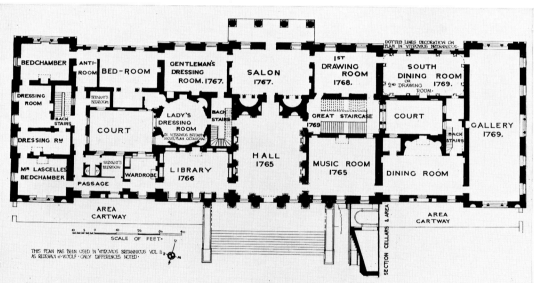

110. Principal floor plan as executed and published by Carr. The dates are those of Adam's drawings for the interior. (In each case South is to the top.)

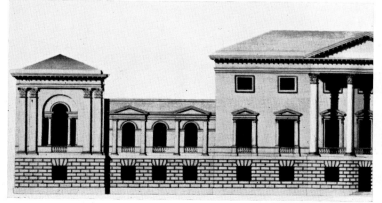

111, 112. Elevation of the south front: (left) by Carr as built, (right) as proposed by Adam.

114. *In the Gallery. A window with Chippendale's 'Trompe l'oeil' valence of carved wood.*

113. *The entrance hall which was completed in 1767. The furniture in 'the Egyptian taste' c. 1815.*

115. *Adam's Gallery and the Reynolds portraits. The ceiling decorated by Rose and Rebecca (c. 1769); the chimneypiece by Sir C. Barry.*

116. *The Music Room, with 'Roman' arabesque panels alternating with Piranesian ruin-pieces painted by Zucchi. The carpet, designed by Adam and probably from Moorfields, repeats broadly the ceiling pattern.*

117. *The principal Staircase looking east. The original plans show successive single flights only. Introduction of the central lower flight produced a somewhat constricted effect in the width available.*

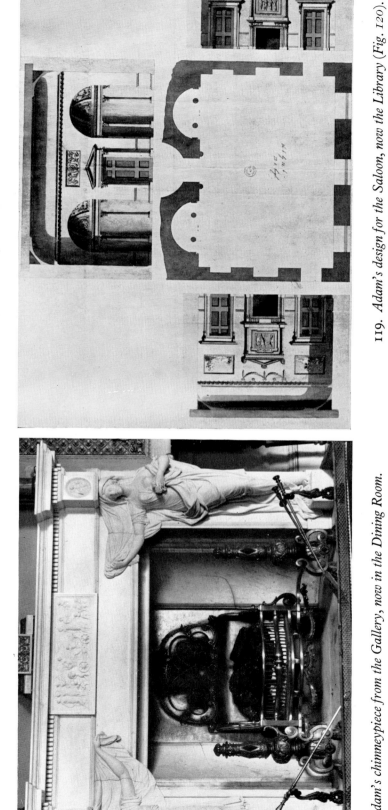

118. Adam's chimneypiece from the Gallery, now in the Dining Room.

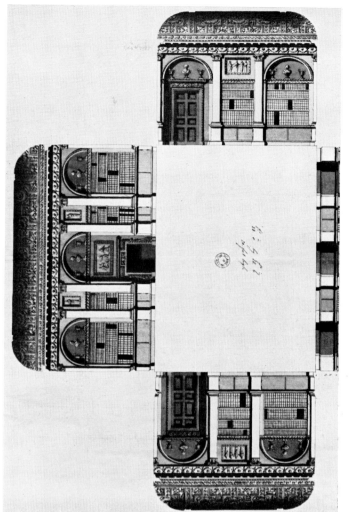

119. Adam's design for the Saloon, now the Library (Fig. 120).

120. The Saloon as converted to the Library in 1843.

121. Adam's design for the Library, 1765 (see Plan, Fig. 110).

chimneypiece (Fig. 118) was also introduced from the Gallery —one of the type with full-length sculptured figures which Adam regarded as ideal for important positions in his earlier houses and used at Hatchlands (Fig. 87) and Croome. The very notable Chippendale furniture remains *in situ*.

The Harewood Gallery (Fig. 115; 75 ft. by 24 ft.) is best comparable to that at Corsham, 1760 (cf. *E.C.H.*, *Early Georgian*) and was finished after 1769, the date of the ceiling design. This employs the same principle of repeating small components to emphasize the length as does Adam's gallery at Syon, and was executed by Rose and Rebecca. The walls were designed to display the handsome series of Reynolds's family portraits interspersed with splendid mirrors. 'Such a show of magnificence and art the eye hath scarce seen', averred a visitor in 1787, mentioning specially 'on one side 4 most superb plate glasses 10 ft. high and another over the chimneypiece. The whole has been supplied in one year by one Chippendale, St Martin's Lane'. The four remain[1] between the windows (Fig. 114), of which the gilded curtain-boxes have *trompe l'oeil* valences of carved wood. This baroque feature, unique at the date, was no doubt to obviate the corrosion of dust at this height beyond broom's reach. Deceptively simulating deep blue drapery, the effect can be

[1] The console tables, long regarded as by Chippendale, are now established as the work of his son in 1797.

compared with the reality at Corsham where the draw-up curtains with which they will have been fitted still survive. The remaining accounts with Chippendale and Haig are dated 1772–75, totalling £6,326, but include the amount (nearly half) of an earlier 'bill delivered'. None of Adam's drawings for the furniture have been discovered, probably because Chippendale never returned them, but there can be no doubt that the architect was responsible for much of it and for the new refinement in the later furniture at Harewood as compared with Chippendale's earlier rococo contributions in his *Director* style.

The suite of reception rooms in the S. front were subsequently altered in many respects though retaining much of Adam's and Chippendale's. The Saloon, in the centre, was converted into the Library by Barry; but Adam's ceiling and apses, their design (Fig. 119) dated 1767, remain amidst the later painted decoration (Fig. 120), and the two chimney-pieces with overmantel reliefs are intact (Fig. 123). The ceiling cove has vases alternating with candelabra, which, with classical reliefs over the doors and columned screens across the apses, are shown in the design to have produced the desired Roman effect. The great library table supplied by Chippendale *c.* 1770 will have stood originally in the room to the left of the hall designed for that purpose (Figs. 121, 124).

In the State bedroom suite beyond the saloon the 'gentle-

122. *In the Dining Room. Rosewood inlaid Sideboard, Wine-cooler, and Pedestals mounted with ormolu.*
By Chippendale from Adam's design c. 1770.

man's dressing room', now the second library, retains its principle features; but little remains of the 'lady's', which has become a passage. A description of it in 1819 mentions Ionic pillasters supporting a dome decorated by Zucchi and blue and white furniture. The bedroom of this suite is now a sitting room and contains a notable collection of early water-colours, besides Chippendale's inlaid satinwood commode of 1773, perhaps the masterpiece of his later style. The younger Chippendale was employed 1796–97 and supplied numerous mahogany wardrobes, etc. to be seen in this part of the house.

The main Staircase (Fig. 117) is contained W. of the Hall between the N. and S. suites, being lit from the court. Carr's and Adam's plans both show a single flight rising up each side successively, but Mr Lascelles evidently wanted a double ascent. The space is restricted, but room was found for a central lower flight, giving each a width of 6 ft. A more delicate design for the balustrade exists (Bolton, I, 168); yet that used, of wrought metal with honeysuckle ornament and minutely carved handrail, makes of this staircase, with the arabesqued walls, one of the finest by Adam in a country house.

On Lord Harewood's death without children in 1795 the estate went to his nephew, son of the Barbados official, who was created Earl of Harewood in 1812. Jewell's *Tourist's Companion* of 1819 refers to 'recent alterations', instancing the

124. *In the old Library (cf. Fig. 121).*

Entry Hall 'in the Egyptian taste with marbling by Mr Hutchinson of London'. This has in its turn vanished, though there remains some attractive furniture probably by the younger Chippendale in that style.

Other subsequent comments on Harewood reflect changing taste but also recognize the failure of the collaboration here to achieve synthesis. 'Too much sameness . . . two rows of large square rooms with costly beds, glasses, chairs and tables' (Wesley, 1779); 'Nothing within interests the mind, no productions of the arts unless indeed the labours of gilders and upholsterers. Taste and fancy turn away with satiety' (R. Warner, 1802). On the other hand we can now recognize Chippendale's contribution as 'among the few masterpieces of English furniture comparable in technical brilliance with the finest achievements of French cabinet makers'[1]—here to be seen in the settings for which it was designed.

It was the inadequacy, as the romantic Late Georgian age saw it, of Carr's elevation and Brown's setting for the pic-turesque capabilities of the site, which prompted the 3rd Earl to engage Barry, when a second bedroom storey was needed, to Italianize both. The S. portico was removed, a richer silhouette and texture imposed, and the tiers of terraces built against the south slope.

123. *Chimneypiece in the Library, originally Saloon (cf. Fig. 119).*

[1] Oliver Brackett, *Thomas Chippendale.*

KEDLESTON, DERBYSHIRE

Built for **Sir Nathaniel Curzon, Baronet, 1758–68**
Architects **Brettingham, Paine, Adam (1761)**
Master Mason **Joseph Hall of Derby**
Sculptors **Collins, Spang**
Decorators **Rose, Bartoli, Linnel, Hamilton, etc.**
Owner **Lord Scarsdale**

Sir Nathaniel Curzon, 5th Baronet, created Lord Scarsdale 1761, recorded that he replaced a Queen Anne brick quadrangular house, and removed the adjacent village, between 1758 and 1768. His employment of Brettingham for the initial stages of the house suggests that his immediate inspiration was Holkham, the previous generation's outstanding achievement in the synthesis of Palladian ideals with English feeling. That he so soon replaced him by Paine, and Paine by Adam, may imply, in view of the result, that he aimed at a more picturesque synthesis with the monumental than he found the two former architects able to perform. As a travelled connoisseur he was certainly conscious of the aesthetic trend towards emphasizing visual values, to which his successive changes of architect gave effect.

Brettingham supplied or concurred in Palladio's Villa Mocenigo plan with four pavilions linked to a square centre by quadrant corridors at two levels. The latter (as at Stoke Bruerne) curve to a terminal window before joining the pavilions instead of being linked to their rear as was customary. The N.E. wing, built 1761, was and is a self-contained house in which the owner could reside during construction of the remainder. Paine, who had used a similar plan at Nostell (*E.C.H., Early Georgian*), states that he took over Brettingham's wings of which the two that were built (N.E. and N.W.) resemble normal Palladian houses. The form and largely the plan of the central mass is Paine's contribution and typical of his development of Burlingtonian classicism. That is most evident in the plan. As at Nostell he provided informal entrance to a sub-hall through a basement arcade, that supports the great Corinthian portico, between the pair of returning ascents to the *piano nobile*. At that level he proposed a spectacular composition: a columned hall on the portico's axis, which continued through the further pillars between a pair of semicircular staircases, contained in a top-lit domed hall, to a round Drawing Room. Externally, with its semicircular colonnade, this would have had the appearance of the Temple of Vesta flanked by the southern quadrants joined to wings containing the chapel and stables. Within, the axial *enfilade*, with the interposed staircases ascending in shadowed spirals, would have been impressive.

Curzon's rejection of it in 1761 is likely to have been due to the time and cost factors as much as to the aesthetic and, possibly, to the competing preoccupations of Paine. The equanimity with which the latter, in his book[1], stated that he had begged to be excused from completing it owing to the pressure of other commissions, was no doubt in part due to his engagement in that year to rebuild Worksop (Fig. 7) where he proceeded to elaborate his Kedleston scheme. 'The

[1] *Plans . . . of Noblemen's & Gentlemen's Houses . . .*, vol. I, 1767. (Vol. II, 1783).

125. *The north front.*

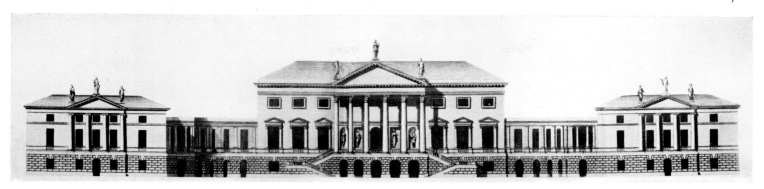

126. *The north front: Paine's and Brettingham's designs revised by Adam.*

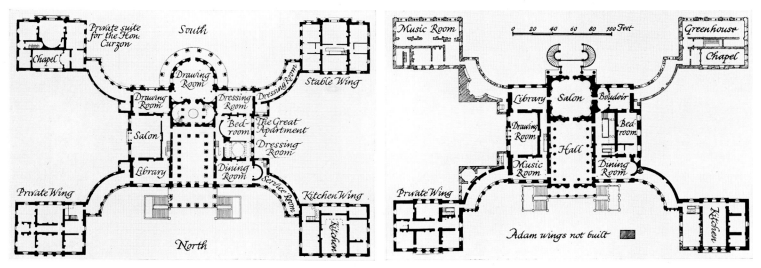

127. *Paine's plan of the main floor.*

128. *(Above, right). Adam's plan.*

129. *(right). Section through Hall and Saloon from 'Vitruvius Britannicus', vol. IV.*

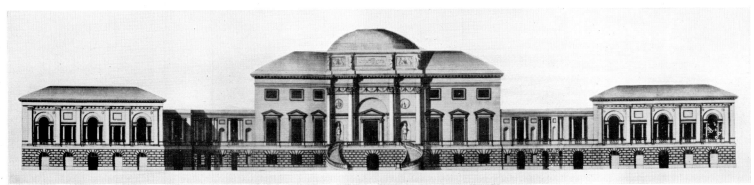

130. *Adam's complete design for the south front from 'Vitruvius Britannicus', vol. IV.*

132. *The centre of the south front.*

131. *The north portico.*

133. *The Great Hall with columns of Derbyshire alabaster 25 feet high.*

134. (left) One of the hall chimneypieces: relief figures by Spang.
135. (above) Tablet candelabra in the Saloon.

136. The Drawing Room chimneypiece, with supporting figures carved by Spang.

137. Cast iron stove in the saloon.

138. *The Saloon. It is a rotunda of 42 feet diameter, 55 feet to the eye of the dome.*

noble owner,' he continued, 'placed this great work in the hands of those able and ingenious artists, Messrs. Robert and James Adam'—with whom, it is agreeable to know, he remained on friendly terms.

Since 1760 Adam had been supplying designs for internal decoration and furnishings, in much the same capacity as already at Shardeloes, Croome, and Harewood. Progress was therefore not interrupted and, although Joseph Hall of Derby was already raising the N. front, there was time for Adam to lighten the wall in the portico, shown blank by Paine over the niches, with roundel reliefs carved by Collins. He also revised the columnation of the great Hall, but Paine's arrangement of the rooms E. of it was not changed. The whole S.

front could be designed anew, Paine's central staircases be eliminated, and the W. side replanned to contain a less costly ascent to the visitors' bedrooms. In the result, a great circular room was retained but set back within the S. front, where its rotundity was expressed only by the flattened dome. In his full scheme for this front (Fig. 130) the wings and quadrants were also completely redesigned, developing the Venetian window motif which had been limited to the return face of the quadrants. 'We can see clearly enough', Mr Lees Milne has remarked, 'how Adam meant to achieve effects of "movement" in the contrasting convexity of the dome and concavity of the quadrants and perron (which shows strong affinity to Carr's at Tabley), in the advance and recess of light

139. *The Drawing Room. Adam's design for the ceiling is dated* 1760.

140. *(left) The Venetian window and a doorway of the Drawing Room, of green Derbyshire alabaster.*

and shadow, sharply defined and accentuated by the projecting columns'. Though the wings were never built, and Adam's conception consequently fails of its full effect, the central mass is nevertheless the closest that he came to realizing in a country house his Piranesian conception of dynamic monumentality. But whilst acclaiming the power and beauty of what stands, we should not forget how many of its elements originated with Paine or, possibly, Sir Nathaniel.

Not least among these, it is generally overlooked, was the Hall, of which the columns were supplied and worked by J. Hall for £1,184 in 1760. But whereas Paine proposed fourteen columns, there are sixteen, arranged with a freestanding pair at the N. end and engaged columns at the S. instead of *vice versa* as in Paine's plan. The change, which is not to the advantage of the effect as seen on entry, may have been connected with Adam visualising the chief approach as by his perron and circular saloon from the S. The only precedent for the use of Derbyshire alabaster on such a scale as in the columns was the tribune at Holkham, but the effect here of the green-veined fluted shafts some 25 ft. high and 2 ft.

141. *The Dining Room: paintings by Zucchi and Zuccharelli; sculptors, Spang and Collins.*

6 in. diameter is proportionately more powerful. Their weight is relieved by the lightness of Joseph Rose's arabesques in the ceiling cove (not executed till the '70s, and claimed by G. Richardson, one of Adam's draughtsmen for ceilings, as his own design). The floor, kept clear of furniture, is paved in grey Hopton marble with a great circular star in the centre. In the aisles the two exquisite fireplaces combine delicate sculpture by Spang with consummate metal work (Fig. 134). Above the niches, containing casts, the panels are painted in *grisaille*; and the doors, faced with *papier maché*, early products of the Birmingham firm of Clay, are similarly decorated.

It is possible that the idea of the hall, though incorporated by Paine in his plan, had been originated by Adam whilst acting only as decorator. For in his book on Spalato Adam emphasized the Roman conception of the *atrium*, consecrated to the honour of ancestors, leading directly to the *vestibulum*, sacred to the gods. His revised plan embodies the relationship exactly, yet Paine's also seems to have been inspired by a notion of it. Supreme both in its artistry and, as the Tory Dr Johnson complained, in its apparent uselessness, this hall, adapting archaeology to neo-classical design, may stand

as the climax of the Whig Ideal: 'in the best taste' but, as Walpole commented, 'too expensive for Lord Scarsdale's estate'. It was Adam's fate to make his debut at the top of an economic decline. Only at Syon did he have an equal opportunity to realize his vision on such a scale and with such precious materials, and there too he was halted.

The Saloon, a perfect circle of 42 ft. diameter and 55 ft. high to the top of the dome, compares with Borra's contemporary oval saloon at Stowe. It is perhaps Adam's most consummate room—and least typical. His team of artists and craftsmen, already assembled, applied their skills to perfecting simplicity, not elaboration: W. Hamilton in the paintings of ruins, Rebecca in the grisaille panels, the Carron Works in the cast iron 'altar' stoves, evolved by Adam for heating; pilasters of verd-antique scagliola by Bartoli, the doors and frames shaped to the curve of the walls. The candelabra beside them (Fig. 135) epitomize the infinite care applied.

Comparison of the plans shows that the uses, and on the W. side the arrangement, of the other rooms were altered by Adam. But the Dining Room (Fig. 141) remained at the N.W. corner linked to the kitchen wing. In its decoration Zucchi and Zucharelli contributed the applied paintings, Spang the

142. *The State Bedroom.*

chimneypiece, Collins reliefs beside the alcove, and J. Stuart, it is said, the design of the wine cooler of Sicilian jasper standing within it. The furniture of the alcove—made to display the silver, much of which the architect also designed —survives intact. On the tall pedestals are metal urns, on the sideboard a tripod ormolu incense burner and metal plate-warmer in the shape of a vase.

The dining room stucco is in Adam's best manner of moulded enrichment, and several years later than that of the E. rooms erected to Paine's plan, the drawings for which date mainly from 1760. There the ceiling of the Drawing Room, and its chimneypiece with supporting figures by Spang, are still in his first style. The classical doorways and Venetian windows, executed in green Derbyshire alabaster, may well be due to Paine, but Adam's drawings exist for the wholly rococo mirrors. The furniture includes the four famous rococo sofas embodying merfolk with dolphin feet made by Linnel elaborating Adam's design of 1762. In the Music Room, decorated with landscapes in inset frames, the organ is also from a drawing of 1762. The library has a

ceiling of recessed circles and octagons like that of the gallery at Croome.

The State suite in the W. side was replanned by Adam more compactly and so as to substitute a boudoir for Paine's dressing room. The latter is an unsatisfactory room divided into two sections by a columned screen that looks almost like a Victorian caricature of the Adam style; the ceiling is of the light pattern which Walpole criticized as of 'too great same-ness', and the walls have lost their blue damask. But the State Bedroom, though in the same style, has the remarkable rococo bed, originally hung with gold lace, its posts formed of palm trunks. If designed by Adam, the only counterpart in his *œuvre* is the tea pavilion at Moor Park.

In the park, Adam designed the characteristic fishing pavilion, the handsome three-arched bridge, and a drawing exists (1761) for a picturesque Roman ruin possibly intended in connection with it. In the old church, immediately W. of the great house and all that survived on the site of the village, is a notable sequence of sculptured monuments culminating in that of the Marquess Curzon, uncle of the present peer.

143. *The park from the east: from a painting by N. T. Dall, c. 1769. On the left are 'The Arch of Hadian' and 'Temple of the the Winds'.*

SHUGBOROUGH, STAFFORDSHIRE

Enlarged by **Thomas Anson**, *c.* **1760** and **Viscount Anson, 1792–1806**

Architects **James Stuart, 1760–70; Samuel Wyatt, 1792**

Decorators **Rose; N. T. Dall**

Owner **The Earl of Lichfield**

Overlooking the junction of the rivers Trent and Sow between Stafford and Cannock Chase, the setting and also the contents of Shugborough illustrate notably, despite subsequent alterations and losses, the contribution of 'Athenian' Stuart and the Society of Dilettanti to the development of rococo into neo-classicism. The square three-storey block forming the centre of the house was built by William Anson in 1694 to replace the manor house acquired by his grandfather seventy years before, which may have incorporated a medieval dwelling of the Bishops of Lichfield. Of his sons George, the younger, became the celebrated Admiral and circumnavigator; and Thomas, who succeeded in 1720, an enlightened patron of the arts and sciences. In 1734, two years after the founding of the Society of Dilettanti for the encouragement of 'Greek taste and Roman spirit', he himself travelled in Asia Minor in search of antiquities, but lacked means further to indulge his tastes till 1762 when his brother's death endowed him with a fortune.

The Admiral, who employed Brown to landscape Moor Park (cf. *E.C.H., Early Georgian*), occasionally contributed to embellishments at Shugborough, where a Chinese House, still existing, was built *c.* 1747 from drawings made in Canton by Sir Piercy Brett, one of his officers; and there is some evidence that, besides a pagoda in the park, Stuart's reproduction of the Arch of Hadrian was begun before 1762. Thomas Anson, as a member of the Society that financed the publication of *The Antiquities of Athens*, was already acquainted with Stuart, with whom he continued on friendly terms, at his own death in 1773 bequeathing him an annuity

of £100. Enriched at the age of sixty-six, he immediately employed Stuart to build a London house, 15 St James's Sq., to add wings and a greenhouse-sculpture gallery at Shugborough besides landscape features; and engaged Nollekens, Jenkins, Dick and others in Rome to assemble collections of sculpture, painting, and medals.

The Ionic order with which Stuart graced the front of 15 St James's Sq., in itself a prototype, is accepted as the first manifesto of the Neo-classical movement in England, except for his Doric temple at Hagley (1758, cf. *E.C.H., Early Georgian*). In letters to Anson (1764) he states that Scheemakers is carving the prototype of the Ionic capitals, 'in which I do for the honour of Athens interest myself very much'. At Shugborough he erected versions of the Arch of Hadrian, the 'Tower of the Winds' and 'Lantern of Demosthenes', derived from his and Revett's drawings, besides more rococo objects. The greenhouse, at right angles to the W. front, had a lofty Order and balustraded parapet, with an *exedra* in each pedimented end; it was remodelled probably *c.* 1790. In the work on the house itself for which Stuart can be deemed responsible, Roman and rococo predominate over Athenian, recalling that Stuart was an eclectic decorator before he turned antiquarian, and as an architect did little to adapt his Grecian knowledge to English usage. Indeed all the Greekness at Shugborough that at first sight one supposes to be Stuart's proves to be due to Samuel Wyatt. However, the wings as added by him (Fig. 145) reveal that independence, which characterized rococo design, from the Palladian Orders, and something of the neo-classical conception of pure geometrical forms based on principles of proportion. Yet their domed bows, originally covered in lead, derive rather from French usage by way of Isaac Ware. The only specifically Greek touch was the wings' cresting of terracotta *antifixae*.

The whole exterior was refaced by Wyatt, who added the portico. A series of paintings by N. T. Dall *c.* 1769 shows Stuart's wings as of half their present depth and joined to the

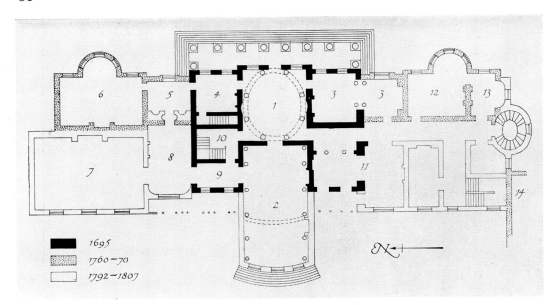

144. *Ground Floor Plan, showing additions by Stuart, 1760–70
and S. Wyatt 1752–1809.*
1. *Entry Hall.* 2. *Saloon, originally Dining Room.* 3. *Library.*
4. *Bust Gallery.* 5. *Ante-
room.* 6. *Great Dining room.*
7. *Drawing Room.* 8. *Ante-
drawing room.* 9. *Ante-gal-
lery.* 10. *Staircase.* 11. *Garden room.* 12. *Sitting room.*
13. *Boudoir.* 14. *Kitchen
wing.*

main block by single storey links. The S. wing contained
Anson's private rooms connected with the scenically con-
ceived Library (Fig. 152); the N. wing a great Drawing Room.
In the W. front a large bow of five windows lit the Dining
Room. Stuart's letters also refer to the addition of the kitchen
wing and of the stables to the S.

The two dilettanti evidently agreed that the interior of the
house should reflect the glory that *was* Rome, as Piranesi was
revealing it. A complete series of his engravings was in the
Library, and Stuart commended to Anson the quality and
interest of the plates in *Della Magnificenza* (1761). But it was
to be the romantic rather than the exemplary aspect of Rome
that was to form the background to the collection of sculpture
and old masters. Thus the dramatically devised Library has a
markedly Piranesian character, whilst the Drawing Room
struck the same note in the tempera ruin-pieces.

But apart from them the latter room (Fig. 148) is Palladian
in treatment. True, the deep cove of the ceiling has medallion
heads of Greek (and a Chinese) deities, and its centre is
filled with a large relief modelled from Guido Reni's 'Chariot
of Apollo'. But the candelabra ornament in the ceiling's
cove is a motif found at Mereworth thirty years earlier, and
the chimneypiece by Scheemakers is surmounted by an overmantel of the kind that Flitcroft frequently used. The gilt
console tables and the picture frames are still wholly Kentian.

The temperas must have been designed for the room,
which, however, did not become the Dining Room till 1795,
when Wyatt, doubling the depth of the wing, added the
present Drawing Room along its west side. Buried in the
dividing wall have been found windows, but these must have
been immediately blocked and covered over, since the seven
paintings were obviously conceived for their present positions.
Dall did also paint a decoration for the 'greenhouse'. Stuart
wrote in 1770 that Mr Dall had shown him 'the designs for
the pictures in the greenhouse and library' [sic]. The subject
for the former was:
'a view of the Temple of Minerva Polias with caryatids on
the principal ground, and in the distance what remains of the
Odeum of Pericles, both of them subjects engraved for my

second volume. They compose admirably well and will have
in my opinion a great and pleasing effect. We agree this will
be best executed in oil as it will then be safe from the moist
effluvia of the orange trees.'
So there can be no question of any of these temperas having
previously adorned the orangery. The letter shows that Stuart
to some extent collaborated with the painter in the choice of
subjects to be included in these fantasies. But they were
evidently drawn largely from Piranesi's *Della Magnificenza*.
Stuart's letter also dates Dall's work to 1770, which is confirmed by his having exhibited a 'View of Shugborough'—
no doubt one of those still here—at the Society of Artists in
1769. Nicolas Thomas Dall, elected A.R.A. in 1771, died

145. *The east front, c. 1775. Wash drawing by Moses Griffiths.*

146. *The west front, c. 1769, with Stuart's orangery and 'ruins'. Watercolour attributed to N. T. Dall, c. 1770.*

1778, was a Dane who came to England about 1760, being principally employed as scene painter at Covent Garden. These temperas, painted thinly and vigorously in monochrome on coarse canvas, show him an admirable draughtsman with a theatrical sense of the sublime. The use of ruin pieces in a decorative scheme is comparable to the rooms designed by Adam *c.* 1765–67 at Harewood (Fig. 116) and Nostell with ruin compositions by Zucchi.

At Nostell, Joseph Rose was employed by Paine and Adam successively for the stucco; and he subsequently worked at Shugborough for Wyatt. This possibly justifies ascribing the stucco of this room and the Library to him, on the strength of a curt remark of Stuart's in 1766, 'Rose thanks you for the money'. The fine character of the work tends to support the inference. But the woodwork in the Dining Room is carved with rather heavy egg and scallop enrichment. Stuart endorsed bills of John Adair, dated 1763–69, for carving and gilding numerous frames, besides models of capitals, etc. for repetitions in stone or lead.

The Library consists of two halves: the room S. of the Entrance Hall, and the link to the S. wing. The running of these together involved burrowing through the outer wall of the older house, and was made the occasion for the wide, flattened 'Piranesian' archway. Five feet through but only 8 ft high, the coffered arch is carried on little Ionic columns, and the airiness of the composition was cleverly exaggerated by placing mirrors at the sides of the *antae* to give the illusion of continuous book-space behind them; a device repeated beside the similar arched recess at the S. end. The apparent length of the whole, actually less than 40 ft, is increased by the perspective of the arch and by the part in the link being slightly narrower than the N. half. The scale throughout is so carefully handled that the effect given is of spaciousness, despite the richness of the partly gilt decoration. The ceilings have large central reliefs—of Fame and Minerva respectively—and medallions of philosophers and the arts and sciences—the quality of which is indicated by Fig. 151. Medallions after the antique occupy the spaces between the

147. *The east front as remodelled by Samuel Wyatt, c. 1792.*

148. *The Great Dining Room, originally the Drawing Room, attributed to J. Stuart, 1764–70. The chiaroscuros in tempera by N. T. Dall, c. 1770.*

149. *The Great Drawing Room, by S. Wyatt, c. 1795.*

150. (*Above*) *Bust of Admiral Lord Anson by L. F. Roubiliac* (?) 151. *Detail of Library ceiling.*

152. *Thomas Anson's Library, looking south. James Stuart, architect, c. 1762.*

arches above the shelves in the N. half, which are surmounted by busts ranging from notable antiques—a Hercules and an Emperor—to 19th century portraits. The detailing is essentially rococo. No documentation exists, but the quality of the stucco may confirm the tentative attribution to Rose made above. The 'Romantic classicism' of the conception can be taken as typical of Stuart *qua* decorator.

All Anson's books, together with most of his pictures and sculptures, were dispersed in 1842, though there remains his copy of Wincklemann's *Lettre sur découvertes à Herculaneum* (1764). One of Stuart's letters witnesses to his catholic taste—he has 'a singular book to bring you: *Eloge de Moukden*, a translation into French by Père Amiot, a missionary, from a poem by the present Emperor of China'. This rococo element was given free reign in the landscape park, which, resembling the contemporary Kew Gardens in its introduction of varied features, formed an integral part of

Anson's and Stuart's expression of the period's varied enthusiasms. It lies outside the scope of this volume, but a notion of its contents is given in Dall's landscape (Fig. 143), whilst the *chinoiserie* mirror seen in Fig. 157 is one of several formerly in the Chinese House, of which the rococo ceiling is now in the garden hall. Among relics of Anson's circumnavigation is a leg of the rampant lion which formed the *Centurion's* figurehead, and an armorial dinner service of 197 pieces presented to him by the merchants of Canton. Others are contained in the *chinoiserie* mahogany cabinet (Fig. 156) of which the design figures in Chippendale's *Director*, 1754.

Pennant says of his 'much respected friend Thomas Anson' that 'I saw him about thirty hours before his death, listening calmly to the music of the harp, preparing for the momentary transition from an earthly concert to an union with the angelic harmonies'. Shugborough was inherited by

153. *The west front as remodelled by Samuel Wyatt*, c. 1792.

his sister's son, George Adams, who took the name of Anson. His son George succeeded in 1789 and married the daughter of Coke of Norfolk, thus allying the Ansons' moderate Whiggism to one of the pillars of the party's advanced wing. In 1806, by the influence of Fox, the Viscountcy being prepared for the Admiral when he died was conferred on him.

In 1792 he engaged Samuel Wyatt to enlarge and modernize the house. The central block was much as it had been built in 1695, and a permanent weather-proofing and facing of its brickwork was required. But the adding of a storey to the links, probably by George Adams Anson, had evidently made the original pediment and pilaster treatment of the old front inadequate as the central feature of so long a façade.

His choice of a successor for Stuart, who had died in 1788

after years of chronic toping and gout, to carry out the work and to complete 15 St James's Sq., was appropriate. Samuel Wyatt, elder brother of James, was a Staffordshire man associated with Stuart—he had contracted for the carpentry of Greenwich Hospital Chapel in 1779—and had built the big adjacent houses of Doddington (1770, p. 160) and Hooton (1778). His style here is studiously Athenian as compared to his simultaneous building of Trinity House, and interesting for the facility with which it is used. The Ionic portico (Fig. 147), built to the width of the centre block without pediment, was a stylistic innovation that successfully gives unity to the over-long façade. By transferring the parapet balustrade from the centre to the wings, Wyatt shifted emphasis to them whilst carrying their cornice-level across the centre by the flat entablature of the portico. Vertical accent is confined to the

154. *The Entrance Hall, S. Wyatt*, c. 1792.

155. *The Staircase*, 1793.

156. *Chippendale mahogany cupboard. The design is in his 'Director' (1754).*   157. *From ante-drawing room to Saloon.*

colonnade, the attic storey above it being reduced to relative insignificance. The columns' construction is singular. Each consists of an oak tree clad with twenty-four facets of slate retained by lead fillets, the capitals cast in Coade stone. The whole exterior was also cased in polished slate which was then painted and sanded, with incisions to simulate ashlar masonry. (As early as 1749 the same problem seems to have troubled Thomas Anson, for Lady Anson wrote from Wimpole: 'Mr Flitcroft says the time for sanding is after the third painting is laid on'.) Stuart's domes in the wings were also slated, and a further bow, containing a side entrance, was effectively added to the end of the S. wing. At the same time the wings were doubled in depth.

The Entrance Hall (Fig. 154) was remodelled to the oval form of which Wyatt was fond by a ring of scagliola pillars. Previously it had displayed Anson naval pictures by Scott, and in the 1842 sale catalogue was full of antique sculpture. The remaining pair of casts in the alcoves were actually among Thomas Anson's earliest purchases, a letter from Nollekens, 1765, specifying '2 centaurs in plaster, £25'. The Staircase (Fig. 155) was renewed, for which Messrs. Underwood supplied the cast metal ornaments in 1793, and the small rooms communicating to the N. wing remodelled. The ante-room to what now became the Dining Room (Stuart's Drawing Room) contains busts by Roubiliac of Lord and Lady Anson (cf. Fig. 150).

The new Drawing Room (Fig. 149), added to the N. wing, is slightly longer and little less magnificent than Stuart's. The coved ceiling was decorated by Joseph Rose, who received £800 in all, the chimneypiece being by Richard Westmacott and the seat furniture costing £264 by 'Smith,

upholsterer, of Cavendish Sq.'. The 1842 catalogue lists paintings here by Pannini, G. Poussin, a Claude formerly in Dr Meade's collection, and a Vandervelde (*Calm with Shipping*), besides the two large Guido Reni still in place. It also contains Reynolds's portraits of Mrs Adams and Admiral Sir C. Saunders; the two *Meets of Lord Anson's Hounds* by Webb of Tamworth (1827) pertain to the next generation. Accommodation was further increased in 1803 in expectation of a visit by the Regent, by extending the original Dining Room to form a Saloon on the centre axis, which Wyatt provided by the expedient of bringing forward the three central bays as a kind of axial wing ending in a segmental curve (Fig. 153). The decorators were J. Alcott, Bernasconi, and Rossi (chimneypieces).

The 2nd Viscount was created Earl of Lichfield in 1831. Postmaster General under Melbourne when penny postage was introduced, he was hospitable and addicted to all field sports: his hounds, which he gave up on appointment as Master of the Buckhounds, are the origin of the Atherstone Hunt. These and political expenses much reduced an estate worth £10,000 a year at his accession so that in 1842 the London house was sold, with all contents, and much of that of Shugborough. Happily the fixtures were not offered, and items of historic interest were bought in by Lady Lichfield. Subsequently the 2nd Earl acquired much excellent French furniture, the bulk of which has, however, been sold recently. Much of interest remains, though relatively little, unfortunately, of the contemporary collections that would have rendered Shugborough representative artistically, as it is architecturally, of the Dilettante impetus to the neo-classical movement.

SYON HOUSE, MIDDLESEX

Reconstructed for **The Duke of Northumberland**

Architect **Adam, 1762–c. 1770**

Decorators **Rose, A. Kauffman, T. Moore** (others not
  identified)

Owner **The Duke of Northumberland**

In his conversion of the medieval and later quadrangle of the
former convent of Syon into a neo-classical palace, for which
Henry (Smithson), 1st Duke of Northumberland, approached
the brothers in 1761, Adam recognized the opportunity to be
as great as the need for that synthesis which his temperament
and studies equipped him to apply. 'The idea was to me a
favourite one,' he tells us.[1] The Duke, 'a person of extensive
knowledge and correct taste, possessed the wealth to execute
a great design', and 'resolved that the apartments be executed
in the antique style', but to preserve the existing walls and
levels. These created many 'difficulties with which I had
to struggle'. His solution was so to 'manage' them, so as to
'increase the scenery and add to the movement';[2] thus to
create a progression of state rooms 'thoroughly neo-classical
in that it contains a variety of geometrical shapes contrasting
happily, and each originating in a classical prototype.'[3]

[1] *The Works of Robert and James Adam*, 1773.
[2] ibid. [3] Summerson, op. cit., 265

158. *The entrance gateway, with 'artificial stone' enrichments*, 1769

Their relationship and the quality of their decoration are such
that Syon is one of the country houses of England 'which can
unquestionably hold its own with the greater palaces of the
Continent'.[1]

It is noteworthy that no more than superficial alteration
was contemplated of the plain, somewhat grim, exterior of
the building which, despite its chequered intervening history,
preserved the form of the conventual cloister founded by
Henry V.

Its towers and battlements, though scarcely picturesque,
already carried associations too venerable to sanction replacement, even by a Percy (in name but not by blood) seeking
to re-establish the historic family's prestige.

Syon, retained by the Crown after the convent's dissolution,
had often proved a sinister possession for its occupants, pre-
luding sudden ends to Queen Catharine Howard, Protector
Somerset, John Dudley, Duke of Northumberland, and his
daughter-in-law Lady Jane Grey—who here had given her
fatal consent to ascend the throne. The Protector had
initiated alterations, but they were not resumed till James I
had granted Syon to the 9th Earl of Northumberland. He
caused a survey to be made by Moses Glover, 'painter and
architect', who with Christmas and Jansen was also responsible for the front of Northumberland House at Charing
Cross—long surmounted by the famous lion now re-erected
at Syon. The E. front (Fig. 159) probably dates from this time
since it contains the Long Gallery, a Jacobean feature,
carried on a Renaissance arcade. Inigo Jones supervised
unspecified repairs in 1632. The situation, looking eastward
across the river to royal Kew and screened from London's
approach by an ancient park, gave an idyllic quality to historic walls that the eye of taste accounted significant enough
without further embellishment.

No more than the trees of the domain were visible to the
passenger along the Oxford highway, for whose benefit the
colonnaded screen with arched entrance was erected in
1769[2] (Fig. 158). This 'lace-work gateway', as he called it,
caused Walpole as soon as 1773 to complain that neo-classic
'grandeur and simplicity are not yet in fashion'. Its ornate
grace pleased Adam himself and, at the outset, enunciates the
third element in his synthesis, and in the Syon symphony:
classic form, romantic overtones, exquisite ornament.

In the majority of his works circumstances were accountable
for the third element predominating, and at Syon especially.
In his full scheme the inner court was to be filled by a vast
domed rotunda. Had this been built permanently instead of
as the 'temporary Pantheon' described by a visitor in 1768, it
would have centralized the whole plan and created 'sublime'
illusions of extent by its circular colonnade within its peri-
meter, besides making 'grandeur and simplicity' dominant.
Linked to it there was to have been a suitably grand entrance
in the N. side.

As it is, we enter from the W. in the middle of the Hall,

[1] Lees-Milne, op. cit., 107.
[2] An artificial stone (Holt's?) was used for the enrichments,
notably the renaissance scrolling of the main pilasters, but proved
defective and had soon to be partly replaced in the newly perfected
Coade stone, which shows lighter (see *Introduction*, §V).

159. *The south and east front, with the 17th century arcade.*

which probably occupies the site of the refectory. Its design, almost a double cube of 33 ft., is based on a Doric basilica with apsidal ends. The forceful scale of the ornament exemplified in Fig. 163 derives from Piranesi, with whose engravings Adam's dramatic plate in the *Works* stresses the connection. The colouring, so large an element in the Adam synthesis, is here restricted to black and white; but 'movement', set up by the diagonals in the ceiling, is given scope and 'additional pictoresque' in the treatment of the S. end. Here steps to the anti-rooms ascend behind the screen of columns spanning a wide arch that echoes the *exedra* in the other end. The arrangement was in fact an afterthought, necessitated by old levels found during construction, the first proposal having been for a narrower arch with straight steps.

The solution witnesses to Adam's ready empiricism and still enabled him to draw attention to the 'noble effect and increased variety' produced by the end recesses being 'one square, the other circular'. Ante-rooms planned at either end, he continued, were 'for the attendance of servants out of livery, tradesmen etc.' Only the south one was built, which he described as 'decorated with columns of verd-antique marble'—a studied understatement for perhaps the most gorgeous room in English architecture (Fig. 164).

The twelve precious antique columns, recovered from the bed of the Tiber, are so placed as to square the oblong space without the deception being at once apparent. On three sides they support salient entablatures, carrying gilt statues; but on the S. they are set 8 ft. from the wall and carry a con-

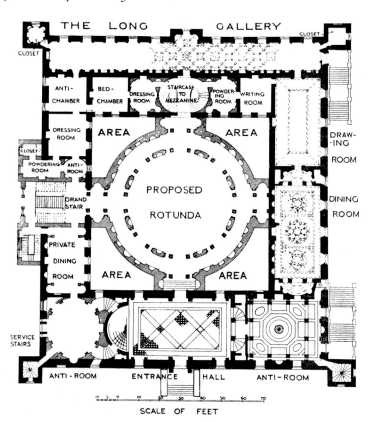

160. *Adam's plan, 1761. Unexecuted and non-existent work shown hatched. North point to left. (A. T. Bolton.)*

161. *The Entrance Hall, looking south, with the ascent to the Ante-room.*

162. *Entrance Hall, looking north.*

163. *Detail of south west angle of Entrance Hall.*

164. *The Ante-room, looking south west. It was designed round the twelve superb antique columns of verde antico marble.*

tinuous beam, also with statues surmounting the columns. The 'narthex' so formed faces the entrance from the hall and, although the mind may question this trick of picturesque empiricism, it is accepted by the eye, charmed by the greens, blues, pale terra-cotta and gilding of the colour scheme, which are intensified in the patterned scagliola floor. Each inter-columnar section of wall is occupied by chimneypiece, door, or window. But on the N. side (Fig. 166) superlative gilt trophies were modelled by Rose inspired by those at the Villa Madama. Adam's anticipation, in this neo-classic *tour de force*, of its decorative perversion in the *Empire* style is emphasized by furniture of that period brought from Northumberland House.

Columns and recession are also used to manipulate the proportions of the Great Dining Room (Fig. 166) to a triple cube of 21 ft. (66 × 21 × 21 ft.). In contrast with the Ante-room it is parchment coloured. The '*rosso antiquo*' in the statue niches is a later addition that gives an emphasis not intended to those figures, making Cipriani's frieze-panels in chiaro-scuro look a little feeble, and weakening the effect of the antique relief in the overmantel. Acting on his principle of eliminating drapery from dining-rooms, Adam did not provide even for curtains, their place being taken by shutters in the deep enriched window recesses. The room was one of the first completed, and the ceiling resembles that of the library at Shardeloes.

'Next is a splendid with-drawing room for the ladies, or *salle de compagnie*, varied from the others', to quote Adam's description, 'by the form of its ceiling which is wood and painted in compartments' (Fig. 169). Also, we might add, by

165. *In the Ante-room looking towards the Hall. Gilt bas-reliefs by Joseph Rose.*

166. *The Great Dining Room looking east. Chiaroscuro panels by Cipriani. The 'rosso antico' background in the niches was inserted later.*

167. *The Dining Room chimneypiece.*

168. *Detail of the Great Drawing Room doorway.*

170. *The ceiling. Composed of 'paterae' with red or blue grounds painted by Angelica Kauffman.*

171. *Ormolu by Matthew Boulton in the chimneypiece of the Drawing Room.*

172. *The Gallery looking north. Neo-classical design adapted to Jacobean proportions.*

174. *The 'Round Closet' at the north east corner of the Gallery.*

173. *A corner of the Gallery, showing the scheme of decoration in detail.*

176. *Chimneypiece of 'Bossi' work, from Northumberland House.*

175. *The square 'Chinese Closet' at the south east corner of the Gallery.*

177. *The chimneypiece and a section of the Gallery.*

178. *The private Dining Room in the north range. Decorated* c. 1864, *to contain pictures brought from Northumberland House. Reynolds' portrait of the first Duke hangs above the sideboard.*

its wall lining of a crimson Spitalfields silk relieved by a silver-grey pattern, said to be the first produced by that factory. As an experiment, for he never repeated it, Adam tried to reproduce in the ceiling the effect of Raphael's and da Udine's vault decorations at the Villa Madama. It is laid out in small octagons containing *paterae* with red or blue grounds painted on paper by Angelica Kauffman—which Chambers called 'a myriad skied dinner-plates'. There is an alternative design for a modelled plaster ceiling related to the superb Moorfields carpet signed by T. Moore, 1769. In the magnificent doors and doorcases and the chimneypiece he introduced another new English product, Matthew Boulton's ormolu, applied on a ground of inset ivory in the doorcase pilasters (Figs. 168, 171).

The colour sequence so far has been black and white, blue and green, white and gold, crimson: the rooms themselves ratios of cubes. The next differs entirely (Fig. 172) and exercised Adam's power of synthesis to the full, for it was a Jacobean Gallery 136 ft. long, 14 ft. wide and high. To orthodox eyes these proportions were grotesque. Adam resolved to rationalize them by applying the gallery to a purpose akin to its original one: 'for the reception of company before dinner and for the ladies to retire to after it—for the Drawing Room prevents the noise of the men being troublesome.[1] It is (therefore) finished in a style to afford great variety and amusement'. The problem was to devise an architectural ratio of 'movement' for this passage. He first tried dividing the wall-space into a succession of wide, low arches, but de-

cided on a closely-grouped unit of four pilasters[1] with wide intervals centred on the doors and fireplaces (Fig. 177). Thus a sense of spacing and variety is obtained in the perspective, and, in effect, the traditional Jacobean use of pilastered wainscoting is synthesized with neo-classicism. Similarly the ceiling consists in repeated circles held in a framework of octagons and squares which leads the eye down the vista and tends to expand its actual width. The circles are echoed in small medallion portraits in the frieze. The soft opalescent colouring repeats the clear but gentle hues of the paintings and is predominantly grey. From either end opens a closet in a corner tower, one round, one square, exquisitely Roman and Chinese respectively, as a further item of 'amusement' (Figs. 174, 175).

The quality and cost of these rooms suggests why the Duke stopped short of the central rotunda and curtailed the decoration of the private apartments in the N. range. These remain as they were when Adam was called in, except for 19th century alterations. A corridor was added here in 1824 serving three rooms looking into the court. Of these the Green Drawing Room contains a magnificent chimneypiece of 'Bossi' inlay and ormolu from Northumberland House (Fig. 176), over it a portrait of the infant Edward VI, recalling the short possession of Syon by his Lord Protector. The private Dining Room (Fig. 178), with full length portraits of the Duke and his Duchess, Lady Elizabeth Seymour, by Reynolds, was decorated about 1864 by 'Charles Smith of Upper Berkeley Street'.

[1] '62 pilasters by Pergolesi, 3 gns. each', is entered in the 1st Duchess's Syon house-book. M. A. Pergolesi, *d.* 1801, published decorative designs 1777–92; but there is no confirmatory evidence for his work here.

[1] Cf. Lady Lyttelton's similar case at Hagley, *E.C.H., Early Georgian.*

G

MERSHAM LE HATCH, KENT

Built for **Sir Wyndham and Sir Edward Knatchbull**

Architect **Adam, 1762–72**

Decorators **Rose, Carter, J. Gilbert, Alexander and Shrimpton, Chippendale**

Owner **Lord Brabourne**

Mersham, near Ashford, is notable as the only English country house entirely built by the Adams, and for the complete documentation of its decoration. Further, its relative modesty and simplicity make it particularly representative of the Adams' influence on the evolution of the normal country house, in contrast to the 'palaces', towards the end of their great 'first period' (*c.* 1770). The Mersham letters

were fully edited in *English Homes*, VI, by Avray Tipping, whose account is here condensed.

Le Hatche accrued to the lands of the old Kentish family of Knatchbull in 1485. The 6th Baronet, Sir Wyndham, who had inherited as a boy, in 1761 procured a report on the old house from Cole, the Ashford builder, who advised that it was past repair. But some materials could be used again; and he recommended that bricks be made on the site for 12s per 1,000 as compared with 18s if bought, that the estate yielded suitable oak, and fir for scaffolding, whilst 300 tons of Portland stone could be shipped to Hythe, each sloop carrying about 70 tons. A square block of three storeys with a bow commanding the view northwards was contemplated, for which Adam, consulted in 1761, produced a design. Owing to its urban appearance, however, and the difficulty in dis-

179. *The north front from across the lake.*

98

180. (above) *The central bow of the north front. The colonnade was added when the door became the main entrance.*

181. (above, right) *Detail of the original entrance in the south front.*

182. (right) *Plan of principal storey as built.*

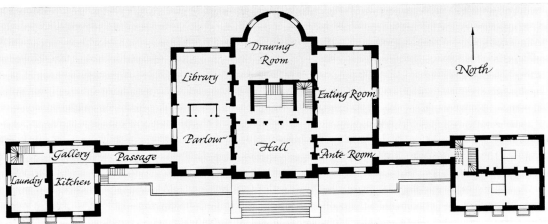

posing of kitchen and domestic smells in so restrictive a plan, he advised the addition of wings. Foundations, on the northern slope exposing a basement that is buried on the S. (entrance) elevation, were dug in 1762, although the 'new design' incorporating wings was not completed till 1763. This scrupulously observed Sir Wyndham's wish that the house should be 'kept entirely plain'. Indeed Mersham follows the basic type of Georgian country house, to which Adam imparted the neo-classic qualities of directness and

simplicity—aptly illustrated by Fig. 180. But in the same year the young baronet died.

His uncle and successor, Sir Edward, though aged sixty, decided to go on with the house. By 1766, when, somewhat to his dismay, £8,000 had spent, payments to decorators began, Rose estimating for the stucco of the principal rooms: for the Hall £82 9s. 9d., the Drawing Room ceiling £111 4s. 8d., and Dining Room £141 17s. 11d. Next year Thomas Carter was supplying chimneypieces the two of stone in the Hall for £60 including carriage and packing, the one of marble in the Drawing Room for £210. Zucchi, who sent in a detailed bill in French, provided the Hall overmantel paintings in 1768. The wood carving, for doorcases and overmantels, came from John Gilbert, totalling £469 14s. 11d. Such an item as the imposts of the Dining Room chimneypiece (Fig. 186) cost only 36s. each and the whole frieze enrichment 46s. The wrought iron for the Staircase (Fig. 187) and front entrance (Fig. 181) was supplied from Adam's designs by Alexander & Shrimpton at £150 and £125 respectively, but the cast members by the Carron Iron Co. Four letters of Robert Adam's to Sir Edward between 1770 and 1772—written as he says when deeply engaged in 'the affair of the embankment at Durham Yard', i.e. the Adelphi crisis—are given in full by Tipping. They show the pains taken by Adam personally with the smallest details of his buildings. One relates to procuring lead figures of appropriate character for the niches in

the Dining Room (Fig. 185), which Hoskins of St Martin's Lane would cast for 12 guineas ('the common price for that size'). Adam was even asked to design a 'sash of drapery' for an Apollo who raised Sir Edward's blushes. Elsewhere he refers to a drawing sent to Cole for the Drawing Room ceiling 'which I have coloured in the way I think will have the best effect and will serve to direct the Painter, (but) I do not think any of the Countrey hands could do it as it ought to be'.

The Drawing Room contains a tablet recording Sept. 13, 1762 as the date of the first stone's laying and 1765 as that of the roof being 'completely covered', 'Robert Adam Esq., architect, Thos. Cole Master Builder'. It was the last room to be completed, but others were in use from 1767 when furnishing began. This was mainly in the hands of Chippendale, the Mersham letters and accounts throwing direct light on his character and methods. The first account is of 1767–68,

183. *In the Hall, looking north east.*

totalling £905 13s. 8d., of which two-thirds is for new furniture, the rest for repairing and upholstering old, and for paper-hanging. Besides elaborate pieces, he supplies quite simple furniture and such utensils as carpet brooms for the 'Dining Parlour'. A sideboard table costs 12 guineas, 10 chairs with open carved backs £25, a large oval glass in a frame 46 guineas, the total £137 17s. od. The 'alcove Bedchamber' had a 'Domed Bed with carved cornise and vases', japanned white and blue, and hangings costing 4s. a yard. The walls of this room were hung with 12 pieces of 'strip'd Verditure' set off with '6 doz. Borders'. The dressing room was an example of the fashion for lining walls with engravings in printed paper borders and with festoons and other decorations in the same material. Unfortunately it has not survived, but there is one that does at Woodhall Park, in connection with which Chippendale's bill for the Mersham room is given (p. 182). Several of the Hatch bedrooms had 'Chintz Papers'; one, which cost 6s. a piece, is called 'a fine Strawberry Sprig', suggesting that the pattern may have been named after Horace Walpole, who was using wallpaper extensively at his Gothick villa (cf. E.C.H., Early Georgian).

Another account carries on to Feb., 1770, and relates chiefly to furnishing and papering another Bed and Dressing room. For this Chippendale had estimated £196, so that Sir Edward objected to the charge of £267 4s. 7d.: 'As to the man who put up and coloured the Green Paper he was not above two days at work and did it extremely bad, went away and left part of his work to be done by the other man . . . I could have employed a Person in the Country who would have done everything just as well . . . The Walnut Tree plank you had here you have not given Credit for and you have two old Glass Sconces which have never been fitted up, belonging to us'. Chippendale, a little before sending in his second bill, had been pressing for settlement of the first. 'I am sorry,' he wrote, Jan. 12, 1770, 'that my necessity obliges me . . . but it is the time of year when money is much wanted to support Credit.' Up to July, 1769, payments amounting to £800 had been made, so that £105 was outstanding. On the back of the letter Sir Edward drafted his reply: 'Mr Chippendale . . . As I receive my rents once a year so I pay my Tradesmen's Bills once a year which is not reckoned very bad pay as ye world goes: so that when the time comes round that shall be pd also'. The matter was finally cleared up in 1771, when other letters concern a defective mirror and Thomas Haig explains that his partner is away in Yorkshire, doubtless in connection with his work at Harewood and Nostell.

Chippendale himself and a new mirror reached Hatch next year, and more furniture was ordered: the eating-room curtains, of 'Blue mixt Damask 7s. a yard', carved cornices £20, 16 'compass backed chairs covered in blue morocco' at 55s. a piece, and '2 neat Mahogany Compass Tables with term feet and fluted rails £17'. In 1773 further japanned green and white looking glasses were provided, marbled topped tables and 10 'cabriole arm'd chairs Japanned green and white' costing £31 10s., with green striped cotton cases for them at £7. Lady Knatchbull had wanted larger chairs, so Chippendale proposed 'what we call Berjairs', but they would have to be made; regarding covers for them, 'serge is most commonly used but as the room is hung with Indian paper, you might choose some sort of Cotton—suppose a green

184. *The Staircase from main to upper floor.*

striped Cotton which at this time is fashionable'. The Bergères were apparently not ordered, though the striped covers were.

The last bill, for 1778, relates to furnishing the Drawing Room. Sir Edward, aged seventy-four, is more economical than ever and tells Chippendale, who comes to Hatch, though in this last year of his life, that only £100 can be spent, exclusive of curtains and upholstery to be procured. Chippendale nevertheless supplied '10 rich Cabriole arm'd Chairs in burnished Gold at £5 16s. od. apiece', two matching sofas at £15. Making up the curtains, supplying fringes, tassels, and lining cost £40; buff serge covers, for times when the room was not in use, were supplied for £20. Sir Edward was shocked by the total, £282 4s. 6d., and wrote accordingly. 'Sir', replied Chippendale (Aug. 6, 1778), 'you nor no one else could seriously Imagine that those Elegant Goods would come to no more (than £100). What you think exorbitant will bear inspection of any man of Business who is a Judge. I shall submit to whatever you think proper'. Sir Edward's riposte reveals interesting details of the firm's methods. He complained that 'yr man' remained eleven weeks, with board and lodging, besides having two maids who did all the sewing

186. *Adam's design for the Dining Room chimneypiece.*

187. *Adam's first design for the Drawing Room chimneypiece (cf. Fig. 189).*

185. *The Dining Room. Above the chimneypiece, Sir Wyndham Knatchbull who began the building.*

189. *The Drawing Room chimneypiece. Above, Sir Norton and Lady Knatchbull, c. 1610.*

188. *Doorways in the Drawing Room.*

190. *The Drawing Room. Chippendale's letters about the original furnishing (no longer preserved) are quoted below.*

work, and he supposed that the bill 'is made out to answer any charge you may be at on account of your blunders abt the Carpet.'

Sir Edward had no doubt braced himself to the cost of a special carpet to fit the bow-windowed room, perhaps designed by Adam and reflecting the ceiling like that at Saltram (Fig. 256). He also wanted the large mirrors that could now be made of a single plate, like those at Harewood (Fig. 114), so wrote for designs and quotations. Chippendale, Haig and Co. replied (June 23, 1778), giving the lowest price for the plate glass alone as £170 each plus £28 for frames. 'You have likewise a design for an Axminster Carpet to correspond with your Ceiling to go into the Bow: the Expense will be . . . about £100, they will have a painting to make of it at large and the Colours to dye on purpose; but if square like your other carpet it will be proportionately less'.

Chippendale's unbusinesslike methods and apparent expensiveness led to further furniture being supplied by

William Crawford; paper for the bow room walls was procured direct from the noted firm of Bromwich for £12 9s. 0d. and hung by 'Samson ye Upholsterer'; and the carpet was made and supplied by Thomas Moore for £57 12s. 0d. (compared to Chippendale's estimate of £100).

Sir Edward died in 1789, having taken sixteen years to complete Hatch. The principal entrance to the house is now to the basement in the N. bow (Fig. 180), and considerable internal alterations were made by the 9th Baronet between 1819–49. His son, who added his mother's name, Huguessen, of Provender, was created Baron Brabourne by Gladstone at the end of a long political career. The 2nd Baron greatly changed the rooms after 1871, so that none of Chippendale's wallpaper and upholstery remains, and little of his furniture. Their unique documentation can, however, be illustrated by the contents of other houses in this volume.

Since the war Mersham has been leased by Lord Brabourne to the Caldecott Community.

191. *The Rococo Park landscape in 1768. A painting by W. Tomkins (1730–82).*

BROCKET HALL, HERTFORDSHIRE

Built for **Sir Matthew Lamb**, *c.* **1765–8; Lord Melbourne, 1770–80**

Architect **James Paine**
Landscape **R. Woods**
Owner **Lord Brocket**

As a rebuilding, probably on the foundations of an Elizabethan quadrangle,[1] Brocket externally can be considered as belonging to that empirical movement in Georgian architecture of which the so-called rococo style has been claimed

[1] Tipping, in *English Homes*, VI, pointed out that the vestiges of a courtyard plan seem to be represented by the position of the Georgian kitchen and staircase.

to be a phase (*E.C.H.*, *Early Georgian*). It shows many of that manner's attributes: the plain, astylar, brick elevations with sparse stone dressings, the broken skylines, the 'movement' imparted by the diminishing ratio of window-height, the breaking down of the mass by means of those facetted bows devised to secure 'prospect' and sunlight. A pair of these flank the S. front and another subdivides the N. The rococo naturalism of the contemporary landscape setting, depicted in the painting (Fig. 191), emphasises this stylistic aspect of the building, which is the more interesting for being designed by Paine between his monumental essays at Kedleston (p. 70), at Worksop (Fig. 7), and at Wardour (p. 119).

The estate, astride the valley of the R. Lea of which the stream was to be converted into the serpentine lake, had

192. *The southern front. A characteristic 'Rococo' elevation probably based upon Elizabethan foundations.*

193. *Ground Floor Plan. From Paine's 'Plans of Seats', vol. 2.*

belonged to Brockets and Reades before its purchase about 1746 by Matthew Lamb, a successful attorney whose business included that of the Hatfield Cecils and the Cokes of Melbourne (whose daughter he married). He seems to have been content with the old house in its ancestral park till after 1751, when the death of his brother-in-law brought Melbourne to his wife. But since, according to Paine, only two sides of the house were completely finished at the death in 1768 of Sir Matthew (a baronet since 1756), rebuilding may not have been begun much before 1765. The sides completed and fitted up were, according to Paine, the north and east—probably the actual N.W. and N.E. ranges, since the other two contain rooms definitely later. Of these it is the S.E., seen on the right of Fig. 192, that contains the entrance in its raised and pedimented central section, and the S.W. that overlooks the lake. The walls of these were no doubt built, although their interiors were not decorated.

The rooms in the completed sides are 'Rococo Palladian'—for example, the 'common dining parlour' with Ionic columns and compartmented walls; but the plainly treated entrance hall in the S.E. front may also have been serviceable. The conception of the Staircase Hall no doubt also belongs to this phase. It is a scenic composition allied to Paine's staircase effects for Kedleston and Worksop: on the vaulted galleries above three sides stand enriched columns—each with their block of entablature, like Gibbs's at St Martin's—and carry stretched or compressed segmental arches supporting a cupola that lights the whole dramatically. But whereas the design published by Paine shows triple turned balusters and wooden treads, the actual stone stairs have a wrought iron balustrade of the Greek honeysuckle pattern, but unusually large, which Adam used at Osterley and proposed for Harewood. This change was one of those made in the second stage of completion. How marked these were to be is shown by their contrast to the rococo and Palladian detail of some of the bedrooms (Figs. 194 and 195), where the alcove is

treated much as those by Campbell at Compton and Mereworth (*E.C.H., Early Georgian*).

Decoration was resumed after 1770 when the 2nd baronet, the young and fashionable Sir Peniston Lamb, had acquired an ambitious wife, daughter of Sir Ralph Milbank, and, as a supporter of North's government, had been created Lord Melbourne in the Irish Peerage. At their Piccadilly house (now Albany) and later at that in Whitehall, the Melbournes entertained 'the King's Friends' in a style which it became desirable should be extended to Brocket. Hence the greater elaboration of Paine's later rooms in the style that Adam had meanwhile made the rage. Improvements of the park were undertaken, for which the plan exists, stated to be due to 'Mr Wood of Essex', a competitor of Brown's, who also dealt with Hengrave Hall, Suffolk. Paine spanned the resulting waters with a stately three-arched bridge and designed other objects.

The Adam style is paraphrased rather than followed in the ceilings of the 'Morning Room' and 'Drawing Room' flanking the entrance hall (Figs. 198 and 197), the designs for which Paine gives in Vol. 2 of his book (1783); they are, rather, classically refined developments of rococo, lacking the dynamic element found in Adam's. In the Library, at the W. end of the S. front (Fig. 199), he very successfully achieved the 'elegance' at which he now aimed, though the *décor* is no longer complete. The bookcases of painted wood are designed *en suite*, that for the more precious volumes fitted with metal tracery, the scrolls of which were repeated in an overmantel mirror. The ceiling here is distinguishable from one of Adam's by the continued naturalism of the foliage in the angles; possibly one of the artists whom he usually employed executed it. The brass door furniture (Fig. 203), with rams' heads of which one serves as key, may be matched with Adam's at Saltram and elsewhere. Yet if the room as a whole is compared with the library at Nostell, for instance (1765, see *E.C.H., Early Georgian*), its lesser degree of integration becomes apparent.

The right hand half of the bookcase on the right of the chimneypiece opens to reveal a door to the Saloon which, 58 ft. long, fills the centre, including the first floor, of the S.W. front. It is shown in Fig. 200 as before the sale in 1923, when walls and windows were still hung with 'exceeding rich flowered (crimson) damask', probably, like that in the Drawing Room at Syon, from Spitalfields. The arched gilt pelmets of the windows and the pier-glasses between them were little less sumptuous than those at Harewood. Paine's design for the magnificent chimneypiece (Fig. 202), in the V. and A. Museum, is dated 1772 with a note that the frieze is to represent the Rape of Europa. It elaborates the type favoured early by Adam.

The conception of this ceiling (Fig. 200), it seems likely, may also have been influenced by that in the Drawing Room at Syon. But the units, though still of a size to be painted in the studio, are much larger. They consist in 'historical and emblematical paintings of the late ingenious Mr John Mortimer'. 'Our sublime Mortimer' was one of the young men who followed Sir Joshua's ideal for establishing a school of 'historical' painting, and the ceiling's principal subjects—'Night and Morning', 'The Four Continents', 'Flora and Pomona'—are in that neo-classical style which is also

194, 195. *Chimneypiece and bed alcove of a bedroom in the part completed by Paine for Sir Matthew Lamb before* 1768.

196. *The Staircase.*

197. *The Drawing Room ceiling, as decorated after* 1770.

198. The 'Morning Room' ceiling. This, and Fig. 197, are typical renderings by Paine of the 'new classical' style of decoration introduced by Adam.

199. The Library. Paine's book-cases, fitted with brass tracery, were originally painted white.

200. *The Saloon as it remained in 1923. The ceiling decorated by Mortimer and Wheatley.*

reflected in the non-representational panels. After Mortimer's death in 1779 the work was at length completed by Wheatley five years later. At about the same time (1784) Lord Melbourne was considered a 'safe' man to appoint to the Prince of Wales's Household, when Lady Melbourne made herself so attractive to the Prince that he presented her with the great equestrian portrait of himself by Reynolds which still hangs at the end of the Saloon.

Before long her husband shifted his allegiance to the remnant of the Whigs rallied round the Prince, so it was with that party that Brocket was thenceforth to be so memorably associated. It is said that Sir Joshua, who often came down to work on the Prince's and other portraits, would coax the future Prime Minister to behave by giving him a ride on his foot.

It is with the personality of the 2nd Lord Melbourne that Brocket will always be most closely associated. Not a phase of his earlier life but was connected with the place; in particular, as beautifully depicted by Lord David Cecil,[1] with 'the long drawn-out, ironical tragedy of his marriage (to Lady Caroline Paget), from the rapturous, troubled honeymoon to the muted pathos of her last days. . . . The chintz-curtained bedrooms, the gilded, elegant saloon, the leather-scented quiet of the library, the park with its grassy vistas . . . all these were heavy with memories for him'. Though little now remains of the rooms directly associated with the days of 'the Grand Whiggery', the saloon is not greatly changed since the veteran Melbourne there received Queen Victoria for the last time in 1841. After his death the estate passed to his sister Emily, widow of Earl Cowper, and it was at Brocket that her second husband, Lord Palmerston, spent much of his later years. On the death of Lady Palmerston, last of the Lambs, Brocket went to her son, Earl Cowper, who lived at nearby Panshanger. In 1923 it was bought, together with some of the original contents, by Sir Charles Nall-Cain, later created Lord Brocket. His son has re-occupied part of the house since the repair of damage sustained during its war-time use.

[1] *The Young Melbourne*, 1939; *Lord M.*, 1954.

201. *The south side of the Saloon with its original draperies (as in 1923).*

202. (*left*) *The chimneypiece of the Saloon*, 1772.

203. (*below*) *Door furniture of the Library. One of the ram's heads actuates the bolt; the vase below the handle shields the key-hole.*

PEPER HAROW, SURREY

Built for **the 3rd and 4th Viscounts Midleton, 1765–75**

Architect **Sir William Chambers**

Decorators **Alken, Wilton, Hayward**

Owner **Middlesex County Council**

204. *The entrance front. The porch added by Cockerell in* 1843.

In the development of the country house the importance of Peper Harow is its representation of the personality of Sir William Chambers. He directed ripe scholarship to consolidating and refining the English tradition deriving from Inigo Jones, in relation to his firmly held classical principles and familiarity with French practice, to which he brought the best trained mind of his time. His influence was exerted through intimacy with the young King, to whom he had been architectural tutor, and which furthered the foundation of the Royal Academy; through his books and pupils; and above all by his official architecture as Surveyor General, notably Somerset House.

His country house practice was small compared with that of Paine or Adam, for the most part in the shape of adjuncts and alterations. His proposals for Harewood (*c.* 1755) being rejected, the design of its terminal pavilions was adapted to that of the Casino at Marino, near Dublin, *c.* 1780, which best represents his genius. Elsewhere he was apt to be under the necessity of working in 'rococo' for which, although it went against his principles, he showed a marked *flaire* in the *chinoiseries* of Kew, though less in the gothick rebuilding (under protest) of Milton Abbey, Dorset. He contributed to the neo-classical movement by his learned eclecticism and, as Mr Summerson remarks of Somerset House, by his application of the 'French influence to ironing out the bolder terms of English Palladianism'. Peper Harow illustrates this aptitude in a country house of medium size.

205. *The Entrance Hall. The reserve of the white architectural scheme against a flat coloured ground is typical of Chambers's 'Antique' style of decoration.*

206. A doorcase in the Drawing Room.   *207. Wilton's chimneypiece in the old Dining Room.*

*208. The Drawing Room ceiling. As designed by Chambers the decoration was white on a purple ground. The painted devices
were added during Pugin's alterations, c. 1840.*

The property, beside the R. Wey near Witley, was bought in 1713 by Allen Broderick, Lord Chancellor of Ireland, created Viscount Midleton of Co. Cork in 1715. His son, in the year of his death, 1765, procured sketch designs from Chambers for a new house. A copy of the plan, which remained there, is given in Fig. 209; a S.E. elevation has two rows of seven windows and a hipped roof; and one of the N.W. shows the little porch and stretches of blank wall indicated in the plan. This also shows that the principal fronts had the same emphasized centre and Venetian windows that exist. The present porch, however, was added by C. R. Cockerell, 1843.

As the plans were dated March, 1765, it is probable that little building was then done. When the successor came of age in 1775, new estimates were obtained from Chambers for work to cost £8,180 (brickwork £2,253, Portland stone £1,208, floors and roof £1,179). In 1777 an 'Account with Wm. Chambers' specifies the offices as costing £3,200; chambers, basement and garrett £2,585; and for finishing the principal floor £2,340. Extra to them were the bills of Chambers's usual sculptors, Joseph Wilton £202, Richard Hayward £186, and J. Alken £294, the whole amounting to

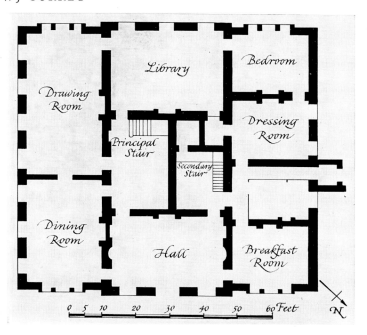

209. *Ground floor plan, from the original by Chambers.*

210. *The serpentine scrolls of the ironwork emphasize the impeccable simplicity of the Staircase Hall.*

211. *The Drawing Room chimneypiece by Wilton. Above it, one of the canvasses by Stubbs painted for the house.*
212. *(right). The Hall chimneypiece elaborates on the Doric mode of the room. It supports a bust of Marlborough.*

£9,912, of which only £894 was outstanding. The need for more rooms was met by substituting for the pitched roof a third storey carrying the walls up into a parapet with balustrade, which, in the entrance front, takes the form of a podium resembling Taylor's central feature at Heveningham (Fig. 336).

The Hall (Fig. 205) is typical of Chambers's restrained formality in applying the Doric mode (the Order itself is absent) to an interior. The cornice's ornament of drapery festooned between paterae and bucrania is supplemented in the chimneypiece with trophies of implements (Fig. 212). Its surmounting pedestal carries a bust said to be of Marlborough, repeated in a medallion above—the other medallions represent bewigged contemporaries. The fine mahogany doors used throughout cost 10s. per foot (or 6s. 6d. if dummies). The chimneypieces carved by Wilton are in the Old Dining Room (Fig. 207) and Drawing Room (Fig. 211). The latter is specified as Chambers's design and as having the pilasters 'feneer'd with verd-Antique and inlaid flutings

of do., the Tablet of Bacchus and Tyger'; the cost £118. Four rooms have ceilings designed by Chambers, of which that in the Drawing Room (Fig. 208) is typical of his manner, though embellished with little devices painted during Pugin's alteration by William Evans. Its original colouring, in six coats, is given as being purple and white. That of the Dining Room was green and white, and of the Library grey with a pink ground. The Hall and Staircase best preserve Chambers's effect of a white design against a plain coloured ground, with, in the latter, the additional grace of the simple scroll-pattern balustrade. The painting by Stubbs seen over the Drawing Room fireplace is one of three 'painted on purpose' to surmount the Dining Room doors. The best bedchambers were hung with 'Indian' papers, in one case specified as 'cut out Indian papers', as at Saltram (Fig. 260). Lady Midleton herself worked several of the carpets and we learn that she 'intends working chairs'; but for the principal rooms she was recommended, probably by Chambers, 'to go to Moore's manufacture near Moor Fields'.

TRAFALGAR HOUSE, WILTSHIRE

Additions for **Henry Dawkins**, *c. 1766–70*
Architects **J. Wood, junr., N. Revett**
Decoration **Cipriani**
Owner **The Viscount Folkestone**

213. *The west front, overlooking the Avon valley.*

Standlynch House, high upon the steep wooded bank of the Avon S. of Salisbury, was renamed Trafalgar, on the analogy of Blenheim, when bought by the nation for the successors of Admiral Lord Nelson in 1814. Its position is superb, looking west over the loveliest of chalk streams to the slopes of Cranborne Chase, and approached on the landward side through a grandly landscaped park. Under Elizabeth I the Bockland family acquired the old house that lay near the surviving mill and church. Royalists and recusants, they were implicated in the rash but gallant attempt by John Penruddock of Compton to overthrow Cromwell in 1655.

The small but remarkable late gothic church beside the river was rebuilt in 1677 by Maurice Bockland. His son's trustees sold the estate in 1726 to Sir Peter Vandeput, Baronet, of Twickenham, whose ancestor had emigrated from Antwerp in 1568. In 1733 he erected on a new site the rectangular brick house which forms the existing central block. This is characterized by heavily blocked window architraves, whilst above the cornice the attic storey, partly concealing the low pitch

214. *The portico added by Nicolas Revett to the east front, c. 1766.*

215. *The Hall c. 1745; a medallion of Inigo Jones in the over-mantel.*

216. *Murals by Cipriani in the Music Room.*

hipped roof, has square windows with plain moulded archi-traves. The Hall in the E. front is a cube (Fig. 215), possibly paying tribute to the similarly proportioned room at Wilton by the roundel bust of Inigo Jones in its two-storeyed chimneypiece. In contrast to the Palladian-baroque decora-tion of the walls, the ceiling is of elaborate rococo that can scarcely be earlier than 1745, as is also the flat ceiling of the single-storey saloon. Unless it is an uncommonly early in-stance of the style, it suggests that alterations were made *c.* 1745, when possibly the attic storey was added to enlarge the accommodation. The main staircase, lit by the Venetian win-dow in the S. end, has triplicate ballusters and mahogany dado, with a ceiling of Coleshill pattern. It is tempting to assign a hand in the design and decoration to Roger Morris (1695–1749, see *E.C.H., Early Georgian*), but less on stylistic grounds than because he married Vandeput's daughter, Mary.

In 1766 Standlynch was bought by Henry Dawkins, M.P., of Demston, Chippenham, whose brother James (*d.* 1759) had pioneered exploration of Greek sites in Asia Minor in 1750 and assisted Stuart and Revett in their records of Athens. Henry, who shared James Dawkins's interests, added pavilion blocks to N. and S., of two storeys and base-ment connected by long corridors at basement and ground level only, the basements lit by areas on either side to the width of the central building and pavilions. This lengthening of the plan is similar to the arrangement of Buckland (1754, *E.C.H., Early Georgian*) by the younger Wood, who signed the plates of Standlynch in *Vitruvius Britannicus*, V (1771). Here each pavilion is a sizeable house in itself (as one of them has since become). That to the N. contained 'Mr Dawkins's Dressing Room', the 'Lady's Dressing Room' in the middle, and a bedroom; over laundry, wash house and bake-house. The S. pavilion contained the Dining Room in the centre above the kitchen, with a service staircase; a two-storey brewhouse filled the S.E. corner. The note accompany-ing the plans does not mention any pre-existing house nor specify the design as by Wood, but does state that 'the portico with some of the other internal decorations have lately been added by Mr Rivett [*sic*] one of the editors of the Athenian and Ionian antiquities'. Revett (see *E.C.H., Early Georgian*), who returned from Ionia in Sept., 1766, designed the memorial in Chipping Norton Church to James Dawkins (*d.* 1766) and was employed on West Wycombe *c.* 1771, but his contributions to Standlynch are his best authenticated domestic work, and among the few instances of direct Hellenic influences on houses at this period.

For the portico (as in his church at Ayot St Lawrence, 1778) he used the Doric order of the Temple of Apollo at Delos, of which the shafts are fluted at the extremities only. These are set in threes, providing a central projection, and the entablature carries a balustrade surmounted by Grecian urns (Fig. 214). His principal work within is in the N. wing, where the Doric treatment of the corridor vestibule can be assigned to him (Fig. 218), together with the ceiling in the middle room to a radiating pattern introducing the honey-suckle and other Greek motifs (Fig. 217). The Library chimneypiece (Fig. 220) in statuary marble with delicate mouldings and Grecian symbols including a lyre, mask, etc., is presumably his, and possibly the design of the wooden

217. *Ceiling designed by N. Revett in the north wing (room K in plan).*

218. *Revett's Doric vestibules to the north wing.*

219, 220. *Chimneypieces showing Grecian influence.*

221. *The unusual Venetian window.*

222. *The Dining Room bow in the south wing.*

entablature adorned with laurel wreaths added to an earlier bedroom chimneypiece (Fig 219).

The Dining Room in the S. wing is an elongated octagon, the decoration of which, gone over in the 19th century, appears to be originally due to Wood. The Venetian window, of which the curious external treatment is seen in Fig. 221, is surmounted within by seated female figures in relief, which are possibly due, however, to the 19th century re-decoration, when the prediments of the lateral windows and other trimmings were added (Fig. 222).

The walls of the Music Room (Fig. 216) are painted in oil colours by Cipriani, on one wall figures representing the Arts grouped in landscape, another devoted wholly to Poetry, represented by Shakespeare declaiming 'The Poet's eye in a fine frenzy rolling' to a tempestuous sky.

The reason for Henry Dawkins so extending the house is not known for he had no family; possibly he contemplated gatherings of Dilettanti, to whose Society he was elected on his brother's death. At his own he instructed his executors to dispose of the estate, which they did in 1814 to the Trustees under the Act of 1806 for 'purchasing an estate for the successors of the late Vice-Admiral Viscount Nelson'. The sum of £90,000 had been voted for this purpose and a perpetual pension of £5,000 a year granted by Parliament. The Admiral's brother, the Rev. William, was created Earl Nelson but, outliving his son, was succeeded in 1835 by his nephew Thomas Bolton, who took the name Nelson but died within the year leaving a son aged twelve. The Dukedom of Brontë and most of the contents of Trafalgar House passed in 1835 to the 1st Earl's daughter. The rooms are illustrated as during the occupation of the 4th Earl Nelson. The furnishing included many relics of Nelson—pikes, muskets, etc. from H.M.S. Victory are seen in the Hall; but was mostly due to the 3rd Earl and his wife, Lady Mary Agar (*m.* 1845), who bought much at the Fonthill sale. After Parliament's termination of the perpetual pension at the death of the 4th Earl, the estate and contents of the house were sold by auction in 1950.

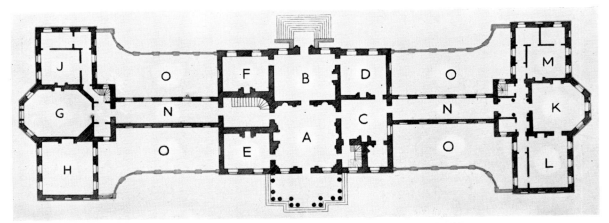

A. Hall. B. Saloon. C. Breakfast room. D. Library. E. Music room. F. Drawing room. G. Dining room. H. Upper part of Brewhouse. J. Bedroom. K. Lady's dressing room. L. Bedroom. M. Mr Dawkins's Dressing room. N.N. Galleries. O.O. Areas.

223. *Ground Floor Plan, from 'Vitruvius Britannicus', vol. V. North point to the right.*

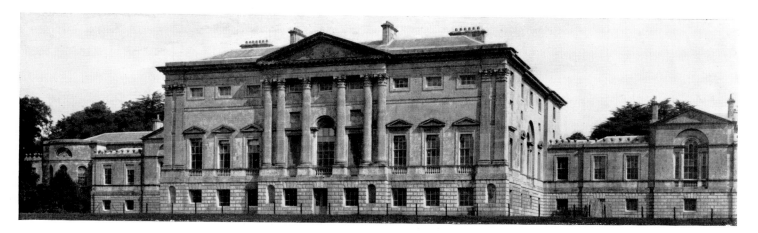

224. The south front to the park and lake.

WARDOUR CASTLE, WILTSHIRE

Built for **the 8th Lord Arundell of Wardour**
Architect **James Paine, 1768–76; Soane, 1788**
Decorator (of Chapel) **Quarenghi**
Owner **The Cheshire Foundation**

Among the wooded hills near Tisbury, John, Lord Lovell, in 1392 built the fortified mansion of Wardour Castle to the unusual plan of a hexagon. The estate was bought in 1547 by Sir T. Arundell and in 1578 the building was modernized for his son by Robert Smithson, between his work at Longleat and at Wollaton. A typical Renaissance arch by him survives in the internal court. But during successive sieges in 1643–44 two sides of the castle were destroyed, after which the family removed to Breamore, Hants., though a small building by the lake adjoining the castle seems to have been adapted for occasional residence *c.* 1720. As Catholics the Arundells were debarred from the usual means by which wealth was acquired in the 18th century: but the marriage of the 7th Lord with the heiress of the Arundells of Lanherne— the Cornish stock from which the Wardour line had sprung— and of the 8th to Mary Conquest, heiress of Irnham, Lincs., enabled the latter in 1768 to re-establish himself on his ancestral domain in the grandest style.

Paine was no doubt recommended as architect by his great recent designs for other Catholic peers—Worksop for the 9th Duke of Norfolk (Fig. 7, 1763) and Thorndon, Essex, for Lord Petre (1764), which latter his design for Wardour closely resembles. It may be significant that these last three Palladian palaces—of which Wardour alone survives whole— were commissioned by Catholics, possibly owing to lack of sympathy with the current trend to a liberal rendering even of the classics, and to religious conviction in the authority of Roman architecture. With his other commissions, these huge buildings rendered Paine unquestionably the leading house architect of the decade. But externally, though deriving straight from English Palladian precedents, they can be regarded as neo-classical in their severe plainness, and re-assertion of the ancient virtues of proportion and simplicity. The new building at Wardour commands a picturesque view of the castle (Fig. 225) beyond a lake, much as at Tabley. But its austerity is uncompromised by any suggestion of syn-

thesis. Nor is there even that brisk subdivision of mass which characterizes Paine's more rococo designs—deriving from Burlington and Holkham, although the latter influenced the planning of these palaces. Yet internally Paine's planning carried Palladianism on towards the neo-classical conception of related geometrical shapes: his section of Wardour (Fig. 228) illustrates this, though to a less degree than his schemes for Kedleston and Worksop. But by the time that he had finished, as Mr Summerson puts it, 'other men and other influences had brought it even further'.

An external ascent to a saloon appears to have been dispensed with from the first, in preference for a monumental internal stair, so disposed as to astonish. The entrance, beneath the single Venetian window in the N. front, is insignificant, and gives into a low Doric columned hall (where

225. Old Wardour Castle, 1392; ruined in the Civil War.

226. *The entrance front from the north west.*

the brass-mounted cast-iron stove is probably the original heating device, Fig. 229). It leads through an arch into a 'Pantheon' where semicircular flights converge on the gallery of the main floor and eight columns carry the dome (Figs. 230 and 231). The square area is reduced to a circle by a girdling corridor on the lower level and by four exedrae on the upper, each containing three doors (Fig. 232). A fifth exedra on the centre axis communicates with the great dining room above the entrance. The detail is exquisite, notably that of the

wrought brass balustrading—still carrying candlestands—and the effect at first floor level is, on its smaller scale, akin to that proposed by Adam for the central Pantheon at Syon.

The contents and much of the mural decoration of the rooms have been dispersed, those illustrated appearing as in 1930. The three middle bays of the South front were occupied by a square Music Room (Fig. 233), its ceiling modelled in Roman arabesques (possibly by the Italian decor-

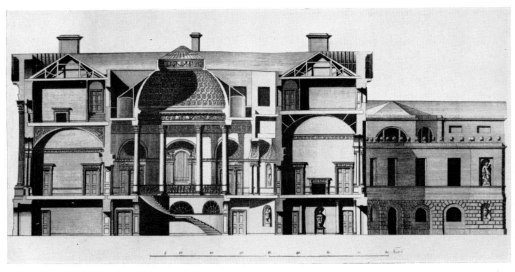

227. *Plan of Principal floor.* I. *Ante-room ('Music Room').* 2. *Drawing room.* 3. *Saloon.* 4. *Common Dining Room.* 5. *Great Dining room.* 6. *Library.* 7–7, 8–8, 9–9, 'a complete apartment'. 10. *Upper part of Chapel.* 11. *Anteroom.* 12. *'Mixtilineal anteroom' to private wing.* 13. *Small dressing room.* 14. 14, *Lord and Lady's bedchamber.* 15. *Breakfast room.* 16. *Lord's dressing room.* 17. *Lady's dressing room.* 18. *Small book-room.* 19. *Upper part of kitchen.*

228. *(below, left) Section through centre. (Figs. 227 and 228 from Paine's 1771 book of Plans.)*

229. *(below) A contemporary stove in the Entry Hall.*

230. *The Staircase, seen through the Entry Hall arch.*

231. The gallery and dome of the Staircase.   232. The head of the stairs. The exedrae in the diagonal segments each contain three doorways.

234. The Chapel; looking to the entrance (west) the design recalls Dance's All Hallows, London Wall (1765-67).

233. The Music Room. The flattened dome ceiling with Roman arabesques contains an 'Aurora' by Battoni after Guido Reni.

235, 236. *The west end of the Boudoir, and its chimneypiece of onyx, 'fleur-de-pêche', and 'lapis lazuli'. At the south west corner of the State suite, 7–7 in plan.*

ator of the Chapel), and the centre filled with a copy by Battoni of Guido Reni's *Aurora*. A rather plain, oblong, drawing room filled the E. half of this front and contained notable rococo mirrors; W. of the Music Room was the state bedroom with a vast domed mahogany bed draped in crimson silk with deep embroidered borders. Beyond, the Boudoir was little wider than its window, its rounded inner end with two inset china-cupboards of satinwood and having an arched recess containing its original settee. This faced an amazing chimneypiece of *fleur-de-pêche* marble inlaid with lapis and onyx and surmounted by a palm-leaved mirror inset with a landscape said to be by de Loutherbourg. Since crimson silk with gold rosettes of *Empire* pattern lined the walls, some of the decoration must have been somewhat later, but the ceiling, and richly elegant quality of the whole, showed Paine's quality as a decorator (Figs. 235, 236).

The Chapel, of which the roof rises above the W. wing (Fig. 234), reveals him in another light, though the concentric domed Mausoleum at Gibside, Northumberland (1760), gave him a greater opportunity for church design—which he seized. The Chapel is a barrel-vaulted hall with lunettes piercing the vaults and originally with both ends apsidal. That to the east has the organ gallery (opening from the

house). The decorator is recorded to have been Quarenghi, a Venetian, who may also have worked the Music Room ceiling. An interesting aspect of the Chapel is the resemblance of its form to All Hallows, London Wall, erected by George Dance the younger in 1765–67, and thus in time for Paine—if he required it—to borrow the idea. But if so, he ignored the revolutionary simplifications that the younger man there introduced, notably the omission of the conventional cornice—which, in comparison, here looks heavy and otiose. This reflection may well have occurred to John Soane, Dance's disciple, when called on in 1788 to enlarge the liturgical E. end. He added a square, flat-domed chancel flanked by apsidal transepts in which the family pews are carried as galleries on scagliola columns. He assimilated the work to Paine's, but the stucco is characteristic of the date. A magnificent marble altar was made at Rome by G. Quirenza and enshrines an antique sarcophagus of *verd antique* presented at the time by the Pope. The Chapel also possesses the Wardour chasuble dating from the later 15th century.

When the 16th Lord Arundell of Wardour was killed on active service in 1944, the title became extinct and the estate passed to Mr Reginald Talbot, son of a grand-daughter of the 9th Baron, from whom the mansion has been acquired by its present owners.

SALTRAM, DEVON

Built for **John Parker**, *c*. 1745, and **Lord Boringdon**,
1768
Architect **Adam**, 1768
Owner **The Earl of Morley**

237. *The south front* c. 1745–50, *of rendered and whitewashed brick, with a Regency porch.*

In its wooded park overlooking the Catwater with Plymouth in the distance, Saltram, like Crichel, is a reconstruction, in two stages, of an earlier house, in this case of such an ancient quadrangle as Cothele. The first stage, *c.* 1745–50, is characteristic Rococo, outstanding in its decoration; the second exemplifies Adam at the end of his great 'Early Period'.

Outwardly, however, it is of singular plainness, the Georgian brickwork rendered and whitewashed against the weather like any seaboard cottage. The porch, added for the same reason in the early 19th century, prompted Tipping to surmise that till then the front had had architraves and perhaps pediments to its principal windows and possibly red brick for its surface—the material that so often and so well consorted with the thick rough slates and lead ridge that the roof retains.

The lower sections of the W. side (Fig. 238) may represent the height of the original house and indications remain of its

rough masonry structure: just to the right of the high central block can be seen the pyramidal roof of a four storeyed tower, like that at Boringdon near by, containing a 17th century

238. *The west side, incorporating parts of the 17th century house.*

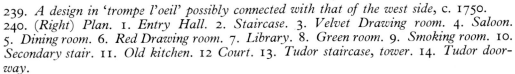

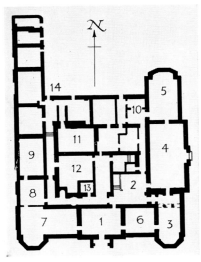

239. *A design in 'trompe l'oeil' possibly connected with that of the west side, c. 1750.*
240. *(Right) Plan. 1. Entry Hall. 2. Staircase. 3. Velvet Drawing room. 4. Saloon. 5. Dining room. 6. Red Drawing room. 7. Library. 8. Green room. 9. Smoking room. 10. Secondary stair. 11. Old kitchen. 12 Court. 13. Tudor staircase, tower. 14. Tudor doorway.*

staircase; and across the little court from which this rises the kitchen has massive chimney-stacks that were heightened in the 18th century as the house grew up. In the mid 17th century, when it belonged to Sir John Bagg, there was living at Boringdon Edmund Parker, whose grandson, George, was to buy Saltram. John, the latter's son, in 1725 married Earl Poulett's daughter Catharine and, after his father's death in

1743, began the changes that were to transform it. The external rebuilding, faced with whitewashed plaster, was probably completed by 1750 and exemplifies Rococo's aptitude for assimilating an existing structure. In the W. side (Fig 238) the centre had probably been raised to its present height during the Bagg ownership under Charles II; but the lower links, and the high 'pavilions', of which that on the right is

241. *The Hall, with exceptionally fine Rococo plasterwork of c. 1750.*

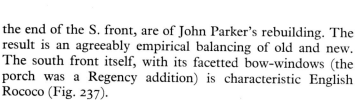

242. (*Above*) *Rococo pastoral relief in the overmantel of the Hall.* 243. *Superport in the Hall. High relief stucco.*

244. *The Staircase, looking north east. The square domed ceiling has rococo decoration.*

the end of the S. front, are of John Parker's rebuilding. The result is an agreeably empirical balancing of old and new. The south front itself, with its facetted bow-windows (the porch was a Regency addition) is characteristic English Rococo (Fig. 237).

The decoration of the Hall within is a notable product of the style (Fig. 241). Over the stone fireplace the bust of a Roman is welded into its background (Fig. 242): a relief in plaster of a pastoral landscape with figures, uncertain in subject but dexterously modelled. With the elegant frame of floral garlands and attenuated Terms, it recalls a similar relief at Gately Hall, Norfolk. The overdoors, with groups of boys (Fig. 243), and the large Mercury who flies across the rococo ceiling, are no doubt by the same hand, which exhibits many of the characteristics of Charles Stanley (see *E.C.H., Early Georgian*); but this work is almost certainly too late to be assigned to him. The quality of the stucco is matched by brisk carved enrichment of woodwork and wainscot, both here and in the Staircase Hall (Fig. 244). The N.E. door from the Hall leads into it beneath an upper landing carried on Doric entablatured columns. The stair itself is of the conventional type; but the ceiling is yet more elaborate

than that of the Hall, with every division—the great cove, a broad flat band, and the lantern—alive with rococo scrolls, amorini, birds and baskets of flowers.

The same artist worked the ceilings of the two S.E. rooms (6 and 3 in plan). The further of these is called the Velvet Drawing Room from the red velvet used not only for upholstery and curtains but for lining the walls (Fig. 245). The rococo wood-carving, too, is of exquisite quality on architraves and above the arched doorway seen beyond the columned screen at the inner end of the room. A date about 1760 for the completion of the room may be suggested by a bill—one of the few extant documents relating to Saltram—of Benj. and Thos. Carter for chimneypieces supplied. That here must certainly be one of them (Fig. 246).

There is reason to believe that Lady Catharine Parker was the moving spirit of these decorations. A *trompe l'oeil* is preserved, painted to look like a drawing fixed to a board, and addressed 'To the Rt Hon. Lady Katharine Parker of Saltram' (Fig. 239). It depicts a house of which the centre block resembles the S. front of Saltram, but of two storeys only and with a portico and a dome, prolonged by wings ending in great gates beneath cupolas. Tipping hazarded that

245, 246. *The Velvet Drawing Room, c. 1760, and its chimneypiece with Reynolds's 'Mrs Parker and her Son'.*

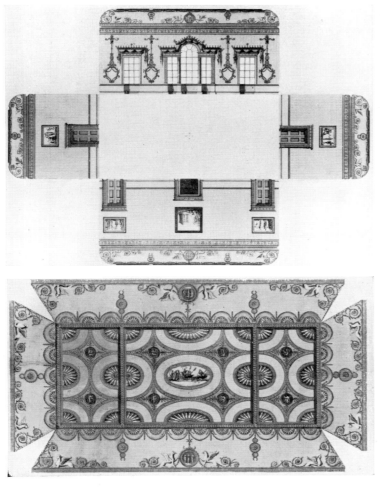

247, 248. *Adam's drawings for the sides and ceiling of the Saloon.*

249. *A doorway in the Saloon.*

250. *Adam's Saloon, looking north. The colouring is pale greys, yellows, and blues. The ceiling differs from the design.*

252. *The Saloon chimneypiece.*

251. *The east windows of the Saloon.*

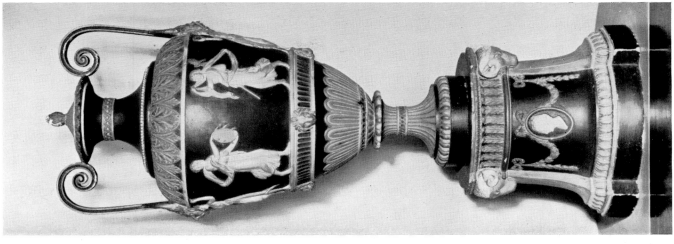

254. The sideboard and north end of the Dining Room.

253. A Sideboard urn.

256. *The Dining Room, 'Adam Green' walls, the enrichments white: with Zucchi's decorative paintings.*

257, 258. *Chinese paintings on glass with 'Chinoiserie' frames in a bedroom.*

259. *One of the four Bedrooms lined with 'India' papers.*

260. *Another, with cut-out scenes of smaller scale.*

it might be a 'fanciful and friendly' scheme by Adam, connected with his actual work at Saltram, though he recognized the stylistic improbabilities. It seems more likely to have preceded the first stage of reconstruction *c.* 1750, and that it related to the remodelling of the W. side, some of the drawing's features (e.g. the bows) having been adopted for the S. front. Its authorship remains a mystery, perhaps linked to that of several other fine mid-century houses in Devon and Cornwall, including Pencarrow and Trewithen, besides Saltram.

In 1768, the year of John Parker's death, Adam was called in by his son of the same name, for designs with which to complete the fitting up of the E. range, the greater part of which had apparently been standing empty. Whether previously intended or not, he occupied the whole centre with a Saloon or Ball Room (Fig. 250) on the great scale that was then being demanded (cf. Crichel, p. 153, Claydon, *E.C.H., Early Georgian*).

The Saloon is entered from the Velvet Drawing Room. The colouring is now buff and grey, to which the pale blue striped damask on the walls has faded, Wedgwood blue in the background of the ceiling (that has been carefully repainted), and the cove Nankeen yellow. The cove and its painted medallions flanked by griffins is as shown in Adam's drawing for the room (Fig. 247). But the flat of the ceiling is an improvement on the drawing for it (Fig. 248) which proposed a repetitive pattern a little reminiscent of that of the drawing room at Syon (p. 92). The window side (Fig. 251) was carried out exactly as to the carved and gilt boxing for the draw-up curtains; but instead of small oval mirrors hanging from elaborate swags, large ones with side-tables, much like those

in the same position at Syon, were substituted, and were repeated on the opposite wall. A more magnificent chimney-piece, with Siena columns, was introduced (Fig 252); and such wall treatment as had been suggested was scrapped for the display of the considerable collection of paintings on which Sir Joshua was advising his friend and fellow Plymptonian. He was also painting Mrs Parker, both in a gracious full length that hangs in the saloon above a Guercino originally belonging to him; and seated (Fig. 246) with her little boy, the future Earl of Morley, who was inserted two years afterwards. In 1775 his mother wrote: 'I wished to have the child added to the picture two years ago . . . but he made such faces it was impossible. This year Sir J. has consented to put him in and though he sat but an hour you would be astonished to see how strong a likeness it is'.

Beyond the Saloon is the Dining Room. Its low length and shape were due to the earlier phase, and the proportions seem to have challenged Adam to devise a synthesis of his own with the Palladian kind of *decor* (Fig. 256). Apparent simplicity and the use of flat colour to impart unity makes the room one of his most satisfying compositions, as it is one of the closest integrated and best preserved. The ground colour is 'Adam green' with the enrichments white, in ceiling, walls and furniture; green, too, is the prevalent hue of the paintings supplied by Zucchi of suitably picturesque subjects. These have plainly fluted frames except the one over the chimney-piece, which alludes to a Palladian type and is similar to those placed in like positions at Osterley and Bowood. In the Georgian bow he replaced two of the windows with niches for painted composition copies of Etruscan urns, and designed the painted but otherwise plain semicircular side-

261. *In the Colopies Bedroom, lined with continuous non-repetitive landscape.*

board. But its attendant urns on pedestals (Fig. 253), like their sisters at Kenwood, are as exquisitely adorned as if minted by Wedgwood. In the ceiling, again, Adam adapted the compartmented Palladian type besides reverting to his own earlier, large-scale range of motifs. Mrs Zucchi (Angelica Kauffmann), who certainly worked at Saltram, probably painted the ceiling vesicas. The whole pattern is closely reflected in the carpet, probably from Moorfields whence also would have come the exceptionally large and rich one in the Saloon—which is not so reflective.

Adam did not go upstairs, all the bedrooms being of the earlier phase, but their outstanding *chinoiserie* decoration is of these years. In one this is confined to paintings on glass in rococo frames (Fig. 257). But four are entirely lined with 'India papers'. In those over the Dining Room and known as the Colopies (Fig. 261), the Dressing Room has a small repetitive landscape design, whilst that in the bedroom is unusual as having pure landscape for its theme. In the S.W. bedroom a third variant is found: separate scenes, some of them repeated several times, and mounted to form a pattern, much as in the contemporary 'print rooms'. Some of the scenes may have been cut from large sheets, but the majority do not suggest

that. A fourth and most unusual kind of paper is that in a small S.E. room (Fig. 259), consisting in repetitions of two sheets, each about $2\frac{1}{2}$ ft. wide by 5 ft. high, on which are groups of Kang-Hsi figures splendidly coloured and boldly disposed. Saltram is also rich in the *garnitures* of chased ormolu, sometimes embodying blue-john, which Matthew Boulton was producing at his Soho works to Adam's design.

The younger John Parker sat for Devon as a Whig from 1762 to 1784 when, transferring his support to Pitt, he received the Barony of Boringdon. Five years previously he had evidently meditated further changes at Saltram, for there is a plan of Adam's dated 1779 for recasting the W. front with a great domed dining room in the centre, and turning the existing one into a library. This latter provision, however, was in fact left to his son—the 'Bor' of Lady Holland's Journals and eventually 1st Earl of Morley—who turned into a pleasant Regency library the room in the S.W. corner adjoining the entrance hall.

The 4th Earl inherited Westonbirt, Glos., through his mother, with Sir George Holford's famous Arboretum. He was succeeded in 1951 by his brother, the present peer.

CLAREMONT, SURREY

Built for **Lord Clive**

Architect **Brown, with Holland, 1770–74**

Mason **H. Wood**   Carpenter and Builder **J. Hobcroft** (?)

Plasterer **W. Pearce**   Smith **Thos. Rawstorne**

Owner **Claremont School for Girls**

The character of Robert Clive (1725–74), than whom 'our island has scarcely ever produced a man more truly great either in arms or in council', is perhaps to be exactly estimated only in context with the houses which he built. In contrast to the chequered glory of his achievements and reputation, and indeed to the buildings of many lesser contemporaries, they reflect both the essential modesty and the delicacy of his nature.

The original designs for Claremont, recently discovered, taken with estimates and price books preserved at Sir John Soane's Museum, and Brown's record of payments by Lord Clive, have settled the long-disputed authorship of this house and thrown light on the relationship to its design of two of the principal neo-classic architects—Holland and Soane.[1] Clive bought Claremont in 1768, from the Duchess

[1] D. Stroud in *Country Life*, CVIII, p. 60, from which much of this account is derived. The drawings, found in 1949 by Lady Mary Clive (by whose permission they are reproduced) at Whitfield, Herefordshire, may have passed into the possession of George

262. *Elevation, endorsed by Clive and Lancelot Brown. As built, except that the frieze of the pediment is plain.*

of Newcastle. The castellated mansion formed by Vanbrugh for the 1st Duke out of his own villa still stood on the level ground below the existing belvedere and adjacent to the existing bastions of the kitchen garden in the landscape by Kent.[1] The great Nabob proceeded to commission designs for a new house from two architects, Brown and Sir W. Chambers. The latter had already rebuilt for him (c. 1760–64) his father's home, Styche, and altered Walcot (c. 1764), both in Shropshire; and had erected Lord Bessborough's Roehampton villa (now Manresa College). Clive's preference for Brown's proposal is said to have provoked the Surveyor General's thinly veiled attacks on Brown in the *Dissertation on Oriental Gardening* (1772).

Brown placed his new house on a rise above the site of its predecessor. He proposed a self-contained block of two storeys with basement, conventional but of simple elegance, midway between Chambers's two manners, the bald and the scholarly. The materials were to be Portland stone, and the white brick which Brown advocated as more economical than ashlar and avoiding the clash of red brick with the green lawns of the landscape. Set off by cedars, his conception, though of no great architectural distinction, has the well-bred ease which was the taste of the age.

The plan, forecasting Holland's for Berrington (p. 184) in its arrangement, can be regarded as Brown's and Holland's joint production and typical of their office. But the appropriation of the western half of the main floor to the owner's private suite is a peculiarity due apparently to Lord and Lady Clive, since it was largely repeated at Walcot. It is also notable for the conveniences afforded—W.C.s, a Powdering Room, and a 'cold bath' (under the S. portico steps). The carefully devised whole illustrates the qualities to which Holland afterwards drew attention in his father-in-law's

263. *The front from the south.*

Clive of Whitfield, Lord Clive's cousin, in connection with his building in 1772 of Mount Clare, Richmond. The presence of the estimates among Soane's papers can be accounted for by his working for Brown and Soane during the final stages of the building.

[1] See Laurence Whistler, *The Imagination of Sir John Vanbrugh*, 1954, for the fullest account of the Vanbrugh building.

264. (left) The perron of the north front.
265. Design for 'best staircase' balustrade (cf. Fig. 268).

buildings: 'No one I ever met with understood so well what was necessary for the habitation of all ranks of society; no one disposed his offices so well, set his houses on such good levels, designed such good rooms, or so well provided for the approach, drainage and comfort and convenience of every part of a place'. In these respects, we may infer, Brown's

capability led him to be preferred to the leading professor of architecture.

Foundations were begun in 1770 and designs were agreed in the following February. The building estimate came to £15,584, and the eventual cost of decoration to £15,882. The mason-carver was Henry Wood; the builder probably John Hobcroft, the carpenter, who had himself designed and built Padworth House, Berks., the previous year. Thomas Rawstorne the Smith's bill for the 'best staircase' balustrade (Fig. 268) came to £880.

The drawings suggest the work of at least two hands, and that Brown was already enlisting the services of his young assistant, son of his old friend Holland the builder. The elevations can be accepted as Brown's alone, and he evidently went some way with the interiors. A scheme for a gothick Library recalling a room at Corsham (Fig. 275) and a design for the Great Room with a ceiling similar to that of the gallery there (Fig. 269), have the rococo qualities of his known decorative designs. Others are clearly informed by the critical and archaeological values applied to design by the 'new classical' school. A chaster alternative for the Great Room, with a geometrical ceiling intended to receive painted decorations (Fig. 270), can be ascribed to Holland; but a much simplified version of his ceiling for the Crimson drawing room at Carlton House ten years later was in fact used.

A third hand may be detected in two drawings for the entrance hall. In 1772 Brown and Holland, now in partner-

266. Principal floor plan based on 'Vitruvius Britannicus', vol. VI. 1. Drawing Room (1855 Library, 1925 Billiard Room). 2. Eating Room. 3. Great Room (1912 Drawing Room). 4. Small Eating Room (1912 Duchess's sitting room). 5. Lord Clive's dressing room (1846 Princess's bedroom). 6. Occasional bedroom (later bathroom). 7. Lord and Lady Clive's bedroom (1846 King's bedroom). 8. Lady Clive's dressing room (1846 Yellow Drawing Room, 1912 divided as bed and bath room).

267. *The Entrance Hall.*

ship, engaged as draughtsman John Soane, then aged nineteen. Years later he recalled that he had drawn for the Bishop of Derry (see Ickworth) a dining room 'in imitation of one of the rooms at Claremont, executed from a design made by me when I was employed by the late Mr Henry Holland'. The design accompanying these remarks, Miss Stroud has observed, shows a room very similar to one of the alternatives for this hall. One is an elaborate essay with Corinthian pilasters, the other an ingenious scheme for an oval arrangement of columns in a rectangular space (Fig. 274). As executed (Fig. 267) the Hall broadly follows this design, but the symbolic reliefs, an inlaid floor echoing that of the ceiling, and the principal doorway taken from Wood's *Ruins of Palmyra*, are probably interpolations by the partners.

The Drawing Room (1 in the plan, Fig. 266) has a typical Holland ceiling with a central circle. Brown made a design for the Eating Room (2) that is remarkable for including a series of great decorative paintings of episodes in Clive's Indian career (Fig. 276). No such paintings are known to exist, though 'a very large picture in the style of Rembrandt painted by Wilson and certainly his masterpiece, representing Lord Clive conducting Meer Jaffier on board our ship', is recorded by Walpole.[1] This could scarcely have been one of

[1] *Visits to Country Houses*: 'Collection of Dr Hurd of Leeds,' Aug. 13, 1772 (Walpole Soc., XVI).

268. *The Staircase and inner Hall.*

269. Brown's rejected design for the Great Room.

270. A design (part) for ceiling of Great Room.　　　271. The Great Room (Drawing Room) in 1923.

272. Chimneypiece of the Great Room.　　　　　273. A doorway in the Great Room.

274. *Alternative design for the Entrance Hall.*

275. *Brown's design for a Gothick Library.*

the 'Claremont set', but Clive or Brown may have had Wilson in mind for painting it. The plasterer's accounts include £20 for 'enrichments to the walls of the Eating Parlour on ea. side pictures'. It is probable that the room, which was re-decorated *c.* 1846, never received these particular paintings. The setting up in 1772 of a committee to investigate the conduct of the British East India Company may well have discouraged such a display, since genteel opinion was hardening against the triumphant transactions of its servants. Clive could profess himself 'astonished at my own moderation', but

his high-strung vitality had been undermined, and two years later the creator of the British Empire in India died by his own hand. By then most of the decorative work at Claremont was complete, if in a simplified style, though Brown's account was not at length settled by the executors till 1780.

Claremont was sold to Lord Galway, then to the Earl of Tyrconnel, and belonged to C. R. Ellis 1807–16. It was then acquired by the Crown for settlement on Princess Charlotte, who died there in child-birth the following year. It remained with her husband, subsequently King of the Belgians, till his

276. *The Eating Room: a design to display paintings (by Richard Wilson?) of events in Lord Clive's career.*

277. *Ceiling of Lord Clive's Dressing Room (5 in plan).*

278. *Ceiling of Small Eating Room (4 in plan).*

death in 1865, his son-in-law King Louis Philippe occupying it in 1848 till his death there in 1850.

About 1882 Claremont became the residence of H.R.H. the Duke of Albany, when Messrs. White Allom effected the first of a succession of 'period' alterations. After the Duchess of Albany's death in 1922 it was acquired by Sir W. Corry[1] for whom repairs and redecoration were carried out by Mr A. J. Davis. In 1929–30 more extensive stylistic alterations were made for another owner. But in 1931 the house was acquired by the present owners. During the war it was occupied by the design department of Messrs. Hawker Siddeley (Aircraft), the producers of the Spitfire.

The 1929–30 redecorations added much that is highly deceptive. The photograph of the Great Room (Fig. 271, now slightly altered) shows it as it was in 1923, when plaster wall panels had replaced salmon pink silk lining, then much decayed, behind which was the bare brick. The doorcases, however (Fig. 273), and the chimneypiece (Fig. 272) are original. In 1929 decorative panels were added above the doors and other ornaments introduced. Rooms 4 and 5, originally the Small Dining Room and Lord Clive's Dressing Room respectively, retain Holland's ceilings (Figs. 277, 278). That of 5 is identical with the library at Berrington (Fig. 381), except for not including painted medallions. Room 8, Lady Clive's Dressing Room, was divided by the Duke and Duchess of Albany, but was restored in 1929. It lacks, if it ever had,

the decorative ceiling expected in so important a room. The staircase (Fig. 268) is shown as in 1923 (compare the design for the wrought iron balustrade, Fig. 265). The approach from the hall to the ascent, beneath an arcade supporting the first floor landing, is interesting both as an early essay in the new style and as the germ of Holland's remarkable development of the theme in the Berrington staircase (p. 382).

A measure of documentary reconstruction has been applied in this instance because of the importance of Claremont in relation to Holland's subsequent evolution.

[1] For what follows I am indebted to discussions with Sir James Corry, Bt.

NEWBY HALL, YORKSHIRE

Built for **Sir E. Blackett**, *c. 1705*
Additions for **William Weddell**, *1767–85*
Architects **Adam (Carr)**
Owner **Major E. R. F. Compton**

Approaching Newby, on the N. bank of the R. Ure between Ripon and Boroughbridge, the first object noticed, after Adam's magnificent lodges (Fig. 281), is the equestrian statue of Charles II (Fig 283), before the E. front and formerly in the Stock Market, London, on the site of the Mansion House.[1]

The three-storey brick house of nine by five bays was built by Sir Edward Blackett (*d.* 1718), M.P. for Ripon 1689–90 and afterwards for Northumberland, whose father

[1] Placed there in 1672 by Sir Robert Vyner, who traditionally bought the statue, representing John Sobieski vanquishing a Turk, in Leghorn, and had the head altered. Gunnis (*Dictionary of British Sculptors*) gives evidence for ascribing the whole monarch and the base to Jaspar Latham (*d.* 1693). In 1737 the statue was removed and given in 1779 to Robert Vyner who erected it at Gautby Hall, Lincs. It was moved here in 1883 by his descendant Henry Vyner, whose wife inherited Newby from her father Lord de Grey.

had made a fortune pioneering Newcastle coal. The date given (Hargrove, *History of Knaresborough*) for its erection is 1705, but from the style could well be *c.* 1690; and confirmation exists for the traditional ascription to Wren. The small quoins and the drip-moulds at each floor level are traditional features associating the building with such late 17th century Yorkshire houses as Halnaby and Sprotborough. The West was probably the original entry front and has a curved pediment in the centre (Fig. 280) above a porch with a similar entablature carried on coupled columns; the same entablatures are repeated in the S. end. These features and their sculpture suggest a local mason of *c.* 1690, no doubt influenced by Wren and Talman. An old painting shows the house with hipped roof surmounted by a cupola. The existing balustrade and cornice are similar to those of the wings added by Adam, when the roof appears to have been remodelled.

William Weddell, whose father bought the estate in the mid-century, was a *dilletante* of exceptional taste who after visiting Rome *c.* 1765 formed a notable collection of sculpture and works of art. For the housing of these he turned to Adam, whose earliest surviving design (for a ceiling) is dated 1767, but the series, probably incomplete, extends to 1776, and

279. *The south side, with Adam's south east wing containing the Sculpture Gallery.*

280. *The centre of the west front (c. 1705).*   281. *Adam's entrance lodges.*

282. *The stable quadrangle, by Carr of York.*   283. *Statue of Charles II originally in the Stock Market, London.*

there is evidence that he had not finished before 1783. 'In his highest (and indeed I think best) taste', Lady Bute told Mrs Delany; a judgment confirmed by the imaginative plastic quality of the Sculpture Gallery designs. It may be that these, at least, are of his Kedleston-Syon phase, *c.* 1763, and so possibly prior to Weddell's going to Rome. The many analogies to work at Osterley imply a second stage *c.* 1767–68, but the final result belongs to the 1770s.

Adam added two wings forming a forecourt on the E. (Fig. 286), which he converted to the entry front with a new porch. The wings, of which the northern was designed to contain the kitchen and agent's rooms, have facetted bays at their ends; and being of half the height of the house they provide 'supporting masses' imparting 'movement'. In the strikingly assymetrical S. aspect (Fig. 279) equipoise is sensitively attained by weighting the wing with a repetition in its middle bays of the square shape of the earlier block on a

smaller scale, further stressed with a portico. In the forecourt there seems to be similar play with related rectangles. The satisfactory effects obtained are good instances of genuine architectural synthesis, achieved through 'empirical irregularity' controlled by classic rule—and the eye of an artist of Adam's calibre. The handsome stables (Fig. 282), long attributed to him, are now known to be by Carr.[1]

The Hall has trophy panels in relief (Fig. 285) resembling Rose's contemporary work in that at Osterley; the mahogany organ case (Fig. 287) can be compared to that at Kedleston. The Staircase (Fig. 288) is very like that at Osterley in arrangement; it rises from an ante-room beyond a screen formed with two *cippolino* columns procured by Weddell in Italy. North of the Hall lay the owner's private suite, but the south range looking towards the river was designed for superb and

[1] Colvin, op. cit., p. 746.

284. The east, entry, front with Adam's wings and porch.

285. The Entrance Hall looking north.

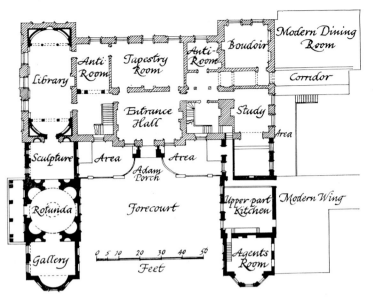

286. *Plan showing Adam's additions in black. North point to the right.*

scholarly entertainment. The original entry hall in the W. front was remodelled for the set of Gobelins tapestries commissioned *c.* 1765 (Fig. 294).

Adam had the handling of four of the six sets of *Les Amours des Dieux* tapestries, designed by Boucher and the Scotsman Nielson, produced for various Englishmen.[1] In the Newby set the colour of the groundwork is fawn (that at Osterley *rose du Barry*). The two panels signed by Boucher

[1] The others were Lord Jersey, Lord Coventry, and Thomas Dundas (a set with grey background installed at Moor Park), Lord Bradford, and the Duke of Portland.

are dated 1766, but it was three years later that Nielson sent, in the cylinder containing the Moor Park set, a pattern of the Newby colouring for Weddell's approval, so that some years must have passed before these tapestries were installed (a design by Adam for mirrors in this room is dated 1771). The Moor Park set cost £6,077, and the chairs, upholstered *en suite* as here, were made to Adam's design by Norman, as these may have been, though in the full Louis XV style. The ceiling, with medallions by Zucchi, is pale blue and pale green, the pattern co-ordinated to the design of the tapestry. Thus the large oval over the fireplace has above it a lunette; in the end sections of the ceiling each medallion comes above a feature in the tapestry. The carpet, at Moor Park and Osterley of large flowing patterns, is here of a repeating but characteristic design.

The whole S. end of the old house, entered through the Ante-room (Fig. 288), was replanned as a dining room with screened apses (Fig. 289). The ceiling, centred on a painted oval of Bacchus and Ariadne, has an ingenious pattern of alternately recessed and *relievo* panels, and the walls, again as in the dining room at Osterley, have arabesque panels in relief. The room's conversion to the Library was probably due to Lord Grantham, who added the present dining room at the N.W. side *c.* 1792. But in 1802 it was still serving its original purpose, when the Rev. R. Warner noticed in the apses 'large transparent alabaster vases standing upon pedestals to receive candles'. Their dim religious light assisted in 'the magic effect with which the mind is impressed when we look through the door at the . . . *penegralia* of the Temple'.

He referred to the exquisite Sculpture Gallery opening in prolongation, which remains exactly as Weddell and Adam arranged it, affording the best example surviving in this country of the beau ideal of the classical *cognoscenti*: the

287. *The organ in the south end of the Hall.*

288. *Staircase and Ante-room.*

289. *The Library, designed by Adam as the Dining Room.*

290. *The central rotunda of the Sculpture Gallery.*

imaginative reconstruction of a Roman interior on the evidence of Herculaneum and the Catacombs. The Gallery has three compartments as expressed in the elevation, of which the central is a rotunda with four *exedrae* and two arched recesses, lit from its coffered dome. In their shapes and sizes the sculptures are so well related to each other, and to the scale of the gallery, as to suggest their having been selected to fit a scheme at least outlined if not completed by Adam not later than *c.* 1765. Equally the effect of his design is much enhanced by the relatively small scale of the sculpture. It may be observed that Adam nowhere applied the neoclassical conception of space-modelling into primary shapes with more moving success. The contrast between the sculpture galleries at Newby and Holkham succinctly illustrates the meaning of 'neo-classical'. The square, rather low, flat-ceiled end-compartments are joined to the rotunda by deep vaulted arches, their soffits heavily coffered in 'true catacomb manner', thus exaggerating the height of the dome. The walls opposite the windows are of varying shades of terra-cotta pink with inset cameos of deep red on white and

grey marble borders; oil lamps are supported on console brackets, and in the pedestals of the larger statues air vents connect with a heating system as at Kedleston. 'Seen from the open library door, the vista through the three compartments (Fig. 291), enlivened by the interplay of light and terminating in the apse with its great bath or sarcophagus of white and purple pavonazzo, conveys a most convincing representation of the catacombs in their antique splendour' (Lees Milne, *The Age of Adam*).

The invaluable Jenkins was Weddell's agent in Rome, procuring the Barbarini Venus discovered by Gavin Hamilton and then regarded as the gem of the collection. The great bath in the apse recalls that Weddell's attachment to Roman antiquities and habits was responsible for his death in 1792, in the Roman Bath in the Strand. Newby then passed to Thomas Robinson, Lord Grantham, who succeeded his maternal aunt as Earl de Grey. His daughter married Mr Henry Vyner of Gautby, who laid out the beautiful gardens which have been admirably replanted and maintained by his present successor.

The Sculpture Gallery and Tapestry Room are illustrated in Figs. 291–294 on the two following pages.

291. *The Sculpture Gallery as seen from the Library door.*

292. *Under the dome of the Sculpture Gallery, looking west.*

293. *The further end of the Sculpture Gallery. A Roman bath of 'pavonazzo' occupies the alcove.*

294. *(below) The Tapestry Room, 1765–1771. The pattern of the ceiling in pale blue and pale green is co-ordinated to the design of the Boucher-Nielson tapestries, the ground colour of which is fawn.*

DOWNTON CASTLE, HEREFORDSHIRE

Designed for himself by **Richard Payne Knight**, *c.* **1775**
Owner **Major W. Kincaid-Lennox**

The empirical spirit throughout these years was being expressed in the development of romanticism and of natural and political science. This quest of fundamentals was leading in architecture to the 'natural simplicity' of neo-classicism, and giving support to the study of gothic, whilst in landscape both its emotional and scientific sides were engaged in the discovery of 'the Picturesque', as visual romanticism was termed. The notion of a synthesis of 'classical' and 'romantic' values as the solution of the aesthetic problems confronting the age is completely if crudely illustrated by this remarkable building, erected, and largely if not entirely designed, by one of the period's most representative minds.

Richard Payne Knight, neo-classical antiquary, Radical Whig M.P., controversialist, and sponsor, with his neighbour Uvedale Price, of Picturesque aesthetic theory, was a product of the early Industrial Revolution in so far as his grandfather was a rich self-made ironmaster. Richard Knight of Madely acquired Bringewood Forest on the Welsh border to supply his furnaces with fuel, and transmitted a strain of obstinate originality to his descendants. Payne Knight's brother was Thomas the Pomologist, an early official of the Royal Horticultural Society; his uncle gothickized Croft Castle; and his young cousin was Thomas Johnes of Hafod. He himself inherited Bringewood when he came of age in

1771, after a long stay in Italy, and seems to have immediately set about building.

The site he chose looks southward over the deep valley of the R. Teme, where it issues from a rocky gorge, with magnificent views over Bringewood into Wales and to the Clee Hill. Describing Downton Castle in his *Analytical Inquiry into the Principles of Taste* (1805), he said: 'It is now more than 30 years since the author built a house ornamented with what are called Gothic towers and battlements without, with Grecian columns and entablatures within, and though his example has not been much followed, he has many reasons to congratulate himself on the success of the experiment, he having at once the advantage of a picturesque object and of an elegant and convenient dwelling, though less perfect in both respects than if he had executed it at a maturer age. It has [moreover] the advantage of being capable of receiving alterations and additions in almost any direction without injury to its genuine and original character'—as indeed has been the case.

The *Analytical Inquiry* brilliantly states the case for rational individualism in the arts and for an eclectic functionalism in architecture. Knight makes clear that at Downton he aimed to evolve a modern type of 'gentleman's house', irregularly planned for convenience, aspect and site, in which, he insisted, it followed the precedent of Roman villas. He maintained that 'the system of regularity of which the moderns have been so tenacious' in planning, being derived from sacred architecture, was misapplied to domestic building. Stylistically, both as regards convenience and harmony with

295. *The south, originally the entrance, front. The further angle tower is Victorian, the small isolated tower c. 1785.*

296. *The north and west sides, with Bringewood Forest beyond the deep valley of the River Teme.*

scenery—i.e. the picturesque—he considered that 'we are becoming too rigid in rejecting such combinations of Grecian and Gothic' as Claude and Gaspar depicted in buildings in their landscapes, or as are equally 'naturalized' in this country in 'the fortresses of our ancestors transformed into Italianized villas by Inigo Jones'. He saw no inconsistency in mixing styles, 'uniting the different improvements of different ages in the same building'. If it were intended to be an Englishman's house, it should imitate neither Greek temple, Gothic abbey nor feudal castle, yet might draw on all. It was the visual principles of planning and design that mattered, not the 'servile copying of effects'.

If Knight had built when he wrote the *Inquiry*, he would probably have freely adapted Elizabethan. But in 1775 he could accept domestic Gothic and sacred classical models as ingredients for an undigested compound (rather than a true synthesis). Yet already, in his early twenties, he was bent on demonstrating the efficacy of irregular planning; and, though he afterwards refused to admit that there was any such thing as 'pure Gothic', his Castle is not least interesting for the faithfulness with which the spirit and some details of medieval structure are reproduced. These must have been carefully studied and drawn. Since there is no evidence that he himself sketched or drew (on his next Italian journey in 1775 he took J. R. Cozens as his draughtsman), it is possible that he employed an antiquarian artist such as John Carter (1748–1817) to collect medieval details. But there seems no doubt that, broadly speaking, he was his own architect. The closest parallel is to Adam's 'castle' of Culzean, the development of which from an original tower began only in 1777. Whilst the interior of Culzean is superior, the external conception falls far short of Downton, whether considered as 'picturesque', gothic, or neo-classical; and time has fulfilled Knight's contention that a country house should primarily be planned for convenient living.

In the *Inquiry* Knight advised introducing (or restoring) 'the hanging terrace of Italian gardens which, if the house is placed with sloping ground before it, enriches the

foreground and serves as basement for it to stand on', thereby remedying the 'bare and bald' appearance of Brown's landscape settings by contributing 'supporting masses'. The battlemented terrace along the S. front (Fig. 295) which illustrates this principle, was not however part of the original conception, since it does not figure in an estate plan of *c.* 1780. This, and an accompanying perspective drawing, is the only

297. *The north west towers. The porch is Victorian.*

298. *The circular Dining Room. 'Porphyry' columns; green, yellow, and red marbled walls.*

299. The Drawing Room, looking towards the round lobby in the south west tower.

300. Marble and porphyry doorway in the Drawing Room.

301. The Morning Room. The chimneypiece inset with porphyry and ormolu.

302. *In the Library.*

contemporary documentation. It shows the main entrance from the S., at what is now the bay window of the Morning Room (2 in plan Fig. 303) and nothing E. of the tower marked 10. Moreover it shows only one of the drum towers at the N. end of the W. range (Fig. 297).

Knight went on building intermittently—a late addition was the isolated tower at the E. end of the terrace, where he retained rooms after making over Downton to his brother Thomas. It cannot be doubted that he completed the N.W. entrance with the second tower and the arch linking it to its twin; but the porch appears to be mid-19th century, as do the various Gothic oriels, arcades, and traceried windows (which seem to have plain arched heads in the drawing). The 'chapel' with Gothic windows on the N. front (Fig. 296) is known to be c. 1860, and probably the S. front also was then extended, though in its present form its further section is of c. 1870 when it was rebuilt after a fire.

But although all of the 'castle' is not due to Knight, the greater part is, and his conception was not affected. The S. front itself, balanced on either side of the central 'keep', is effectively assymetrical and was no doubt designed to be seen diagonally from the approach climbing from the river bridge towards the octagonal S.W. tower. This projects from the W. front (Fig. 296) in which it also plays the visually important role of supporting the mass where the ground falls to the valley and distance. In the view from the N.W. the composition is exceedingly effective, the strong masonry of the drum towers adding a sense of conviction to the simple shapes.

These are ingeniously related to the wholly classical interior. The 'keep' in the S. front is entirely filled by a sombrely magnificent 'Pantheon' Dining Room (Fig. 298), top lit through the dome, of which the vault is coloured pale blue, red and gold, as well as by a single round-headed win-

dow. Above the oak dado the walls are marbled green and yellow with red borders, and on the diagonals they swell into four *exedrae* containing a 'basalt' figure (of Coade stone painted) between porphyry scagliola columns with gilt and green bronzed capitals. An ormolu colza-oil chandelier hangs from the dome over the specially woven circular carpet, said to be Viennese, of porphyry red and green.

Knight evidently made considerable purchases of porphyry in Italy, for in the Drawing Room the columns of the doorway (Fig. 300) are antique prophyry shafts, the caps and entablature of statuary marble, the whole probably imported.[1] At the end (Fig. 299), in the rotunda contained by the S.W. tower, a window is similarly framed, but the large columns are scagliola. The Morning Room (Fig. 301) with a Doric frieze sombrely painted, has a Statuary chimneypiece with inset porphyry panels on which are *appliqué* delicately wrought ormolu masks and garlands. In the west side the Library (Fig. 302) has one wall entirely lined with specially designed bookcases, and a pair which contained Knight's folios flanking the doorway. The remainder of this range is filled with a ball room redecorated in Victorian Gothic, and there is a Tudor-Gothic staircase in the angle formed by these ranges. But on the walls throughout still hang the bulk of his catholic but discriminating collection of paintings: three outstanding Rembrandts, Gaspars, Ruysdaels and Salvator Rosas, a great study of a horse by Vandyck, an early Turner and a group by his favourite English painter, Westall. There is also the series of watercolours commissioned by Knight from T. Hearn of the wooded and craggy gorge below, which exerted a greater immediate influence on taste than the Castle itself.

[1] The following note shows he employed Flaxman, though it probably refers to his London house in Soho Square. Flaxman in 1781 suggested to Wedgwood 'an ornamental frieze' (for Etruria Hall) with 'the Lions and Foliage you admired so much in the chimneypiece I was carving for Mr Knight' (quoted by Gunnis, *Dictionary of British Sculptors*, p. 147).

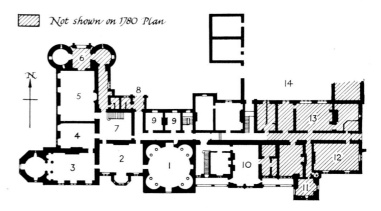

303. *The Ground Floor, from a plan of c. 1870.* 1. *Dining room.* 2. *Morning room, originally Entrance hall.* 3. *Drawing room.* 4. *Library,* 5. *Ball room.* 6. *Porch.* 7. *Staircase.* 8. *Entry.* 9. *Chapel (over).* 10. *Business room.* 11. *Smoking room.* 12. *Servants' hall.* 13. *Kitchen.* 14. *Stable yard.*

304. *The south front, with stone dressings to the cement facing.*

CRICHEL, DORSET

Built for **Sir William Napier, 1742; Humphry Sturt,** *c.*
   1765 and *c.* **1775**

Architects **Unknown**

Painted decoration (*c.* **1775**) **Biagio Rebecca (attrib.)**

Owner **The Hon. Mrs G. G. Marten**

The Crichels lie between the Gussages and the Tarrants
among the chalk valleys running northwards from Wimborne
to Cranborne Chase. The manor house of More Crichel
newly built *c.* 1615 by Sir N. Napier, was burnt down in 1742
in the time of Sir William Napier, 4th Baronet. On the same
site he built the oblong house which twenty years afterwards
was almost entirely buried in great 'rococo' enlargements.
But the principal rooms were not decorated till after 1773,
probably later. There are thus three periods of work, the two
latter possessing distinctive qualities which, in the complete
absence of documentation, inevitably raise interesting
questions of attribution.

As rebuilt after 1742, the house was a rectangle of three
storeys fronting E. and W., of which the E. was the entrance,
extending some 70 ft. with seven windows, and had sides of
some 50 ft. with five windows. Each had a central pedimented
doorway, of which that on the S. side was linked ornamentally
to its surmounting window. This, with two storeys of its
façade, can be seen beneath the portico in Fig. 306, and shows

that it was a modest brick and stone building of George II
type such as the Bastards or Francis Cartwright of Bland-
ford might have designed. Its area was the central rectangle
in the plan, Fig. 308. The existing Staircase Hall (4) was the
entrance hall, which led through to what is now called
the Vestibule (8). This originally contained the main staircase with the back stairs beside it; for not only does its
landing, carried on columns, survive (Fig. 309), and the arched
window that rose from the stairs' half landing (Fig. 311), but
the arms of Sir William Napier and his mother Catharine
Allington form the heraldic ornament of the ceiling, and the
rococo decoration of the upper walls remains unaltered.
When Sir William's successor removed the stairs, all he did
was to insert niches for statues in the lower portion. The
doorways are original and possibly even the rococo landscape
panels. Little if anything else of that period remains in the
adjoining rooms, the uses of which given in the plan are those
of the time it was published in the 1774 edition of Hutchins's
Dorset. In the present century the two S. rooms, which had
been run together, were given a good copy of a rococo
ceiling to form a Sitting Room, as was also the Dining Room
('breakfast room', 9 in plan) which could mislead the unwary.

Sir William Napier was succeeded by his brother, who
died without issue in 1765, when Crichel went to the son
of their aunt Diana, Humphry Sturt, a neighbour. Coming
of a family endowed a few generations back by a City alder-
man, he inherited the possessions of the last Lord Allington

305. *Centre of the east front, with the former entrance.*

306. *The portico spanning the old south front.*

and himself married the heiress of Charles Pitfield of Hoxton. Thus he was a wealthy man and, through his wife if no more, as closely connected with London as with Dorset. Among the meagre pointers available, this may be significant as regards his building operations.

Eight years later, in 1773, he was well forward with them. Hutchins, who died that year, makes no allusion to the alterations, but the editor of his MSS. in the following year obtained a plan and drawing of the enlarged house. And in 1773 Mrs Harris, mother of the 1st Lord Malmesbury, reported: 'Mr Sturt has added much. . . . It will be a very fine thing when finished: a number of very large rooms. It being joined to the old house it is not so complete as one could wish'.

What Sturt had done was this: to add two blocks abutting on the S. and N. ends of the W. front, but leaving the centre of the latter visible between them (an entrance hall now fills the lower part of this recess); and to erect a great new range 120 ft. long in front of and overlapping the old E. front. The rooms in this, and in the S.W. block, were as high as two storeys of the old house, and since they were to be surmounted with a chamber floor, and the S. front to be continuous, some means must be found of lighting the old S. rooms thus engulfed. This was made the occasion for Crichel's most distinctive feature: the great loggia to join the terminal additions, and, containing two storeys of the earlier elevation, to carry the chamber floor across and over it on Ionic columns (Figs. 304 and 307).

There were Palladian precedents for this empirical solution, for example the Villa Cornaro with its recessed portico in two tiers; and at West Wycombe Sir Francis Dashwood (*E.C.H., Early Georgian*) was similarly hiding a three-storeyed house behind two tiers of colonnade. But the rest of

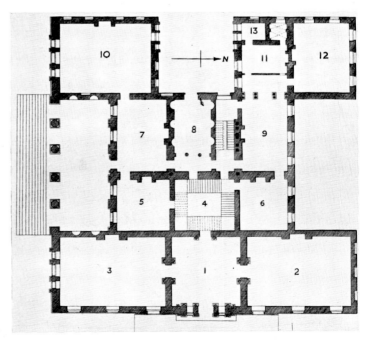

307. *Beneath the portico.*   308. (*to the right*) *Plan, from Hutchins' 'Dorset', 1774. 1. Hall. 2. Dining Room. 3. Drawing Room. 4. Principal stair. 5–6. 'Bed-chamber'. 7. Dressing room. (5 & 7 now combined). 8. Vestibule. 9. Breakfast room. 10. Library. 11. Writing Closet. 12. Common Eating Parlour. 13. Evidence Room.*

the elevation of the S. front (Fig. 304) shows little evidence of learning. The small Corinthian order over the portico has quite an Early Renaissance prettiness, whilst great play is made on the lower floor with Venetian windows, their arch much rusticated: one each side of the loggia and two in the W. end. In these and the new E. front all the windows have full entablatures; moreover their friezes, and that of the loggia, have the peculiarity of being 'cushioned'—all of which was archaistic in 1765. The new E. entrance (Fig. 305), reached by converging steps over a rococo basement, is by a heavily proportioned Venetian window under a queer pediment surmounted by another window of which the arch had to be four-centred to fit under the meagre cornice. These dressings are in yellowish stone, except the loggia columns which are of Portland; the pilasters added beneath it are in the white cement applied over all the façades. Another oddity is the angle pilasters surmounting the quoins of the lower storey.

As seen from the Italian garden laid out by Harold Peto on the gentle slope to the lake, the whole effect is as charming as a baroque villa on the Brenta by some pupil of a disciple of Palladio, but so curiously inept for the age of Adam and Paine as to suggest the work of an uneducated yet original mind. It affords a close analogy to the large-scale addition made between 1768 and 1771 to Claydon, Bucks. (*E.C.H.*, *Early Georgian*) by that otherwise unknown *entrepreneur* named Lightfoot, on whose egregious character Sir T. Robinson's letters to Lord Verney throw light. Not only do both undertakings contain rooms of exceptional size and height added to a smaller, older nucleus; but the same addiction is found to rusticated Venetian windows, full entablatures, the pulvinated frieze, and the same rudimentary pedi-

309. *The Vestibule, originally containing the Staircase.*

310. *The East Hall.*

311. *Upper part of the Vestibule.*

312. *The Dining Room looking north. The ground colour of walls and ceiling is blue-grey and of the painted 'cameo' medallions
faded purple.*

313. *The Great Draw-*
ing Room. The ceiling
with paintings by Re-
becca (?) is indifferently
related to the walls,
originally lined with
silk. The arched window
frames (left) are modern.

314. *The corridor and*
the head of the staircase.

ments. Lightfoot was apparently a contractor for building and decoration with premises in Southwark, who in 1771 took up a mortgage in Jamaica from Lord Verney—which possibly accounted for his subsequent disappearance. Much dissatisfaction was caused by his business and building methods at Claydon. It may be coincidence that at Crichel an interval occurred in about 1771, after the building of the shell of the additions and before their decoration in a wholly different style, and that those additions have stylistic resemblances to Claydon. But the analogies and circumstances are perhaps close enough to justify tentative identification of the Crichel contractor with Lightfoot.

The new rooms, incomplete and their decoration possibly not begun in 1773, may be dated 1775–80. One of the earliest was probably the East Hall (Fig. 310) of which the Palladian doorcases and wall treatment have the conservatism of the exterior. But a new influence is evident in the painted panels of the ceiling in bronze-gold on pale green.

The change in taste is fully apparent in the great Dining Room, lying N. of the hall (Fig. 312). Except for the recessed arch in which the door is set beneath a *grisaille* lunette, the straw-coloured walls are flat, relieved only by medallions painted with reliefs on a blue-grey ground and framed in very delicate stucco festoons. The chimneypiece has grey porphyry columns and its tablet is remarkable in being painted by Reynolds with an emblematic 'relief' in *grisaille*.

Strong ornamented ribs divide ceiling from cove—as in that of the hall at Kedleston (Fig. 133), forming segmental corners treated fanwise. This motif could be matched in the anti-room of Portman House, London (1775–82) by J. Stuart. Tradition here ascribes the medallion paintings to Biagio Rebecca, which is confirmed by their similarity to his known work at Heveningham (p. 165). The ground of ceiling and cove is of blue-grey with white reliefs, which in

the coves take the form of candelabra. Between these are painted 'cameo' medallions of which the ground, like that of the ribs, is faded purple. On the flat of the ceiling the circular wreaths are of finely modelled naturalistic vine-leaves. The exquisite whole retains its original colouring untouched. But the scheme can be criticized for the wall-treatment being insufficient to support so magnificent a ceiling and which, indeed, looks as though it may have been conceived independently.

If this were so it would argue against the room as a whole being ascribed to a leading architect, and in favour, perhaps, of one of Adam's ceiling men having been employed, particularly George Richardson. He claimed to have designed the hall ceiling at Kedleston, to which this has analogies, and published his *Book of Ceilings* in 1774. Another possibility is Joseph Bonomi, employed by Adam 1767–c. 1772, but at the relevant dates working on his own or with Leverton, since this ceiling contains motifs found in drawings among the Adam collections which are believed to be by him.

The other great room in the E. front, the Drawing Room (Fig. 313), is as fine and more elaborate, but not all original; the walls were lined with silk; and the arched window-frames are relatively modern. The mirrors, especially that over the chimneypiece (Fig. 315), are profusely rococo and will have been procured earlier, perhaps in connection with a pre-1770 scheme not executed; and since they were discovered during the last century in an attic, they may not even have belonged to this room. The barrel-vaulted ceiling has four types of inset paintings, probably by Rebecca, contained by bands of exquisite plaster enrichment no less delicate than that of the frieze.

Both the Library, in the S.W. addition (Fig. 318), and the Boudoir, on the first floor above the loggia (Fig. 317), have unusual ceilings in which inset paintings are again the leading

315. *Overmantle mirror in the Drawing Room.*   316. *The first floor corridor.*

feature, but the walls are in each case plainly treated. The decoration of the Staircase hall was also completed at this time. The staircase itself, no doubt erected *c*. 1765–70, has the Corinthian newel-columns and diversely turned trios of balusters usual before 1760, the probability being that they were copied from and partly re-used the Napier staircase previously in the vestibule (the surviving gallery of which communicates with the new stairs at their half landing). The doorcases and colonnade on the upper landing are similarly of an Early Georgian kind (Fig. 314). But the coffered cove of the staircase ceiling with fanned corners, which rises to the skylight, and the particularly pretty stucco ornamenting of the upper corridor (Fig. 316) are of the later phase.

Avray Tipping firmly attributed all the post-1775 decoration to James Wyatt owing to its resemblance to Heaton and Heveningham, where Rebecca was also the decorator. The treatment of the staircase ceiling is certainly close to that at Heaton, and other affinities can be noted. Moreover in 1772 his fashionable triumph in the Pantheon would make him a likely choice to Sturt for completing the Crichel rooms. But all the resemblances are in the details and motifs of the work by craftsmen and painters, which tend to recur whether they were engaged by Wyatt or Adam or Leverton; and there is little indeed of architectural character of which we can say that it is unmistakably Wyatt's and no other's. Moreover, although all records have vanished, it is scarcely conceivable that all recollection of so celebrated an architect's presence

318. *The Library.*

should also have been lost whilst that of the painter survived, howbeit dimly. The conclusion therefore is that, as in the first stage of his remodelling of Crichel, Humphry Sturt continued to employ relatively obscure individuals, possibly as more amenable to his own ideas. In the second phase these men were artists who had worked under leading architects, but capable on their own of producing *ensembles* that are among the outstanding achievements of the period.

Humphry Sturt died in 1786. His grandson was created Lord Allington in 1876, but on the death of the 4th Baron in 1940 when the title became extinct, Crichel passed to his only daughter and is now a girls' school.

317. *The Boudoir over the portico.*

319. *The old house burnt in 1742.*

320. *From the north. To the right of the main block is the service wing, with the stables on the extreme right.*

DODDINGTON HALL, CHESHIRE

Built for **the Rev. Sir Thomas Broughton, Bt.,** 1776–98

Architect **Samuel Wyatt**   Decorator **Biagio Rebecca**

Owner **Sir Evelyn Delves Broughton, Bt.**

At the battle of Poitiers Lord Audley so distinguished himself that the Black Prince awarded him an annuity, which he divided amongst his four squires. One of these was John Delves of Doddington, five miles S.E. of Nantwich where, advancing rapidly in the King's favour, he received licence to crenellate a tower in 1357. A second licence was given to his successor in 1403, and one of them probably refers to the structure now standing in the park (Fig. 324). Till 1777 this was incorporated in a brick quadrangle, probably rebuilt by Sir Thomas Delves, 1st Baronet who died in 1648. The central feature of this older Hall was a porch embellished with statues of the Prince, Audley, and the four squires. These sculptures, with pierced balustrading and other remnants, now adorn the tower. On the death in 1727 of the 4th Baronet, Doddington passed to his grandson Sir Brian Broughton of Broughton, Staffs., who added the name of Delves; and by 1766 had devolved on his younger grandson Thomas.

The Rev. Sir Thomas Broughton (he dropped the Delves) reigned till 1813. He pulled down the old house and it is recorded on his tomb that he built the new one out of income, which accounts for its not being completed till 1798. Before 1776, the date of the executed plans, Brown had been

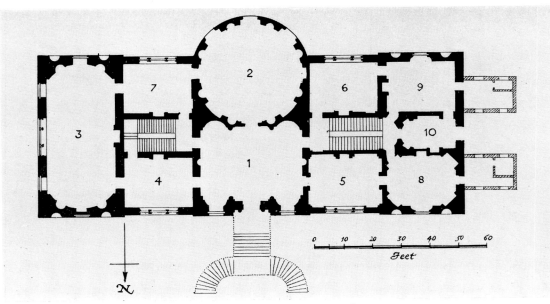

321. *Samuel Wyatt's plan for the principal floor, dated 1776. 1. Hall. 2. Saloon. 3. Dining Room. 4. Ante-room. 5. Library. 6. Dressing Room. 7. Drawing Room. 8. Dressing Room. 9. Bedroom. 10. Wardrobe.*

322. *The south front and bow.*

323. *The entrance front. Coade stone medallions in the lunettes.*

324. *(below) The old tower. The statues and balustrading adorned the 17th century house.*

324(a).*(below,right) Roof of the service wing. The skylight is over the stairs shown in Fig. 326.*

325. *The circular Saloon looking north. It is decorated in the style of Biagio Rebecca*

326. *(left) Service stair and trolley-way in the wing.*

327. *(below) A typical bedroom fireplace.*

paid for making a design, besides for advising on the treatment and enlargement of the mere, some fifty acres in extent, the west side of which was chosen for the new site. The preference given to Samuel Wyatt, then aged thirty and beginning to make a reputation in London, may well have been influenced by his father's old-established Staffordshire connections, which would enable him to keep a watch on a work intended to be spread over a lengthy period.

It also spread, as time went on, over a wide area, a long service wing extending from the main block in a curve westward (therein resembling James Wyatt's segmental wing at Dodington, Gloucestershire; (*E.C.H., Late Georgian*), which is further prolonged by the stables (Figs. 320, 324 (a)). These do not appear in the 1776 designs which, confined to the main body, are to a plan that, with variations, is typical of the Wyatts and of Samuel especially. Its most characteristic feature is the circular bow surmounted by a low dome in the S. front, which, used by Adam at Mersham in 1762 (p. 98) was adopted by both the Wyatts as a regular component of their plans (see Introduction, §3). Main entry being by a *perron* to the first floor, a grand staircase could be dispensed with but, curiously at this date, was instead duplicated, there being an identical stair each side of the hall, with the back stairs adjoining to the west. The whole of the E. end, commanding the view of the mere, is devoted to a great Dining Room— at the furthest possible distance from the kitchen in the service wing, so that the device was adopted of a railed trolley-way (Fig. 326) connecting the kitchen to the foot of the service stair in the basement. Most of the ground floor was devoted to servants' bedrooms, the basement—on the level of the ground floor of the wing—containing cellars. There are trolley-ways in tunnels under the courtyards of Alnwick and Petworth for the transport of meals, but few are to be found in houses of this date. On the second storey the heads of the staircases are connected by a spinal corridor that narrows to pass the dome of the Saloon, which has two semi-circular bedrooms above it.

The walls, faced with grey ashlar, of which the finely jointed slabs measure up to 5 ft. by 2 ft., present the monolithic appearance at which neo-classicism with its restraint of ornament aimed. The fenestration serves as patterning texture, supplemented only by the rustic basement, slight string courses, and panels of carved swags, whilst the circular motif set up by the S. bow is carried through by the arched windows in the ends. (The plan reproduced shows these Venetian windows disposed otherwise). On the main floor their lunettes are pointed by Coade stone medallions of Hellenic symbols painted white on a black ground. The whole delicately moulded mass reposes on completely level lawns stretching outward to the level park turf and mere, merging with rounded tree forms. A more tranquil unity would be hard to find.

This is also the note of the internal treatment, for the most part, emphasized as it is now by the removal of family possessions. It speaks much for the decoration's architectural qualities that the rooms are at little disadvantage for their emptiness. We can the better appreciate the neo-classical *meiosis* of the Hall's modelling (Fig. 329), the restrained adequacy of ornament in Dining Room and Library (Figs.

328. *In the Dining Room.*

328 and 330), and indeed the proportioned elegance imparted to each bedroom by a simple but epigrammatic fireplace (Fig 327).

The great exception to this architectural quietism is the round, saucer-domed, Saloon of 36 ft. diameter (Fig. 325) the decoration of which can be ascribed to Biagio Rebecca. As in his Cupola Room at Heaton (Fig. 14), the walls are divided by pilaster strips into sixteen bays alternately broad and narrow. Each of the latter contains a slender pier-glass while the broader bays are disposed as follows: in the N. segment the door from the entrance hall is flanked by re-

329. *From entrance hall to west staircase.*

330. *From library to entrance hall.*

cesses originally containing fitted seats, the three corresponding S. bays contain windows, and the Drawing Room door in the E. is faced by the chimneypiece. Concave with the walls, the statuary marble and somewhat saccharine mantel, its shelf supported by languid nymphs, is probably of Italian origin. The walls are painted in gradations of French grey with gilt enrichment showing up the brightly hued decorative insets. Each pilaster has a 'cameo', white on a deep blue ground, over and under which are delicate grotesques of varying pattern. Over each pier glass is a roundel and in the other eight bays an oblong panel gaily coloured. Similar paintings by or attributed to Rebecca, which Mr Gordon Nares has pointed out depict in some cases the same incidents, are at Harewood, Heaton, Heveningham and Crichel. The conception and treatment of this exquisite room undoubtedly derives from that at Heaton, which may be preferred for its firmer masculinity. The deficiency of this room in that respect can be exemplified in the two motifs employed in the dome. The concentric rings of gilt foliage con-

trast a little feebly with the more forceful hexagon pattern in the surrounding cove, of which one is conscious of the wish that more use had been made. Similarly, the satisfactory, alternating, rhythm set up by the pilasters and pier-glasses is almost lost in the over-pretty small scale ornamentation.

The gist of this criticism can also be applied to distinguishing between the qualities of Samuel and James Wyatt: whilst the former reveals a better balanced and it may be a finer sensibility, he lacked the *flaire* and impulse of his brother's versatile genius.

Sir Thomas Broughton, having devoted twenty years to thus building Doddington, filled it with thirteen children, having married thrice (one lady to whom he proposed marriage adduced fourteen reasons for declining, one of them personal, the others obvious), and survived completion of his great work fifteen years. The present owner is the sixth in descent from him but, whilst he maintains the family connection with the place, the house is now leased to the Goudhurst College for Girls.

HEVENINGHAM HALL, SUFFOLK

Rebuilt for **Sir Gerard Vanneck, Bt.**
Architect **Sir Robert Taylor, 1778**
Completed and decorated by **James Wyatt, before 1784**
Painter **Biagio Rebecca**
Landscape **Brown, 1781–82**
Owner **The Hon. Andrew Vanneck, M.C.**

The ancient port of Dunwich near Heveningham often sent to Parliament one of that family (pronounced Henningham) and, having decayed into a valuable 'rotten borough', was probably the chief attraction to Sir Joshua Vanneck, Baronet, of Putney, in acquiring this country property in 1752. A merchant banker of Dutch ancestry, his firm's interests included control of the French tobacco trade and the floating of Whig government loans. But he was content with the modest Queen Anne house with which the old hall had been replaced after the last Heveningham had sold it to one John Bence, c. 1707. It stood somewhat low in a pastoral valley watered by a little stream, and was of red brick in three storeys, apparently of seven bays to the N., but of nine to the S.—where it still forms the recessed centre of that façade (Fig. 337).

Sir Gerard, 2nd Baronet, succeeding in 1777, was already Member for Dunwich, and quickly turned to the veteran city architect, Sir Robert Taylor, for converting Heveningham into his 'Seat'. The first proposal was to add to the W. end of the Bence house a large household wing returning southwards. But as the ground rises rapidly to the S., this L-shaped plan was abandoned for one that nowhere much exceeded the Bence house in depth (45 ft.) but extended its frontage from 80 ft. to 260 ft. The brick shell was kept, and the line of its N. front was continued by two-storey wings to pavilion blocks on the same alignment. But since the E. extension was to contain large reception rooms, the depth of both was increased slightly southwards.

Thus an elevation was produced akin in its continuity of

331. *Sir Robert Taylor's north front seen across Capability Brown's serpentine river.*

332. *Sir Robert Taylor's model, showing the north front. The central block incorporates the earlier house. The building as executed follows the model exactly, but for the revision of the east side.*

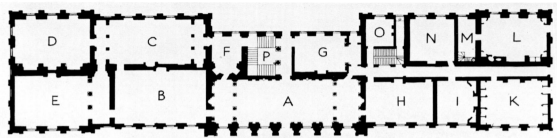

333. *Taylor's Ground Plan. A. Hall. B. Dining Room. C. Gallery. D. Library. E. Eating Room. F. Anteroom. G. Common Parlour. H. Dressing Room. I. Steward's Room. K. Servants' Hall. L. Kitchen. M. Pantry. N. Housekeeper's Room. O. Butler's pantry. P. Principle Staircase.*

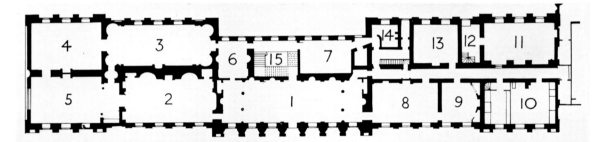

334. *Wyatt's plan, as existing. 1. Hall. 2. Dining Room. 3. Saloon. 4. Drawing Room. 5. Library. 6. Etruscan Room. 7. Study. 8. Morning room. 9. Print or Small Dining Room. 10. Servants' Hall. 11. Kitchen. 12, 13, 14. Offices. 14. Principal Staircase.*

335. *The Hall as intended by Taylor. Engraving by T. Malton, published 1791.*

plane to a street terrace in London or Bath, and Taylor handled it very much as he had Stone Buildings, his palatial range of chambers for Lincolns Inn, then in course of erection. The pedimented pavilions and continuous arcaded basement, with the balustrade carried along the wings, differ little from Stone Buildings except in size. Similarly, too, in the S. front he could even forego a central feature (except for an increase of its height). But in the N. front such modish reticence was precluded, if for no other reason by the need to enlarge the scale of the existing house. Going to the opposite extreme, he encased this, with the maximum emphasis, in a colossal colonnade resting upon deep rusticated arches and carrying a massive enriched podium (Fig. 336). This frontispiece, solidly accomplished like all Taylor's work, is in essence an exaggeration of Chambers's contemporary treatment of the N. front of Somerset House, like it deriving from Inigo Jones. But hints from the garden front of Versailles may have contributed to this device for centering an over-long façade. Throughout, the facing is of a 'Roman cement', with the keystones, capitals and statuary of Coade stone. The general scheme is repeated on the S., except for the centre, and is carried round all three sides of the W. pavilion; but the end of the E. pavilion varies it to introduce broad tri-partite windows in the ground floor, where the rooms are wholly due to Taylor's successor. An engraving after Hearne published in Watts's *Views*, dated 1780, shows the exterior completed. At the same time Brown landscaped the valley, creating in it a serpentine river, and replacing the

337. *The south front.*

old garden southwards with informal pleasure grounds, depicted in two of the best preserved of his surviving plans.[1] The stable yard, etc. is probably due to Brown also.

Attribution of Heveningham's completion to James Wyatt rests, apart from the evidence of style, on the A.P.S. Dictionary which, however, gives 1797–9 as the date of the work. Tipping concluded that the change to Wyatt was likely to have been due to Sir Joshua Vanneck soon after he succeeded his brother Sir Gerard in 1791, Taylor having died in 1788. This chronology, though it prolonged into the 1790s the period during which Wyatt was developing the Adam style, was convincing.

It is now known, however, that the whole interior was finished before 1784, though the actual date, and the reason, of Taylor's supercession remain unknown. In that year François de la Rochefoucauld visited Heveningham and wrote a detailed account in his journal.[2] He noted that there had been 'a very old house' of which '10 or 12 years ago Sir Gerard had all the partitions pulled down and constructed a hall'. This 'is splendidly lofty and has a number of pillars, all extremely dignified and magnificent and completely faced with stucco. When I was there it needed a few statues, but these will no doubt be added'. After seeing the Breakfast room and Small Dining Room 'where Sir Gerard dines when he is alone,' he recrossed the Hall and entered the Dining Room, than which he thought he should never see a more

336. *The centre of the north front.*

[1] Reproduced by D. Stroud, op. cit.
[2] *A Frenchman in England.* Edited by Jean Marchand, translated with notes by S. C. Roberts. Cambridge, 1933.

338. *Wyatt's Hall. Ceiling, walls and floor are completely integrated in this masterly design.*

340. *The staircase balustrade. The ironwork enriched with cast lead ornaments, the whole painted white and blue.*

339. (*above*) *The south hall door. The ground colour is apple green with white reliefs, yellow scagliola columns, the floor of white stone inset with red and black marbles.*

341. *The Etruscan Room. Pale green, the mouldings white, the figures Etruscan red.*

342. *The Saloon. Painted by Rebecca in 'trompe l'œil', the reliefs in shades of green on a biscuit ground.*

344. *A corner of the Saloon.*

343. *The Saloon chimneypiece.*

345. *The Dining Room; pale blue and white, with the reddish brown of jasper in the 'cameos'.*

346. *The east end of the Dining Room. Comparison with the west end, Fig. 345, shows Wyatt's skilful variation of his theme in the handling of each wall.*

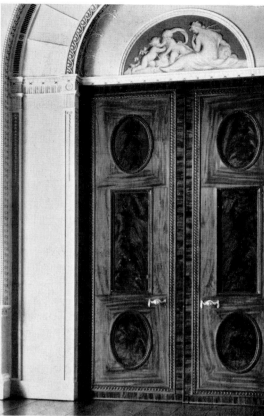

347. *Tripod candelabrum in the Dining Room.*

348. *Detail of doorway in the Dining Room.*

349. *Relief candelabrum in the Dining Room.*

beautiful room, had he not then entered the Library 'which at once blotted it out of my vision'. The Drawing Room was not finished, by which he probably meant the Saloon, since the Drawing Room decoration was in fact, never begun. There can thus be no question that Wyatt must have designed these superlative interiors not long after his completion of Heaton (begun 1772), and some time before 1784. They therefore in fact as well as in style belong to his brilliant early 'Pantheon' period, before domestic tended to take second place to institutional and largely gothic work in his practice.

They illustrate not so much how fully he had assimilated the Adam technique as, by their vigour and reserve of treatment, how he developed it, substantiating the contemporary verdict that 'he employed the antique with more judgment'. There is a good deal of Chambers's discrimination, allied with invention that definitely negatives the view that James Wyatt was no more than an imitator. They confirm, rather, the contention that his adventurous but uneven genius required, in order to reveal its best qualities, to be controlled by and synthesized with classical scholarship.

Taylor's rejected design for the Hall (Fig. 335), and a plan for the rooms differing slightly from those executed, shows that Wyatt was certainly not collaborating with but replacing him. Taylor, it can be inferred, had got so far as putting in the floors, so that Wyatt had to make the best of finite but empty spaces. To provide a Hall proportionate to the large reception rooms intended, Taylor had formed in the N. side of the old house a space 68 ft. long by 22 ft. wide and some 26 ft. high. At each end of this he had thickened the dividing walls to

get fenestral symmetry (which accounts for the difference between internal and external dimension); and at each end he had ceiled a bay at 13 ft. to be divided off with a screen of columns at both levels. The gallery with which he would have surrounded the central area (five bays long), though one side gave access to bedrooms, would have detracted from both the height and width of this space. Wyatt, perhaps recalling Adam's handling of the 'great room' at Kenwood of almost identical size (63 ft. by 25 ft., though slightly lower), eliminated the gallery and seized on the void above the windows in which to strike a semicircular vault, unifying the whole central space. He evidently heightened the cornice level (to 15 ft.) and used a taller Order; but there was not depth in the end bays for an *exedra*, as at Kenwood, so he walled off these end spaces above the columned screens (Fig. 338).

In representing the vault as carried on a series of arched ribs, their haunches filled with the kind of concave fan groining that he used at Heaton, one may detect the influence of his study of gothic. If so, it is an interesting instance of gothic-classic synthesis, giving the much-used fan motif a 'structural' purpose. The three-dimensional composition was cleverly developed between the ribs by two series of lunettes, in the vertical and the horizontal plane: the vertical having an oval medallion (the same motif recurring above the screens); and the horizontal having a half roundel of the alternating patterns used for the rounds in the ceiling's central compartments.

In the walls the pilasters connect the arched ribs to corresponding bands in the marble floor, which repeats the ceiling's rectangular lines in red and black marble on a white stone ground, and completes a colour scheme as soberly rich as the design. On walls and ceiling the foundation colour is apple green, the pilasters yellow Siena scagliola, the capitals and enrichments white. The flat surfaces of the ceiling are white, with the rounds and the fans in shades of apple green. The main ribs, and the medallions in the lunettes, have the green as background to the white relief. The chairs and tables, no doubt to Wyatt's design, are painted to match; the doors, the higher of 12 ft., are of a pale finely figured mahogany as throughout his rooms. This superb space has been analyzed in detail as being J. Wyatt's surviving masterpiece as an interior designer and perhaps, after Adam's Anti-room at Syon, the finest room produced by English neo-classicism.

The staircase was probably retained by both architects in the same position as that in the Bence house. But Wyatt re-arranged its going from Taylor's proposal, carrying it up the three internal walls, so to leave the windows clear, and also a passage-way to the west rooms on both floors, necessitated at the upper level by his omitting Taylor's hall gallery. Since it leads only to bedrooms, the staircase is relatively modest, but its slender iron balustrade is delicately enriched with cast lead foliage, urns, and 'Wedgwood' medallions, the whole painted white and blue (Fig. 340).

The room to the W. of the stairs was the 'common dining room' (latterly study), and all beyond it has remained much as Taylor arranged it for Sir Gerard, probably whilst work was in progress on the centre and E. wing. Beyond the morning room next to the Hall (H), which was proposed, curiously, as 'dressing room', is a square room (I), now the small dining room, with one side partitioned in a shallow curve, and decorated with prints less elaborately framed than the examples at Woodhall and elsewhere. To the E. of the Staircase and opening also from the Hall, lies the Anti-room to the reception suite, still contained in the Bence house. Taylor had apparently proposed two corner fireplaces here, suggestive of a waiting room, but Wyatt created a *salle de passage* for effect only (it has no fireplace). Designed in the Etruscan manner (Fig. 341), it reproduces the character of a Roman room, as deduced from Pompeii, more convincingly than the so-called Etruscan rooms at Heaton (p. 14), Osterley and Woodhall (Fig. 363). The walls are pale green,

350. *The Library, looking east.*

351. *The Library window treatment, with curtain-blinds.*   351 (a). *The Library chimneypiece, with flanking cupboards.*
The over-all colouring is pale green, the reliefs white against purple brown.

with white wood or plaster enrichments, patterned with figures from vases in the appropriate red and admirably painted by Biagio Rebecca. The room is completely detailed, the furniture being *en suite* and including in the niches candelabra that represent in painted wood a classical tripod carrying a vase, with the metal candle branches attached to ram's heads at the angles.

Next to it in the S. front Taylor had placed a 'gallery' (3) with the 'library' (4) beyond it, and the N. front the 'drawing room' (2) with 'eating room' (5) beyond—the service of the latter having to pass either through 3 or 2, but either way the whole length of the house. Wyatt's rearrangement was slightly more practical and, as in the hall, he cleared most of the spaces which Taylor had cut up with columns into Palladian rectangles, remodelling them as neo-classical compositions making play with semicircles and segments. Two factors may have influenced his treatment of them. One was the intention that painting should be the main decorative medium, with plastic enrichment subordinate. The other was the fact that the height, some 15 ft., given to these rooms by Taylor, left nearly half that height above the heads of his ground floor windows. The ways in which this headroom was to be incorporated into the room-spaces largely conditioned their handling.

In the Saloon (Fig. 342) he used the extra height for a segmental vault, its curve repeated in the ends and in the alcoves which they contain. And since the decoration is almost entirely in *trompe l'oeil*, actual relief is restricted to the entablatures (alternating urns and figures in ovals) of the walls and doorways. Rebecca filled in this outline in tones of green on a biscuit ground, with a dexterity extended to the chimneypiece (Fig. 343) and interfenestral furniture. The elaborate arabesque panels, the ceiling groups and mouldings, and the band of running boys framing it, could have been disturbing if painted in polychrome, but so sensitive is the tonality that the room is a soft golden unity, the painting serving as texture.

Parallel to the Saloon is the Dining Room (Fig. 345). Taylor had thickened the wall between it and the hall to obtain fenestral symmetry, and Wyatt further reduced the room's area slightly by similarly thickening the S. wall. This enabled that moulding of the rectangle into compensating curves, which took the place of the Orders in the neo-classical conception. The alcoves with which he could thus flank the fireplace are echoed in a feigned alcove between the doors at the W. end (Fig. 345) and by the treatment of the doorway at the E. end, between rectangular niches (Fig. 346). These concavities sufficiently offset the cubic character of the room, and so far occupied its height that its ceiling could be flat. Within this white three-dimensional frame-

352. *Centre-piece of the Library ceiling.*

work the decoration is of an exquisite elegance, subtly varied. The alcove arches, for example, have no entablature, so that their profile is pure; but in the soffit is a delicate guilloche, and the feigned alcoves have the slimmest of pilasters carrying the suggestion of an arch above the radiating ribs of a fan (Fig. 346). Within, its successive semicircles seem to recede to the lunette—a feigned cameo with jasper ground. On the other hand the true alcoves have arabesque reliefs and the fan motif, threaded with the reddish jasper colouring. This originates in the large cameo above the chimneypiece, diminishing echoes of which point the wall surface and the filigree-fine candelabra in relief (Fig. 349). The same colour picks out the garland and guilloche motifs in the ceiling, and enters into the tripods that occupy the rectangular recesses, likewise providing the ground of the moulded chair-rail. The side tables in the alcoves, of similarly painted deal, have legs identical to those of the mahogany dining table and chairs, ordered, if not designed, by Wyatt. This exquisite room was damaged by fire in 1949 but has been restored exactly.

A third variation on these closely related themes—nearly all the motifs of which can be matched in Adam's later rooms (e.g. Home House)—is applied to the Library (Fig. 350). In both the E. rooms Wyatt was able to insert in their end wall one of his characteristic tripartite windows derived from the Venetian type, here rising higher than Taylor's

windows, and contained by pilasters. These echo the columns opposite, inherited from Taylor and retained because they carry the upper wall of the pavilion. (Reference to the plan shows how, to secure access from 3 to 5, the latter room had been prolonged by means of these columns.) Wyatt actually reduced the height of the N. windows slightly with a cornice which, serving as boxing for the looped-up curtain-blinds here seen in place, also corresponds to that of his shelving. By this means he gained space for a lunettte over each bay, and for the ceiling to be given a cove. His treatment of the bays, with slender pilasters, is a variation of that in the Dining Room, as are the candelabra reliefs, in this case of classical figures (Fig. 351). Here also he thickened the walls, but the depth was not wasted, for where shelving ends the apparent solids form cupboards, as beside the fireplace (Fig. 351 (a)). The colour of the walls is pale green, with the reliefs white and the recessed surfaces purple brown, this last deriving from the porphyry of the chimneypiece and columns. It is also the ground of Rebecca's cameo medallions which, on the walls, depict poets (cf. Berrington, Fig. 381) and in the ceiling Apollo (Fig. 352). This chimneypiece and that in the Dining Room are among the few of marble introduced at Hevening-ham by Wyatt, who generally played down the decorative importance of the English fireplace.

The fourth reception room—the Drawing Room (4)—although a design probably by Rebecca exists for its decoration in bright Kauffmannesque polychrome—was never undertaken. It is not known why Sir Gerard failed to complete the last lap of his splendid course, unless it was due to failing health.

His brother and successor in 1791 had already employed Wyatt, or proceeded to do so, for building Roehampton Grove, Putney. He was created Lord Huntingfield in the Irish peerage (1798), but continued to represent Dunwich till his death in 1815. Exactly a century later the death of the 4th Lord was followed by a sale of the contents of Hevening-ham. The 5th and present Lord Huntingfield bought back many of the pieces designed for the house, and later inherited others, such as the 'Thomas Hope' library table, which pertain very appropriately. Subsequently he sold Hevening-ham intact to his brother, the present owner.

353. *The Orangery, designed by Wyatt.*

WOODHALL PARK, HERTFORDSHIRE

Built for **Sir Thomas Rumbold, Baronet,** 1778–82
Architect **Thomas Leverton**
Decoration (Print Room) **R. Parker,** 1782
Owner **Mr T. Abel Smith**

Clive's A.D.C. at Plassey in 1757, Thomas Rumbold, had been born and brought up in the East India Company's service and at thirty-four was already rich when he came home in 1770. He bought Woodhall Park, north of Hertford, for £87,000 seven years later, but returned to India as Governor of Madras in 1778. Though he was responsible for the capture of Pondicherry, for which he received a baronetcy in 1779, on reaching home in the ensuing year he was arraigned for disasters that had followed his departure. The case, largely due to the wealth he had earlier acquired, failed, but adds to the similarity of background between Woodhall's building and that of Claremont. There was likewise a large pre-existing house, known as Woodhall Watton, the ancestral home of the Boteler family, but half the old mansion had been burnt down in 1771.

Thomas Leverton (1743–1824) was almost of an age with Holland and J. Wyatt and since 1771 had acquired a practice in and around London with houses for well-to-do citizens. His successful adaptation of the Adam-Wyatt neo-classical style, notably in No. 1 Bedford Square for Sir Lionel Lyde (*c*. 1775), may be partly accounted for by J. Bonomi having shifted from Adam's to Leverton's office about that time. The remarkable distinction of parts of Woodhall shows that a highly accomplished hand was concerned in its design, which was exhibited at the R.A. in 1778 as then building, and published in Richardson's volume of *Vitruvius Britannicus*, 1798.

The house is built in the then admired white brick, here of a warm varied hue, relieved by stone dressings. The centre block is given the vertical proportion of a London house by the height of the ground storey (beneath which is a submerged basement), emphasized by its windows descending to floor level. This also imparts an effete, vestigial look to the engaged portico over the original entrance in the S. front (Fig. 354). The central block was flanked at half its depth by single-storey screens connecting to pavilions. On the northern (and later entrance) front, these projected forward and the screens receded segmentally to the plane of the centre. Leverton's elevation and plan (Figs. 357 and 358) can be contrasted with the appearance and arrangement since 1794 (Fig. 355; plan Fig. 359) when the screens were much altered, receiving an added storey and on the N. front were largely rebuilt. But the S. ends of the pavilions survive (Fig. 356), retaining Leverton's Venetian windows and careful punctuation, which was extended across the screens in partly dummy fenestration—since only the space behind the eastern screen was roofed. This contained *inter alia* the upper part of the kitchen (the remainder being in the basement); most of the western space was devoted to a basement court. The plan of the centre block shows the entrance hall flanked by a

354. *The centre of the southern, originally the entrance, front.*

breakfast room (D.), and the drawing room (L.), communicating with the dining room (K.) which was placed as far as possible from the kitchen (G). The room (A) containing the central window of the N. front, though curtailed by the length allotted to the dining room, was called the saloon in deference to tradition, and in 1798 it became the entrance hall. The main staircase and service stair, both top-lit, with a waiting room beside the latter, fill the remaining internal space.

The ground floor rooms are rendered particularly agreeable by the extra height given them by Leverton's departure from Palladian dogma in the elevation. Thus the original Entrance Hall (Fig. 361) could be much loftier than usual with entrance halls; indeed be accorded the ratio of a cube and a half, enabling the external arcade-motif to be repeated round its walls, so emphasizing the architectural unity. The ceiling and floor design, consequently, needed not to repeat each other for that purpose; but in this classical space the inner door (unlike most others in the house) could be allowed its entablature. In the Staircase adjoining (Fig. 362) the height of the lower storey relative to the area available (17 by 30 ft.) caused the arrangement shown in the published plan (double flights ascending either side of the hall door to a half-landing along the N. wall) to be replaced with a single flight climbing round from the E. to the W. end. This is the arrangement usual in a London house, which it resembles, except that the space is entered in its sides.

355. *The southern front as altered in* 1794.

356. *The south end of the west pavilion.*

357. *South front as designed by Leverton and built* 1777–82. *From 'Vitruvius Britannicus', vol. VI.*

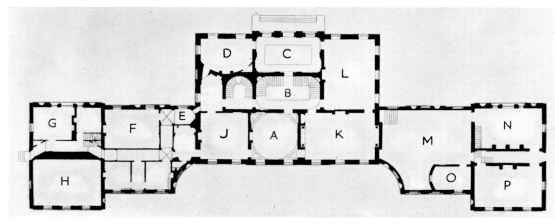

358. (*left*) *Leverton's Ground Plan. A. Saloon. B. Staircase. C. Hall. D. Breakfast Room. E. Lobby. F. Billiard Room. G. Upper part of kitchen. H. House-keeper. J. Library. K. Eating Room. L. Drawing Room. M. Open Court. N. Brewhouse. O. Dairy. P. Laundry.*

359. *As rearranged,* 1794. 1. *Portico.* 2. *Entry.* 3. *Stair.* 4. *Garden Hall.* 5. *Breakfast Room.* 6. *Lobby.* 7. *Print Room.* 8. *Schoolroom.* 9. *Upper part of kitchen.* 10. *Little library.* 11. *Eating Room.* 12. *Drawing Room.* 13. *Lobby.* 14. *Billiard Room.* 15. *Great Library.*

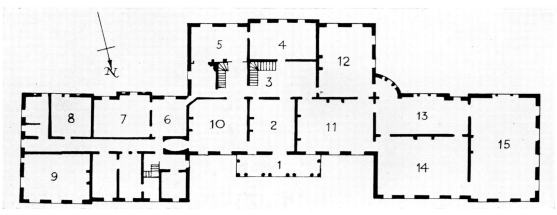

360. Upper part of the staircase hall looking east. Delicate stucco arabesque and 'chiaroscuro' paintings.

The oval and rectangular panels of the lower walls yield to richer decoration in the better lit upper storey (Fig. 360). Here the square below the round dome has at either end arched extensions some 6 ft. deep, their coffered soffits recalling Holland's similar recourse to Piranesian effect in the same context at Berrington (p. 184). Fans in the lunettes and stucco arabesques in the wall panels are supplemented by painted insets—the larger *chiaroscuri* original and skilful; the vesicas modern and less so. The graceful wrought balustrading, painted bronze and gold, is similar to the pattern used by Leverton in the smaller space of No. 1 Bedford Square, but here the longer expanses caused him to alternate the vase-shaped motif with arabesques between plain uprights for variety. All combines to produce delicate neoclassical texture that is emphasized by the plain arching of the eight doorways—four of which, including two *en l'aire*, are dummies.

For the little Saloon, 24 ft. deep by 22 ft. wide (Fig. 363), Leverton, or perhaps Bonomi, elaborated the treatment applied to the hall at No. 1 Bedford Square: a fluted saucer dome enriched with 'grotesques', but here coloured and extended to all the surfaces as a version of fashionable Etruscan decoration. The Wyatts were exploiting the style familiarized by Sir William Hamilton's collection of antiquities, brought to London in 1772, and Rebecca was painting the best example at Heveningham (Fig. 341). In this instance, however, Raphael's rendering of the style in the Vatican *grotteschi*, which had already inspired Kent and Adam, is more in evidence, though 'Pompeian' colouring on white ground is adopted. The panels and medallions representing the Cupid-Psyche story are painted on canvas and applied.

The chimneypiece has similar painted panels with some scagliola inlay; but a better example of the technique is in the room over the hall (Fig. 368). In that the inlay of very thin pieces, almost flakes, of coloured marble is of the kind called 'Bossi work' after the craftsman who worked in this medium chiefly in Dublin *c.* 1775–85.

None of the other rooms display a style that can be regarded as characteristic of Leverton so completely as these. But in the Little Library the recessed shelving is carried round it and, disguising the doors (Fig. 370), shows the same delicacy of touch and fitness; also the elongated type of console bracket which he borrowed and exaggerated from J. Wyatt. Neither Dining Room nor Drawing Room had, or have retained, the Adamesque ceiling one would expect from Leverton's Bedford Square houses, and which at Woodhall was 'reflected' in a splendid Moorfields carpet (cf. Tipping, op. cit., p. 213). The doors throughout the ground floor are of veneered cross-banded mahogany set in flat decorated architraves without entablatures. The fineness of the sculpture in the Drawing Room chimneypiece (Fig. 369) suggestively recalls that Flaxman is said to have been employed in his early days by Leverton; it also illustrates the fashion for using the imposts as panels for arabesque in relief (cf. Berrington, Fig. 388). The design of the mirror is interesting as transitional from the highly enriched to the rectangular pier-glass type. In the Dining Room, otherwise severely plain, the delicate free-hand modelling of the vine trails in the sideboard recess introduces a touch of rococo naturalism (Fig. 367).

An outstanding instance of another decorative mode is found in the East wing room called Billiard Room in

362. *The rise of the Staircase looking east.*

361. *The Garden Hall, originally the entrance hall.*

364. *The Print Room, 'Designed and finished by R. Parker', 1782.*

363. *Leverton's 'Saloon': 'Pompeian' colouring on white ground.*

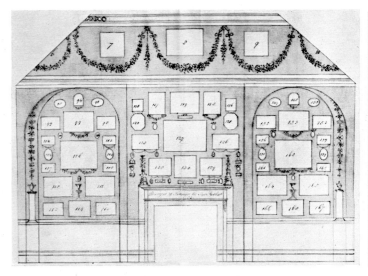

365. R. Parker's design for the east end of the Print Room.   *366. The same as it is.*

Leverton's plan (Fig. 364). Similar 'print rooms' in which engravings are arranged in specially printed strips and festoons to a carefully marshalled scheme, are to be found at Rokeby, Heveningham, Stratfield Saye, the Vyne and Ston Easton, and there was one at Mersham-le-Hatch. This example is not only the most elaborate but the plans for it exist (Fig. 365), 'Designed and Finished by R. Parker, 1782',[1] with the prints numbered to correspond to a catalogue of their subjects. The larger engravings are not only framed but appear to hang by ribbons from nails with ornamental heads, from them depending miniatures or swagged chains. There are also busts, plinths, candelabra, etc., and the decoration is extended to the ceiling cove, every item being printed and cut out. Such variety of components implies considerable demand, or their cost would have been great, whereas the detailed account

[1] Probably to be identified with James Parker, pupil of Basire, and engraver of plates in Boydell's *Shakespeare* (J. Lees Milne, op. cit., p. 160).

by Chippendale for the Hatch room in 1767–68 (cf. p. 101) shows that they cost little. Chippendale's bill is given here for comparison with Parker's work:

	£	s.	d.
To size Paste and Hanging . . . with 2 Papers	1	5	0
Lumberland and Cartridge Paper		10	6
Verditure and Colouring the Room	4	6	0
180 ft. of Papie Machie Border Painted Blue and White	4	10	0
Pins and fixing up the Border			
Cutting out the Prints, Borders and Ornaments and Hanging them in the Room complete	14	10	0
To 506 Printed Borders @ 2	4	4	4
103 ditto Festoons @ 3	1	5	9
91 ditto Corners @ 2½		18	11½
11 Bustos, 18 Sayters and Lions Masks @ 4		9	8

367. The east end of the Eating Room.

368. Chimneypiece of 'Bossi work' in an upper room.

369. *The Drawing Room chimneypiece and mirror.*

370. *A corner of the Little Library.*

39 Rings and 12 Masks @ 1½		6	4½
74 Knots @ 1½		9	3
11 Vases @ 6		5	6
28 Baskets and 8 Sheets of Chains		12	0
18 Patteras and 3 Pedestals @ 2		3	6

All Chippendale's items can be found at Woodhall, except the 'Sayters' (satyrs) and 'Lions Masks', and the papier maché border used at Hatch as edging between wall-paper and dado, cornice, etc. Here that is a broad flat band of paper. The cost, exclusive of engravings, amounted to about £33 at Hatch where the room was probably a smaller one than this, which Leverton's plan gives as 26 ft. by 20 ft.[1]

The year 1782, in which this room was decorated, is probably that of Woodhall's completion, and also witnessed the 'Bill of pains and penalties' brought against Sir Thomas Rumbold in connection with the Mahratta insurrection that followed his return from Madras. A second marriage at this

[1] In 1954 the Minister of Works granted £200 for the repair and safeguarding of this room which the public is permitted to inspect by appointment.

time led to his disinheriting his son by the previous one and, on Sir Thomas's death in 1791, to the sale of Woodhall for the benefit of his widow.[1] The purchaser, who gave £125,000 in 1794, was Paul Benfield, another Nabob of spectacular wealth. This was to disappear in the banking crisis precipitated by the threatened French invasion in 1797—which nearly ruined the builder of Berrington too. Benfield is stated by Clutterbuck to have been responsible for the alterations to Woodhall, by which three large rooms were added on the west, and both the 'screens' heightened.

After Benfield's bankruptcy Woodhall was bought in 1801 for £180,000 by the banker, Samuel Abel Smith, with whose descendants it remains. In the mid-19th century they added a low portico to the former saloon door, which had become the front door, and laid out formal gardens before the southern front. But the interior continued to retain its character and contents to the notable degree represented in the photographs. After a period of disuse before the last war, Woodhall was leased to its present occupants, Heath Mount School.

[1] See *Recollections of a Diplomatist*, by Sir Horace Rumbold, grandson of the disinherited heir.

BERRINGTON HALL, HEREFORDSHIRE

Built for **the Rt Hon. Thomas Harley**
Architect **Holland, 1778–81**
Landscape **Brown, 1775–81**
Owner **Lord Cawley**

Berrington Hall is the most complete surviving example of Holland's earlier style. The park, two miles N. of Leominster, slopes westward to the valley of a tributary of the R. Lugg, commanding a wide prospect of the Welsh Marches and Radnor Forest, where lie Brampton Bryan and Eywood, the ancestral homes of the Harley family. The estate, originally belonging to the Cornwalls of Burford, was bought *c.* 1774 by Thomas Harley (1730–1804), a younger son of the 3rd Earl of Oxford and great nephew of the Tory statesman. He had made a considerable fortune in the City by financing (with Drummond) the payment of the British army in America, and as an army clothing contractor, and was joint founder of a banking house. Aged thirty-one he was elected M.P. for the City, and in 1763, as Sheriff, was responsible for the historic burning of No. 45 of the *North Briton* edited by Wilkes. His vigour in handling the ensuing riots and solicitude for the distress caused by the freezing of the Thames during his Lord Mayoralty (1764), earned him appointment to the Privy Council, a distinction almost unique for a Lord Mayor. In 1774 he stood as Tory candidate for Herefordshire, a seat which he won in 1776 and held till he retired shortly before his death in 1804. His only son died in 1764, but he had three daughters of whom Anne in 1781 married the son of Admiral Lord Rodney, eventually inheriting Berrington. Allusions to

371. *The portico, facing west.*

this marriage in the decoration of some of the rooms, and the enhanced degree of the decoration compared to the original estimate, imply that much work continued after 1780 immediately preceding Holland's reconstruction of Carlton House (begun 1783). Berrington thus fills the gap in his development between Brooks's Club-house, 1776–78, and his *début* as the Prince of Wales's architect. No less significant is the novelty of the plan, disposing the multifarious services

372. *From the south west.*

373. *The south wing.*   374. *The central window of the north side.*

of a country house to a geometrical form clearly inspired by neo-classical ideals (Fig. 393, p. 194).

In 1775 Capability Brown recorded visiting Lord Oxford at Eywood and Mr Harley at Berrington,[1] when it is probable that the site and possibly the outline of the plan were determined; also that the architect should be Holland. But it was only in 1778 that 'Henry Holland junior' produced designs with an estimate of £14,500 for the building.[2] The care

evidenced for comfort and soundness of construction recalls Holland's tribute to Brown in this connection (cf. Claremont, p. 135). The front faces S.W. (to be termed West in this description), but the approach is from the E., entering the pleasure grounds through a lodge in the form of an arched gatehouse (Fig. 375), whence it sweeps round to the portico

[1] D. Stroud, op. cit., p. 171. The plans for the lake, park, etc., then determined were not put in hand till 1781.

[2] The brick core is to be faced with stone dug in the park. Among items of interest are 'to build the dry area round the house; roof

with Westmorland slates; the partitions in bed-chambers and garrets to be partly noggined and part filled with sawdust; a strong counter-floor laid to prevent noise and fire; one pair stairs to have mahogany sashes, glazed crown glass double hung; chimneypieces part wood part stone to cost about £15 each; 2 water closets with marble basons and mahogany seats'.

375. *The archway lodge on the approach.*   376. *The east entry to the court.*

377. The front door under the portico.

passing the S. wing (Fig. 373) and originally went on past the N. wing to stables. The wings lie behind but in echelon to the main block to enclose a large courtyard enclosed on the fourth side by a laundry and bakehouse range (Fig. 376) through an arch in which the court was entered. The four blocks were linked by quadrants, those adjoining the main block being originally screens of arches only with no covering. (The S.E. quadrant has since been removed to facilitate access.) The plentiful accommodation in these ranges was additional to a light basement, and to 'an exceedingly large servants' dormitory' in the attic, of the house itself (plan: Fig. 393).

The elevations are of a neo-classical simplicity, the stone throughout the pinkish sandstone of the region. The plainly gabled wings have the most ornament owing to their prominence in the approach, yet this is limited to a great central alcove with coffered semi-dome surmounted by ball cresting, and a blind arch repeating the alcove in their W. ends. The house itself, of two storeys with basement and balustraded parapet, is unornamented except for the rusticated voussoirs of the arched basement windows. Its effect proceeds from the smooth, warm hued, ashlar masonry and the rhythms of the fenestration. Whereas in the wings the lower windows are arched, here it is those of the upper floor, except under the portico, and in the centre of the N. side where the boudoir window is singled out for special treatment (Fig. 374). Set in an arch, this is contained in a kind of round-headed entablature bordered with the tight kind of garland which Gabriel used in the Petit Trianon. In the portico the columns, of an Ionic order that has the stocky proportions of the Tuscan, are spaced with the centre interval of double width. They carry a full entablature, absent elsewhere, and plain except for a band of Greek honeysuckle ornament over the central span. The lun-

ette in the pediments, now a window, originally contained the Harley arms set in similar ornament. The exaggeratedly tall entrance doorway, with little wreathed Coade stone medallions (Fig. 377), evidently derives, with the boudoir window, from hints of *le style Louis XVI*. It is also tempting to detect in some of Berrington's unconventionalities the original mind of Soane, who was at the time still attached to Holland's office.

The Entrance Hall (Fig. 378), with polychrome marble paving echoing the circular ceiling pattern, closely follows that at Claremont (Fig. 261) in which Soane definitely had a hand. The trophies over the doors and the pedimented central doorway are in fact identical. The colouring is duck-egg blue and terra-cotta with gilding; that of the floor blue, white and variegated marbles.

This latter is an instance of the many decorations extra to the 1778 estimate, in which 'hall and staircase are to be paved with stone'. The estimate was admittedly for the carcase only, but in the ensuing items plain internal treatment is definitely specified, in contrast to the great elaboration adopted, in consequence, it is suggested, of Harley's assurance of having a successor worthy of the additional expenditure. The great Staircase was to have 'a neat iron baluster capp'd with mahogany, the cornices with few enrichments, the ceilings plain, the columns wood'. Indeed it is doubtful whether Holland did not subsequently revise the whole staircase hall to more impressive form (Figs. 382–384).

As executed, it is a brilliant exercise in spatial design using mass and recession assymetrically to produce dramatic visual effects. Entry from the Hall is not, as might be expected, through the door beneath the double tier of coffered arches (on left, Fig. 383) but by the one facing that seen at the foot of the stairs, so that the great coffered span carrying the landing is first seen in profile from below, with the luminous void of the staircase to one's right and the enriched recess of the inner archway in shadow to one's left. The contrasting light and shade, and the almost violent distortion of the axis thus effected, are essentially picturesque in the Piranesian sense, and it is easy to detect his Roman engravings as the germ of Holland's composition. The detailing of the ornament, however, is predominantly Greek, as is the pattern of the bronzed balustrade, which is not unlike that employed for the Carlton House staircase. The original colouring is intact. The walls are a grey-white and pale blue with the frames, dados and string course biscuit and olive, picked out in gilding; in the vaulting the coffers are of *terra-cotta* and biscuit. In the upper stage screens of scagliola columns of bistre and slate colour form galleries overlooking the stairs on two sides and an extension of the landing at the head of the stairs, pilasters repeating the arrangement on the blank east wall. The frieze, with a duck-egg ground, introduces coupled dolphins with their entwined tails gilded, possibly a reference to the Rodney marriage. Above, a skylight dome rises from a ceiling of flesh pink, duck-egg compartments framed in mouldings of pastel blue and gilding, and grisaille painted medallions in the angles.

The elaborateness of the decoration is unique in Holland's *œuvre* except for the vanished glories of Carlton House. In quality and degree, the enrichment of this staircase and other principal rooms shows him demonstrating that he

378. *The Entrance Hall. Duck-egg blue with terracotta and gilding. The polychrome marble floor echoes the circular ceiling pattern.*

379. *The Library. Predominantly pale grey-green and bistre, the enrichment gilt.*

380.   *Library shelves and a doorway.*   381.   *The Library ceiling, with 'grisaille' medallions of English authors.*

383. *The span of the landing in the Staircase Hall.*

382. *The Staircase, looking southward.*

could improve on Adam's later style typified at Osterley, and on Paine's 1775 rooms at Brocket, for example. But they are *sui generis*; and although nowhere else did he command the service of one of the leading decorative painters, some of his ceilings can be closely matched at Claremont (1772–74), Holland's first and only previous commission of comparable importance, so identifying his style at this period.

In the Library (Fig. 379), to the right of the entrance hall, Holland's management of shelving, doors and chimneypiece to form an integrated design recalls Adam's library at Nostell, though the pilasters are characteristically attenuated, without plinths (Fig. 380). The design of the ceiling (Fig. 381) is almost the same as one at Claremont (Fig. 277), the delicate scrolling exactly so, but the component circles here contain painted grisaille medallions of the leading English authors from Chaucer to Addison. In the delightful frieze over the fireplace (Fig. 379), Homer (?) receives the tributes of the children of the Muses, and the Muses themselves are portrayed on the larger mural medallions. The colouring is mainly bistre and gilt, with the grey-green of the paintings; the walls duck-egg green, the woodwork pale terra-cotta and flesh, with the pilasters white and gilt. The old Axminster carpet combines carmine-pink and cobalt blue on a beige ground, and the mahogany doors are light golden brown. If Holland employed the same craftsmen as at Claremont, the stuccoist was William Pearce, Hobcroft the carpenter, but the sculptor of the chimneypieces is in both cases uncertain. The painter, according to a sale catalogue of 1887, is 'reputed to be Rebecca the Dutch artist [sic] who spent many years on the work'.

In the Drawing Room, which is on the other side of the hall, the ceiling alone is comparably decorated, but that is more elaborate than any other existing by Holland (Fig. 385). Stylistically it is interesting for the inclusion of high relief modelling, almost in Adam's earlier manner, used for the cupids leading sea horses with blue ribbons. These almost certainly refer to the Harley-Rodney marriage and so date the work to 1781 or later. Rebecca's gaily coloured medallions

384. *Upper part of the Staircase Hall. The columns of bistre and slate colour scagliola.*

385. *The Drawing Room ceiling that celebrates the Harley-Rodney wedding in* 1781.

with Jupiter, Cupid and Venus grouped in the centre, appear to carry on the symbolism. The ceiling's ground colouring is pale French blue, with grey-blue mouldings and lavender in the surround; the reliefs white, as are the walls. The statuary chimneypiece (Fig. 386) with term supporters carries on a convention by alluding in the plaque to Harley's delight in architecture. The steel grate is very unusual for having Wedgwood cameos inset in its spandrils—which miraculously have survived pokers for nearly two centuries! Two interfenestral mirrors of plate glass are contemporary, as may be their pelmets and console tables though with the curtains they are more probably mid-19th century.

Opening out of the Drawing Room and occupying the central bay of the N. side of the house, is the exquisite Boudoir (Fig. 390). In his later boudoirs, at Althorp and Southill, Holland was to capture the Louis XVI style more completely. Here he evidently essayed the manner, notably in the pattern of the door-frames (Fig. 391), but the alcove, with which space is stolen in the north side, was a trick familiar to James Wyatt. Its columns are lapis-lazuli blue scagliola. In the ceiling, picked out with pink, blue and gold, Venus disports with cupids.

386. *Drawing Room chimneypiece. The grate inset with Wedgewood plaques.*

387. *The Dining Room, hung with paintings of Rodney's naval victories.*

The Dining Room, occupying three bays on the E. side of the house, at first sight contains no naval allusions in the decoration. In the centre of the ceiling Rebecca (if he was the painter) set a Banquet of the Gods (Fig. 387), garlanded around with highly realistic floral swags, and the end panels represent Bacchus and Ceres characteristically: themes conventional to a dining room. The chimneypiece (Figs. 388, 389), a work of exceptional delicacy, contains several symbolic if obscure allusions. Originally an inscribed silver plate occupied the place of the central plaque (which is a recent insertion). It bore a relief of the Sacrifice of Iphigenia with the words *Te Arete Athanate* ('To Immortal Virtue') and recorded the gift, no doubt of the chimneypiece, 'to the late Mr Harley by Bell Lloyd Esq', according to *The Leominster Guide* (1808).[1] The sculptured imposts display a vine-wreathed rod supporting (right) a female figure carrying what appears to be a distaff and, in faint relief behind her, Britan-

nia's shield and trident; and (left, Fig. 389) a male bearing a stork with (in faint relief behind) a full rigged ship and a naval fort. These figures may refer to the Rodney marriage (Aphrodite's stork being a symbol of love); or symbolize Commerce and Banking, in which connection the sacrifice and text could refer to Harley's behaviour when, his banking firm having failed in 1797, he discharged his liabilities in full from his private resources. In that case it would be some fifteen years later than the rest of the room. Neither interpretation, however, fully accounts for the symbolism; and the inscription implies that the chimneypiece was installed after Harley's death in 1804.

Harley was certainly much delighted by his daughter's marriage. A suite of rooms was set apart for the Admiral's use,[1] and the principal rooms were decorated much more elaborately than had been contemplated, introducing references to the union. But, if made in 1781, those to naval

---

[1] Bell Lloyd (1729–93) eldest son of William Lloyd of Pontriffith, Co. Flint, and Frances, heiress of Bell Jones, was nephew and heir to Sir Edward Lloyd, 1st Bt., Secretary of War. His eldest son was cr. 1st Baron Mostyn; his second son (d. 1845), also Bell Lloyd, m. 1792 Anne, sister of Thomas, 1st Viscount Anson.

[1] The sale catalogue of Berrington in 1887 states that the bedrooms in the E. side above the Dining Room formed 'the Admiral's suite, consisting of two bedrooms with dressing rooms and W.C., having doors communicating with balcony (i.e. landing) and lobby of servants' staircase'.

388, 389. *The Dining Room chimneypiece, and (right) detail of its sculpture which reveals symbolic illusions.*

390. *The Boudoir. Lapis-lazuli scagliola columns.*

391. *The doorway in the Boudoir from the Drawing Room.*

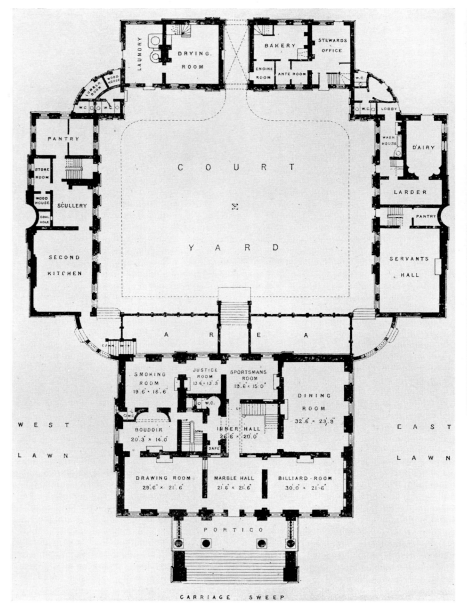

392. *The back staircase.*

393. *Ground Floor Plan as in* 1887. *As described here, west is below, east above.*

glory can only have referred to Rodney's earlier successes, since his crowning victory, the Battle of the Saints, was won in the following year. This celebrated action is depicted in two of the naval paintings by Thomas Luny, dated 1785, that still hang at Berrington, and were presumably brought here by the 2nd Lord Rodney. There are four, of which three are signed and dated 1785. The remaining one (a copy of the picture now in the Royal Maritime Museum and probably made to complete the set when hung at Berrington) is the first of the series chronologically. It depicts the explosion of the Spanish flagship during 'the Moonlight Battle' (Jan. 16, 1780). Those undoubtedly by Luny are: the Battle of Martinique, with Rodney engaging three French vessels simultaneously (April 17, 1780); and the two supreme moments in the Battle of the Saints (1782)—Rodney's breaking of the French line, and the surrender of de Grasse's flagship.

Holland's arrangement of the bedroom floor is shown by the plan to have been disposed with exceptional care. The bedrooms are grouped in twos or threes, and all have varied

chimneypieces. The oval room looking into the portico is, however, more simply treated than its elaborate planning might lead one to expect. The service staircase, contrived between the boudoir and main stairs, is given increased width by the use of the deflected bannisters sometimes found at this date (Fig. 392). It is interesting to learn from the 1887 sale catalogue that in 1851 Berrington was still regarded as 'of so excellent a plan and design that the model was considered worthy to be exhibited in the Great Exhibition'. At the end of the century, a tower was added to the centre of the W. side of the house for water tanks and bathrooms. Though detracting from the character of the courtyard, it saved Holland's plan from more serious interference.

In 1900 the 7th Lord Rodney sold the Berrington estate to Mr, later Sir, Frederick Cawley, Chancellor of the Duchy of Lancaster 1916–18, created Lord Cawley in the latter year. He acquired some of the original and historic contents of the house and these have been supplemented with judicious acquisitions, and the original decoration restored where necessary.

394. *From the south west with the western pavilion and colonnade.*

ATTINGHAM, SHROPSHIRE

Built for **Noel Hill, 1st Lord Berwick, 1783–85**

Architect **George Steuart** (Nash, 1807)

Landscape **H. Repton, 1797**

Owner **The National Trust,** tenants, **the Shropshire Education Authority; Lady Berwick**

The French vogue affected by Whigs in the years prior to the Revolution is evident in this curious house designed by a Scots architect, and is amplified in the contents introduced in the early 19th century. A more specific factor in its unusual plan was the fact that Attingham was designed to incorporate its predecessor on the site, known as Tern Hall. The new name for the great new house was adapted from the medieval spelling of Atcham, much as the title taken by Noel Hill on being made a peer in 1784 referred to Berwick Maviston, a long-vanished hamlet near the present home farm, which one Henry Malveisin had held in 1166.[1] The transformation of the place was completed by Repton's enhancing of the little river Tern (cf. Figs. 409 and 410), spanned to carry the Holyhead road by the handsome bridge designed by John Gwynn's pupil William Hayward in 1780 (erected by the County but 'decorated at the expense of Noel Hill Esq.').[2] Tory opinion of the whole magnifying process, more characteristic of the early than the late 18th century, was expressed by John Byng: 'pass'd by Lord B's great tasteless seat, a thing like the Mansion House, but I visit not such houses. The all around is in most deplorable taste. . . . He does right to begin building a wall . . . to keep out insolence and roguery.'[3]

Tern Hall itself had been built *c.* 1700 by Thomas

[1] Michael Rix: 'New Light on Attingham Hall', in *Country Life,* October 21, 1954.

[2] Atcham Bridge over the Severn two miles E. of Shrewsbury, by Gwynne himself, was built 1769–71.

[3] *Torrington Diaries,* July, 1793.

Hayward, Lord Berwick's grandfather and a descendant of Shrewsbury merchants, to whose wife the Atcham estate had been given in 1680 by her brother Richard Hill of Hawkstone. A wealthy bachelor, and Ambassador at Turin during Marlborough's wars, who later became a priest and declined a bishopric, Hill had bought Atcham not long before. Thomas Hayward, their son, assumed the name of Hill and, marrying the heiress of William Noel, Chief Justice of

395. *In the eastern colonnade.*

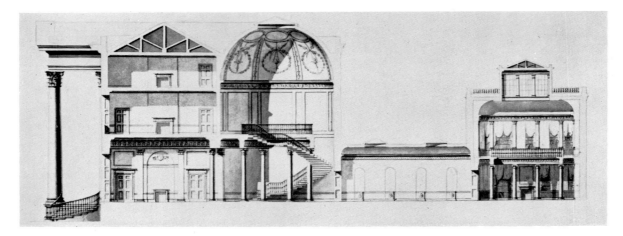

396.   Sectional
drawing by Steuart.
The staircase rotun-
da,   corridor,   and
two storey library
contained in the old
house were not exe-
cuted.

Chester, christened his heir Noel Hill. Succeeding in 1782, Noel Hill immediately began building. Foundations were opened in Feb., 1783, yet his steward could nevertheless note in the following month 'the Militia Officers dined at Tern'. The foundations were in fact being dug immediately in front of the old house, which was to be retained to provide the servants' quarters. The old front, with flanking bows, fits against the back of the existing main building so tightly that, as the plan shows (Fig. 397), the ends of the latter's sides were made to consist in circular rooms in order to dovetail on to Tern Hall, of which the centre made the fourth side of an internal court. Moreover it was to mask the sides of Tern Hall that the colonnades were carried back so far before extending laterally in prolongation of its northern face. At the back of all, a great walled court extends 250 ft. by 150 ft., entered axially through a charming neo-classical gatehouse (Fig. 398) and with pavilions in the angles. Since a magni-

ficent stable quadrangle with standings for sixty horses was built to the N.W. (in 1785), the purpose of this huge base-court, unless in connection with Lord Berwick's militia, seems to have been wholly for grandeur.

The link between Noel Hill and George Steuart, a native of Atholl, is not known. The architect had designed c. 1770 a house in Grosvenor Place, London, and was established in Berners and Harley Streets, possibly erecting some of the later houses on the Cavendish Estate. Since the rebuilding of Barons Court, Co. Tyrone, and the recent demolition of Lythwood Hall, Salop, and Earl Stoke, Wilts. (both c. 1785), Attingham is his only surviving country house; but the remarkable Church of St Chad, Shrewsbury (1790–92), with its oval nave and free-standing tower, testifies to his originality and belief in neo-classicism. At Attingham an extensive appearance, as then visible from Tern Bridge, seems to have been the first consideration. For the central block Steuart

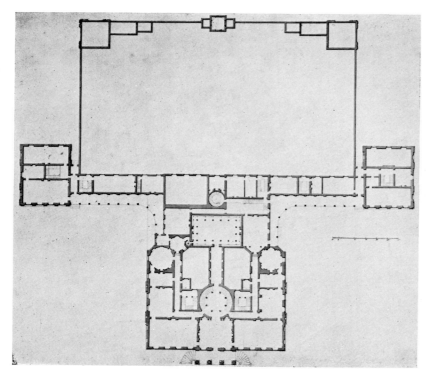

397. Steuart's plan as proposed (north point at top).

398. Entrance gateway to the Great Court.

399. *The Entrance Hall. Steuart's ceiling, chimneypiece and slender grey columns; Nash's mural decoration.*

400. *The 'Outer Library' in the south half of the west pavilion.*

was committed, by the need of using the old house, to the form of a hollow square; and, by the accommodation required, to three storeys with a basement. In the nearer view (whence the low-pitched roofs are invisible) the design relies on an empirical balance of the rectangular masses.

'Comparison with Barons Court and Earl Stoke reveals similarity of handling: a uniform severity of wall surface broken occasionally by slightly recessed arches containing a window (after the fashion set by J. Wyatt) and a tenuousness of pilaster and column. These characteristics occur here upon the side elevation of the central block and of the wings, and in the stable buildings.'[1] A French analogy to a portico of such height (at this date) is the Château de Benouville by Ledoux; Castle Coole, Co. Fermanagh, by J. Wyatt 1788, affords a more conservative rendering of the same themes, with the portico restricted to two storeys. Steuart could, however, point out that its height enabled him to make this a true portico with a functional ridge roof as used by Campbell at Wanstead—the Palladian prototype of his

[1] J. Lees Milne, *Guide to Attingham*, The National Trust, 1949.

401. *The Dining Room: Pompeian red with white enrichments.*

design. The fine ashlar masonry, giving monolithic character, is of the silvery Grinsill stone quarried locally; but to reduce the load on the foundations he used geometrical tiles in place of bricks on the inner frontages.

Steuart's original designs are preserved at Attingham and show that the plan (Fig. 397) was considerably modified in execution. The Entrance Hall 30 ft. square and the flanking Dining and Drawing Rooms 45 ft. by 35 ft. are as intended, and so is the arrangement of the sides. But Steuart proposed, behind the hall, a great circular domed staircase and an axial corridor leading to a two-storey library of collegiate proportions occupying the centre of the old Tern Hall block (Fig. 396). Actually this was used for office accommodation; and a plainer staircase was substituted in a rectangular space divided from the hall by a screen of columns, as at Barons Court. The exact arrangement is uncertain since it was re-modelled in 1807 when Nash closed off the hall and formed the Picture Gallery.

The Hall (Fig. 399) retains Steuart's slender grey scag-

liola columns and pilasters, Adamesque ceiling, doorcases, and inlaid chimneypiece set in a blind arch. But the walls *c.* 1807 were marble-painted and received panels of feigned re-lief in *grisaille*. The combined effect is delightful, perfectly according with the French element in the exterior and the furnishing. French influence may also be detected in the differentiation of the rooms on either side, in which a feminine note predominates in those to the right appro-priated to Lady Berwick and a masculine in those to the left, his Lordship's sphere. Thus the Dining Room, in the latter, is coloured Pompeian red with the delicate enrichments left white (Fig. 401); the carpet illustrated is comparable to those at Syon and Saltram. A Library, anti-Library, and octagonal Study (Fig. 404) succeeded each other in the W. side, but did not suffice to hold the books and antiquities collected, more especially by the 2nd peer. The W. pavilion became the 'Outer Library' (Fig. 400): a room that, remaining substan-tially as designed by Steuart, reflects the revival by Gabriel and Ledoux in France of loyalty to Palladio. The carpet

402. *The Drawing Room: ice blue, the enrichments white or gilt.*

mentioned above is thought to have been made for this de-lightful room. The E. pavilion, designed as a Music Room, became the greenhouse.

Externally these pavilions, having a complete entablature, are the more attractively handled part of Steuart's building, and contrast advantageously with, for example, the per-functory coupled pilasters supporting a section of entablature with which he sought to break the tedium of the side eleva-tion (seen in the same view, Fig. 394).

The Drawing Room (Fig. 402), ice-blue with the enrich-ment of the ceiling partly gilded, is the feminine counterpart of the dining room. The pictures by Angelica Kauffmann, and the notable French and Italian *Empire* furniture, were acquisitions of the 2nd and 3rd Lords Berwick. The chimney-piece (Fig. 403), with very delicate sculpture in its frieze, was supplied, with that of the Dining Room, by John Deval the younger, of the firm of sculptors active since the 1730s. The French vogue is evident in the treatment of the Lesser Drawing Room that comes next (Fig. 405), and is pro-nounced in the exquisite circular Boudoir, at the N. end of the range (Fig. 406), which recalls the *Salon à Coupole* at Bagatelle (1780). While the decoration—with flaming lamps in each segment of the dome ceiling, and slim Corinthian columns set around—is English neo-classic, the arabesque

403. *The Drawing Room chimneypiece.*

404. *The Octagon Room. At the north end of the west side.*

405. *The 'Lesser Drawing Room'. Adjoining the drawing room in the east side.*

406. *The Round Boudoir. At north end of the east side.*

painting of the sides, where not occupied by book cases, sustains a Louis XVI character. It is probably slightly later in date, since Steuart's drawings show these rooms more plainly treated. Possibly Rebecca or Cipriani was the artist, but not Angelica Kauffmann, to whom the decoration was long attributed, since she left England, as Mme Zucchi, in 1781. The 2nd Lord Berwick did, however, sit to her at Rome in 1792 for the portrait hanging over the drawing room chimneypiece, when she also painted the mythologies placed beside it.

Lord Berwick, who first occupied the new house in the autumn of 1785, died in 1789. His eldest son, then aged nineteen, on coming of age travelled in Italy 1792–94, taking as his companion Dr E. D. Clarke who recorded their tour,[1] besides his mother and young wife. Like their Shropshire neighbour, Payne Knight (cf. Downton, p. 148), and the Bishop of Derry (see, Ickworth, p. 239) the travellers took interest in geology and mineralogy equally with amassing antique and modern works of art, and settled for some time at Naples. Among the pictures there acquired is an interesting group of landscapes by Philipp Hackaert, who had been Payne Knight's companion in Sicily and was subsequently the friend of Goethe.

After his return, possibly with his visual sense quickened by travel, Lord Berwick procured Repton to advise on im-

[1] *The Life of Dr Edward D. Clarke*, 1825. Tipping quotes his interesting references to Lord Berwick's art collecting, op. cit., p. 290.

407. *The Picture Gallery formed by Nash in the internal court,* 1807.

408. *Sketch (by A. C. Pugin?) for the Gallery, showing proposed cast iron framework of the lay-lights.*

409. House and river seen from Tern bridge before 'improvement'.

410. Tern bridge and the lake after improvement. From Humphrey Repton's 'Red Book' for Attingham, 1797.

proving the park. His 'Red Book' containing illustrated proposals survives and is typical of his contributions at this time to the scenery of many places. He found the setting of Attingham restricted and flat, reporting that it was 'impossible to annex ideas of grandeur and magnificence to a mansion which appears to have little extent of park belonging to it'. He recommended expanding this eastward across the Tern, the sedgy course of which he proposed to enhance into 'extended waters'; and to break the belt of trees that had been planted to hide the high road so as better to show up the handsome Tern Bridge and admit the views southward (Figs. 409 and 410). His scheme was carried out immediately.

But it was not till 1807 that, to display his collections at Attingham, Lord Berwick engaged Nash to form the Picture Gallery, in the space between the wings behind the present Hall. Owing to its position, top-lighting was unavoidable and Nash proposed supporting the ceiling on heavy oval cast iron lights, to be made at Coalbrookdale. A watercolour at Attingham, probably by A. C. Pugin (Fig. 408), preserves the proposal, but it may have been found impracticable, since the existing solution was substituted—the earliest use in England of coved cast iron frame (Fig. 407). A new staircase was inserted in the narrow space left between the N. wall of the gallery and the S. wall of Tern Hall. Nash constructed a brick wall across which the stair ascends in a single flight then divides and turns back on itself to a landing. He failed to reach first floor level thereby, so that the remaining ascent is devious; but the fluted treatment of the walls and the scale pattern of its dome render this staircase

an interesting early essay on the tent theme which, as Mr Rix has pointed out,[1] Nash was to develop at Brighton, in conjunction again with cast iron framing.

The Gallery contains a notable organ in a mahogany case by Samuel Green, dated 1788, who also supplied that at Heaton. The collection of pictures is chiefly representative of early 19th-century connoisseurship. But the nucleus only is due to the 2nd Lord Berwick whose extravagance, as patron of the arts and society, and in a second marriage to a lady of notable beauty but doubtful family, necessitated in 1827 the sale of the entire contents of the house. The auction, conducted by Robins, lasted sixteen days and fetched high prices, but evidently much was either bought in or failed to reach the reserve. Three years later Lord Berwick died, as had his first wife, at Naples where his next brother William Hill was then Ambassador. It is to the latter, who had lived in Italy *en poste* since 1807, that the majority of the older Italian masters and of the splendid French and Italian furniture are due. As 3rd Lord Berwick he died unmarried in 1842, when a third brother succeeded, from whom the 8th peer descended. Likewise a diplomat and connoisseur he devoted his later years to Attingham and its collections, and his widow resides in part of the house, which his successor, the 9th Lord Berwick, transmitted with the estate to the National Trust in 1947. The greater part of the house has been leased to the Shropshire County Council for use as an Adult College devoted largely to inculcating appreciation of the arts, but enabling public access to the principal rooms.

[1] *Country Life, ibid.*

ALTHORP, NORTHAMPTONSHIRE

Reconstructed for **the 2nd Earl Spencer,** *c.* **1790 (Sir John Spencer,** *c.* **1580; the 2nd Earl of Sunderland,** *c.* **1665)**
Architects **(R. Morris** (?) **1729–33, Sir R. Taylor, 1772). Holland, 1786–91, and 1800**
Owner **The Earl Spencer**

One of the greater 17th century mansions but transformed in the late 18th century, Althorp is an outstanding instance of the fusion of traditional sense with classic style producing a highly satisfying form of domestic architecture. The material to be reconstructed was an Elizabethan quadrangle that had been remodelled under Charles II and renovated in Palladian taste; the synthesising medium the wit of Henry Holland in applying the distilled essence of the new classicism to English usage.

The Spencers were woolmen on the Warwick-Northamptonshire borders in the late middle ages, of whom John, an extensive grazier, at the beginning of the 16th century acquired arms and subsequently knighthood, with the estates of Wormleighton, Althorp and Great Brington. He made the first his home, some parts of which remain; at the second obtained licence in 1512 to empark 300 acres; and to the church at the third added a chancel in which his own and his descendants' splendid monuments are well known. His grandson, another Sir John, is said never to have quite succeeded in possessing 20,000 sheep; but at the time of his death in 1586 he had built at Althorp the courtyard, with wings projecting on its front, in which the house still essentially consists (Fig. 411). Sir Robert, the 5th Knight, was created in 1603 Lord Spencer of Wormleighton, and his grandson, marrying in 1639 Lady Dorothy Sidney, the 'Sacharissa' of Waller's poems, was killed, aged twenty-three together with

411. From the south west, as refaced by Holland.

412. *South view showing the 2nd Earl of Sunderland's gardens, c. 1700.*

his friend Falkland, serving in the King's Bodyguard at the Battle of Newbury, a few months after he had been created Earl of Sunderland. It was Lady Sunderland, according to reliable tradition, who before their son's coming of age in

1662, roofed the courtyard and put in it the oaken staircase, with big newels and balusters of Coleshill type (Fig. 418). The present arrangement of the lateral galleries dates from 1790; and the coffered ceiling that gives the whole a Palladian look from 1877.

The son, the Earl of Sunderland of Restoration history, travelled in Italy during the Commonwealth, sojourned in Holland, and served Charles II as Ambassador at Madrid and Paris, acquiring considerable taste in art and architecture. By 1688, the year that also witnessed one of the more flagrant of the tergiversations which distinguished his political career, Evelyn could note: 'The House or rather Palace at Althorp is a noble pile in form of a half H, built of brick and freestone *à la moderne*; the hall is well, the staircase excellent; the rooms of state, galleries, offices and furniture such as may become a great prince. It is situate in the midst of a garden exquisitely planted and kept . . . with rows and walks of trees, canals and fishponds . . .', as depicted in the contemporary painting (Fig. 412).

413. *Principal part of the Ground Floor Plan as in 1822. 1. Hall. 2. Vestibule. 3. Dining room. 4. Drawing room. 5. Long library. 6. Raphael library. 7. Billiard room. 8. Marlborough room. 9. Corridor. 10. Gothic library. 11. Lord Spencer's bedroom. 12, 13. Lady Spencer's rooms. 14. Housekeeper's quarters. 15. House Steward's room. 16. Kitchen. 17, 18. Confectioner's quarters. 19. Land Steward's room. 20. Waiting hall. 21. Wardrobe room. 22. Butler's quarters. 23. Packing room. 24. Area. The top is North.*

414. *The stables, finished in 1733.*

Sunderland added to the red brick walls of the Elizabethan house Weldon stone Corinthian and Composite columns in two tiers, with a balustrade above them but with no complete entablature. He remodelled every room, but will have retained the Elizabethan gallery in the S.W. wing for his magnificent collection of pictures, lining it with a wainscot of the large oak panels then usual. This noble Gallery, 115 ft. long, 20 ft. broad (Fig. 417), remains essentially as he left it, though the broad oak floor boards are a renovation. At one end hang the Beauties of Charles II's court, painted and signed by Lely, and at the south end Van Dyck's famous double portrait ('Peace and War') of George Digby, Earl of Bristol—Sunderland's father-in-law—and William, 1st Duke of Bedford, Bristol's brother-in-law; for the most part in the type of frame still known as 'Sunderland'. Outside, he

drained, turfed and parterred the moat, which, with a bridge from terrace to forecourt, is visible in the painting. Le Notre is stated to have provided the design of the layout; and the Duke of Tuscany's secretary was told that Lord Sunderland obtained the design for the house 'from an Italian architect'.

His son, a more reliable if less attractive minister of Anne and George I, married secondly the great Marlborough's daughter Anne, their son Charles succeeding as 5th Earl of Sunderland on the death of his elder brother unmarried in 1729; as 3rd Duke of Marlborough in 1733; and to possession of Blenheim in 1744 when Duchess Sarah died. The 3rd Earl, according to Defoe, was projecting great additions to Althorp when he died in 1722; but it was Charles, as 5th Earl, who gave its Palladian character to the Hall (Fig.

415. *Gateway to the walled garden.*

416. *The gardener's house and loggia.*

417. *The Picture Gallery. It runs the length of the west side on the first floor.*

418. *The Grand Staircase, c. 1660, the galleries added c. 1790.*

419. *The Hall, decorated by the 5th Earl of Sunderland before* 1733. *It is lined with paintings by Wootton of the Earl's sports and horses; his sporting tastes are also represented by foxes' masks, hounds, etc. in the frieze below the richly coffered cove of the ceiling.*

420. *The north front as at present, without the extension shown in the plan.*

419), covering its walls with the huge paintings by Wootton of the field sports and horses to which both he and his brothers were devoted. A ducal coronet surmounts the doorway to the Staircase Hall; but a year after the 5th Earl was

421. *Centre of the south front as refaced by Holland in white brick with Roche Abbey stone dressings.*

entitled to wear it (1733) Althorp and the Sunderland estates were transferred to his younger brother Jack Spencer.

Though the additions to the house were not made, a great stable quadrangle was erected S.W. of it, the Weedon gate to the park built, and the walled garden embellished with a classical arched gateway, the axis through which is closed by the delightful loggia and gardener's house (Figs. 415 and 416). These are ascribed to the 5th Earl and certainly the stables were unfinished in 1733. The latter is a square (Fig. 414) with pyramid roof pavilions and two porticos which are miniatures of that of St Paul's, Covent Garden. The gateways and loggia pay similar tribute to Inigo Jones with a force and grace suggestive of Colen Campbell who, however, died in 1729. Their Palladianism has that robust and imaginative quality, half recalling both Vanbrugh and Kent, which is found at Marble Hill and in works with which the Earl of Pembroke and his architect Roger Morris are connected. In this context it may be significant that the latter was at that time building Wimbledon Park for Duchess Sarah and that her disapproval of Morris would, if anything, have commended him to Lord Sunderland.[1]

On the 5th Earl's succession to the Dukedom of Marlborough, Althorp passed in 1734 by a provision of his grandfather's will to his younger brother Jack, a fast-living character but also a considerable collector. But neither he (*d.* 1746), to whom Duchess Sarah left her great wealth, nor his son (created Earl Spencer 1765), made much use of Althorp except for fox-hunting. The latter's mother-in-law, Mrs Poyntz, staying there at the time of his wedding in 1755, found the house had 'a melancholy appearance inside, about two lighted billets in each chimney with tin fenders . . . neither carpet nor screen'. The 1st Earl's architectural

[1] Morris (for whom see *E.C.H., Early Georgian*) was apparently consulted after Campbell's death at Stourhead (see p. 234).

422. *The South Draw-ing Room. (The Old Dining Room, 3 on plan.)*

423. *The Old Drawing Room (4 on plan). Both rooms are as redecor-ated by Holland.*

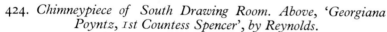

424. *Chimneypiece of South Drawing Room. Above, 'Georgiana Poyntz, 1st Countess Spencer', by Reynolds.*

425. *Chimneypiece of the Old Drawing Room. Above, 'Daedalus and Icarus', by Van Dyck.*

interest was given to the building of Spencer House in London (whence much of the furniture has now been brought to Althorp). When in 1772 part of the roof fell in, Sir R. Taylor was engaged to execute repairs. It was not till after 1783, when George John succeeded his father as 2nd Earl Spencer, that complete renovation began to be considered.

At the beginning of 1780 Brown had given 'some very excellent advice', according to Lady Spencer. But it probably related to Wimbledon, where he laid out the park and not to Althorp. Lord Spencer died later in the same year and the next we hear is in December, 1786, when the new lord wrote: 'We have got Mr Holland here who has brought his plans with him. I have a notion they would be very clever ones . . . but the Quomodo is the difficulty. I must be content with making the apartments we live in weatherproof and saving the house from tumbling down'. As a member of Brooks's Club Lord Spencer was well acquainted with its architect; Holland senior had worked for the 1st Earl at Coombe, 1762–66; and the son had built Battersea Bridge for him in 1772. Holland was now advanced with transforming Carlton House and already engaged on the house at Brighton to become the Royal Pavilion, so that 'the Prince's affairs' tended to interfere with his attendance at Althorp.

The scheme was to case the old walls (as Holland had at Broadlands in 1783, Fig. 21), adding simple pedimented features to the S. and N. fronts, and corridors to the sides

of the entrance court in the former. The roof, possibly due to Taylor, was hipped and reduced in height, having pedimented dormers, but the numerous chimneys, rebuilt in white brick, were retained as an essential element in what thus became a synthetic rendering of English classic tradition. Whilst wholly appropriate to Althorp's Caroline and Palladian antecedents, and according with the current demand for rational comfort, this was also the economical course. Moreover, in the place of the fashionable white brick for the refacing of the walls, Holland used his particular substitute of 'mathematical tiles'.[1] The local Kingsthorpe stone was used for dressings, but for the pilasters and front entrance was replaced with Roche Abbey stone.[2] A big range of offices stretching 170 ft. beyond the portion of the plan given in Fig. 413 was added to the E. extending over the moat. This was now filled in and the wing screened by shrubberies, the landscaping of the whole setting being undertaken by Holland himself. It is interesting to find him thus assuming the mantle of his father-in-law, but it led to

[1] Here called 'rebate tiles'. 100,000 rebate tiles costing £315 were delivered at Lynn by Wm Gooding of Ipswich, Sept.–Oct., 1787; he also supplied 86,000 white bricks for £354 March–June, 1789 (Althorp Accounts). See Introduction, §5.

[2] 'From the neighbourhood of Bawtry, Lord Scarborough's country' (Holland to Lord Spencer, Sept., 1787.) The stone was shipped by river *via* Wisbech.

indignant protests from Lapidge, Brown's assistant, who considered that the work should be entrusted to him.[1] Lord Spencer did not intend extensive alterations. But it is clear that Holland was a forceful character and had no intention of allowing Lord Spencer's 'quomodo' to interfere with his full scheme for transforming the house. In January, 1790, the architect (who was also, of course, a speculative builder in a large way) hints at advancing the necessary capital to his client:

'. . . No doubt but the way to steer clear of all pecuniary difficulties is to defer further proceedings for another year as your Lordship proposes, and the only question seems to be whether it is not worth while to suffer some inconveniences of that sort in order to obtain some conveniences and accommodation . . . I am ready to carry any part of the design into execution whether money is forthcoming or not, upon being allowed Interest on the money while I am in advance, if it would be the least accommodation.'

The shrewd Countess regarded him as 'a rogue in grain'; and, whether or not he charged interest, there was a time when Holland could point out 'I have advanced from my

[1] Extracts from the correspondence preserved at Althorp are given by Tipping, *English Homes VI*, p. 306.

own resources £1,713 and cannot do more to carry on the works, unless it should happen to suit your Lordship to pay me. . . .' Since the work was not executed by a single contractor, Holland had to supervise and pay some hundred firms or individuals. The total cost amounted to £20,257, to which Holland added 5 per cent commission (£1,012). The 'quomodo' was eventually obtained by Lord Spencer selling his reliably rotten borough of Okehampton for £20,000, and Chilworth Manor, Surrey (1798).

The plan (Fig. 413), reproduced from Dibdin's *Aedes Althorpianae* (1822), though revolutionary in one respect, shows that the Caroline disposition was retained in others. The kitchen (16) and offices remained in the S.E. wing, to which the new 'corridor' (17, 19) was assigned to the confectionary department. The Dining Room (3) remained, as at Woodhall (p. 178) and in Taylor's plan for Heveningham (p. 166), as far away as possible, in the S.W. corner; and the butler's quarters (removed in 1879 to enlarge the Staircase Hall) curiously remained tucked into a corner of the former courtyard (22). Next to the Dining Room in the W. side (4, below the Gallery) was the 'Drawing Room used by the family in the morning' (Fig. 423), adjoined by the Long

426. *Holland's Long Library, seen from the south section.*

427. *The Blue Boudoir. The decoration has been transferred from room 12 to room 15 in plan.*

428. *Detail of a panel, by T. H. Pernotin,* 1790.

Library, 'called the evening drawing room' (Fig. 426). Eighty-five ft. long, Holland subdivided it, as later at Woburn and Southill, with screens of shelves bounded by columns (the ceiling was added in the Adam style in 1877). There was a larger Dining Room in the N. range; but in 1800 all the N. rooms were turned to housing the books, of which Lord Spencer had become the most inveterate collector of his time, except the furthest room (11) where he slept. 'The entire length', says Dibdin, his librarian, 'cannot be less than 220 ft.' These not sufficing, the Gallery was fitted with low shelves, and a 'gothic library' (10) was added by Blore to the N.W. in 1820 (demolished 1845).

Lord Spencer's bibliomania originated during the alterations, when books from the old library on the first floor, stacked for rearrangement in the new room below, attracted and held his attention. The majority of the 70,000 volumes ultimately brought together was sold in 1892 and now forms part of the Rylands Library, Manchester.[1]

The state rooms of the Stuart house had been on the first floor and had much impressed the Duke of Tuscany on his visit in 1669. Holland's placing of the reception suite on the ground floor (as in others of his houses) was a reversion to pre-Palladian usage but then an innovation and largely his personal contribution to that planning for comfort on which

his reputation (in succession to Brown) to a great extent rested. The relative lowness of the new rooms demanded also, quite independently of Lord Spencer's finances and, as a Whig, his French tastes, the simplified treatment which Holland was simultaneously evolving. At Berrington (p. 184) and with Brown at Broadlands he had emulated Adam. But at Carlton House Walpole was struck by the 'august simplicity, delicate and new with more freedom and variety than Greek ornaments'. At Althorp in 1789 Holland had not assimilated French neo-classicism so fully as he will ten years later at Southill. But these rooms show him, as in the exterior, adapting Roman and Greek with French precedent to the new synthesis. This is expressed fully in some of the chimneypieces, kept low to offset the lack of ceiling height, as e.g. Fig. 425 where the elongated urn serving as pilaster supports no entablature but a thin shelf. A more conventional one in the Long Library was among those supplied by John Deval and Son in 1790. But that in the old Dining Room (Fig. 424), mounted in ormolu and fully Louis XVI, if not imported, probably dates from Holland's second phase at Althorp *c.* 1801.

On the walls, papers superseded wainscot, even in the Gallery (luckily pasted on framed linen which was removed in 1904). Robson Hale and Co., 'paper hanging manufacturers to the Prince of Wales', supplied and hung these materials, of little colour or pattern where used as background for the arrays of superb pictures (e.g. 'Grey Cloud buff stripe on white satin'), but elsewhere comprising 'Vine

[1] The notable library formed by the 3rd Earl of Sunderland and kept in his London house (on the site of the present Albany) went to Blenheim after his death in 1722 and filled Vanbrugh's great gallery there till sold in 1881–82.

leaf green lines' or 'Richest Rose cluster on yell' (yellow). For the decoration of Lady Spencer's Dressing Room (Fig. 427) the accounts show that one of the group of French artists assembled by Holland for Carlton House was employed. In Sept., 1790, T. H. Pernotin was paid £25 for '4 panels over doors and glass', and £126 for '6 Pilasters, in My Lady's Room', two pilasters being added in the following year. It was transferred in 1877 from the room marked 12 in Dibdin's plan to that indicated by 15, which was nearly the same size. The Blue Boudoir, as it is now called, marks Holland's assimilation of the Louis XVI style since designing the boudoir at Berrington.

There was less renewal of furniture than of decorations, but considerable additions were procured. In 1791 Daguerre, the celebrated Parisian dealer, supplied two secretaires by Weisweiller (£112), two *encoignures* (£52) by C. C. Saunier, and 'une grande Commode en laque' (£100). The chief furniture bill, amounting to £1,224, came from John King, much of it for renewals and upholstery but comprising typical English furniture of the period, notably:

A large Mahogany sideboard made to fit a Recess the legs turned, carved and fluted	£17
2 Mahogany Angle Sideboards, one with a Plate Warmer, the Stonework found by Mr Devall	£36
Large Mahogany Circular Library steps, 9 ft. high, brass wires and green silk curtains, with Mahogany Bookshelf and Seat the Steps with Wilton Carpet, on large brass Castors	£45

The convenience with which this mobile pulpit-like contrivance enabled the great bibliophile to enjoy his treasures reflected the underlying motive of Holland's conversion of Althorp and the opinions which it elicited. Lady Spencer described the altered house as 'the image of comfort—so convenient, so cheerful, so neat, so roomy, yet so compact'. The papering of the Gallery made it for her 'a beautiful lightsome room'. The cheerfulness and convenient planning, which also impressed Lord Jersey in 1792, are thus shown to be the qualities coming to be particularly required of a country house, and which Holland's synthesis supplied. However, a decade later Lady Spencer was altering the chimney in the gallery, by which, she said, 'I hope to have a fire in it occasionally—what has never been possible since Holland altered the house'. Nevertheless she regarded his rebuilding of Wimbledon Park in 1800 as 'the best thing he has done'; and at Althorp he was also extending the library into the north rooms, where hitherto had been the great Dining Room used 'when the weather is hot or the company large'.

The 2nd Earl had supported Fox and continued to oppose Pitt until the excesses of the French Revolution brought him in 1794 to the Tory side and ministerial office. His son, as Lord Althorp, resumed active Whiggism and by 1832 was Lord Grey's right hand man and served under Melbourne. Similarly his great-nephew, the 'Red Earl' (so called from his notable beard) was a leading member of Gladstonian cabinets, and the latter's half brother, who succeeded him in 1910 as 6th Earl, was a Liberal Whip during much of that period. The two brothers, who for so long maintained the Whig affiliations of Althorp, also gave it its present aspect, the architect (1877) being J. MacVicar Anderson. New

429. *The Boudoir chimneypiece. The decoration is in grisaille and gold on a blue ground.*

formal gardens were laid out to W. and N.; the northern addition was removed; and a new great Dining Room convenient to the kitchen built to the E., in front of the housekeeper's quarters denoted in Dibdin's plan 14. Holland's eastern addition in the forecourt (17–19) now fulfilled its destiny as a corridor to the new boudoir; the 'old Dining Room' (3) became an additional Drawing Room, and the whole west and north ranges were formed, with slight alterations, into a continuous reception suite. The 7th Earl, who succeeded in 1922, early turned a scholarly mind to the study of his family's possessions, the chief of which, with its very notable contents, is now accessible to the public regularly in summer.

FARNLEY HALL, YORKSHIRE

Additions for **Walter Fawkes**, 1786–90; furnishing, 1802–10

Architect **Carr of York**

Craftsmen **Rose (?), T. de Bruyn, J. Fisher, H. Hopper, Thomas Carter**

Owner **Major Le G. G. W. Horton-Fawkes**

Farnley, on the north side of Wharfedale between Otley and Leeds, consists in the 17th century and perhaps older home of the Fawkes family, its possessors since the 14th century; and an addition, amounting to a second mansion, built by Walter Hawksworth, a distant kinsman who took the Fawkes name on inheriting Farnley in 1786. The contrast of the parts was accentuated in the 19th century, when the earlier building was dressed up with fragments and fittings of other ancient halls in the vicinity. Thus the sense of synthesis which e.g. at Tabley and Wardour had preserved a romantic old building to compose a picture seen from the new, or at Syon and Althorp led to that aesthetic fusion of old and new which is found so satisfying, here was content with unresolved juxtaposition.

A mere equation of two dissimilar halves seems to have been due in this case to a combination of causes. The new house was wanted entirely for the entertainment of guests, while Walter Fawkes and his family continued to inhabit the old hall. This was preserved partly no doubt from sentimental regard for his benefactor, partly for practical reasons, and partly from regard for the past and in particular for the Cromwellian General Fairfax, for relics of whom several of the rooms became a museum. The Cromwellian bias in Walter Fawkes, it may be supposed, ruled out the Gothick synthesis that one might have expected in such circumstances, whilst his Whig commonsense was reflected in the classicism of his addition—in which there is more of Palladian than 'Neo'. His son, Walter II, added to his antiquarianism the constant friendship and patronage of J. M. W. Turner, a

430. *The approach from the north, showing the Old Hall.*

famous collection of whose works he formed between 1802 and 1825 whilst the painter, besides leaving invaluable records in watercolour of Farnley at that epoch, helped him with the arrangement of his Fairfax museum, so linking Picturesque taste with that for 'antiques'. J. C. Loudon (*Treatise on Country Residences*, ii, 648) illustrates his scheme for landscape improvements made in 1805. The next generation vacated the Georgian house. Major Horton-Fawkes, reversing the process, took Turner's watercolours as a guide for the restoration of the Georgian rooms for his family's use after Farnley had served as a hospital during the last war, and closed off the Old Hall as a separate establishment.

Tradition tells of Francis Fawkes, the last of his line and a childless widower, riding over to call on his nearest relatives, the Vavasors of Weston Hall, when 'a very select party' was

431. *The south, entrance, front of Carr's building.*

432. *J. M. W. Turner's sketch of Farnley from the east.*

433. *The saloon, hung with Turner watercolours.*

434. *The rosette of the staircase balustrade.*

being entertained there. Unwelcomed in his muddy clothes, he proceeded to his cousin Hawksworth, whose good will he tested by asking for an immediate loan of 300 guineas. Walter Hawksworth contrived to produce the sum, in a bag—which was shortly returned unopened and was followed by the bequest of Farnley when the old squire died in 1786. The new house is shown by surviving bills to have been begun that autumn, when large quantities of brick were procured, and

ready for furnishing, decoration completed, c. 1790. Walter (Hawksworth) Fawkes died two years later.

Carr's reputation as the leading architect in the North had rested for thirty years on sober design and sound building. In this late work he acknowledged the trend to neo-classicism by being soberer still. The plan for the building, added to the S. end of the old Hall, is almost a square. The walls are of smooth grey ashlar, quarried on the estate, with an empha-

435. *The Staircase, from the south west.*

436. *On the Staircase, looking south to the Saloon door.*

sized base, a guilloche moulding at first floor level, and Doric frieze surmounted by a balustrade. One of the facetted bows with which he was wont to diversify the sides of his houses here forms the centre of the S. front instead of a portico which would have no use. To relieve the austerity the windows were later framed in entablatures of wood, but since these do not appear in Turner's sketch (Fig. 432) they were evidently not Carr's, and, having decayed, have been removed. The windows of the W. front, however (Fig. 450), have stone surrounds, and the front door in the S. bay retains its original stone Tuscan entablature (Fig. 431).

It opens straight into the Saloon (Fig. 433) which, with the spacious Staircase Hall beyond, forms a spine to the plan having the Dining Room and former billiard room on its E., the Drawing Room and Library on the W. side. The Saloon is an elongated octagon—the windows that flank the entrance overlook Wharfedale, the splayed walls of the N. end have alcoves contained by narrow pilasters. The carved wood chimneypiece has an inner surround of grey and yellow marble which H. King and J. Atkinson supplied with that for other chimneypieces. On the blue-grey walls hang some thirty of Turner's watercolours, mainly of the surroundings and rooms of Farnley, brilliant both in colouring and accurate delineation. One depicts the Staircase from the same position whence the photograph (Fig. 436) was taken—from the half landing on which a door used to open on to the staircase of the old house (Fig. 451).

Carr's Staircase divides to reach the landing, carried on and carrying columns (Fig. 437), whence short vaulted corridors lead to the bedrooms. The lightness of the ornament and colouring—biscuit walls, the enrichments white picked out in blue—show off several notable Turners and Girtins, and also the cantilevered mahogany ascent. Of similar detail to his stairs at Tabley fifty years before, its admirable joinery is enriched with delicate beading under the hand rail and an inlaid whorl where is dies into itself at the foot (Fig. 434).

Another watercolour shows the Drawing Room much as it is (Fig. 439) Though most of the paintings have been changed, Turner's great *View of Dort* (acquired in 1818 for 500 guineas) remains in place. The chimneypiece, of which the central relief is shown in Fig. 440, used to be beneath it in the N. wall but was moved in the 19th century to the E. wall. The shallow barrel vaulted ceiling has broad geometrically treated transverse ribs, and in the lunettes oval coats of arms, Fawkes and Farrer, with the date 1790 beneath. An inventory of 1828 comprises three other paintings by Turner, besides works by Van Dyck, Backhuysen, Guido, Guercino, C. Dolci and A. Carracci. Of those remaining the Reynolds of 'Mary Horneck' over the fireplace, and a de Loutherbourg, *The Sandpit*, are characteristic of the younger Fawkes's collection, the larger part of which has been dispersed for payment of death duties. It was he, also, who furnished the rooms after the death of his father. The Drawing Room still contains the '10 Grecian Chairs, stained ebony' and '2 large

437. *The first floor gallery over the stairs.*   438. *Corridor from gallery to the south bedrooms.*

439. *The Drawing Room. At its north end J. M. W. Turner's 'View of Dort'.*

440. *The Drawing Room chimney-piece (detail).*

Grecian couches to accord' supplied in 1808 by Thomas Carter, 141 Oxford Street, for £125. Much else was acquired from Gillows.

Adjoining in the S.W. corner of the house is the square Library (Fig. 441), having a flat circular ceiling of Adam type raised on pendentives and by lunettes containing arabesque ornament, and four recessed bookcases. Hoppner's portrait of Walter Fawkes II is seen over the fireplace.

These rooms have always relied largely for effect on their contents. But the Dining Room in the E. side (Fig. 442) has an elaborate neo-classical *décor* which, though deriving from Adam, may be taken to reflect Carr's personal taste in its delicacy of treatment, which surpasses that of his Adamesque Denton Hall, *c.* 1775 (Fig. 10). Family tradition may well be correct in assigning the stucco-work, if not the design also, to Joseph Rose, an artist in his own right who designed Sledmere *c.* 1788. Though the room is better documented

than others, this item is missing. It is 35 ft. long by 22 ft. wide, with an identical recess at each end with columns and containing a plaster figure on a pedestal. One of two similar figures on the staircase is inscribed 'H(umphrey) Hopper, London, Dec. 10, 1806.' The remainder of the wall space is divided into panels containing relief arabesques or painted medallions, the whole ceiled with lace-like delicacy (Fig. 443). Walls and ceiling have been repainted in shades of pale turquoise blue, appearing almost green in certain lights, on the authority of Turner's record. The chimneypiece (Fig 445) was carved by Fisher of York, costing 50 guineas. His account, comprising the monument to Francis Fawkes in Otley Church, amounted in 1789 to over £300.

The doors are of mahogany with six raised panels of darker colour crossbanded and inlaid with satinwood. The doorways are framed by half pilasters to the neo-classical pattern used by Carr in others of the principal rooms, where he similarly

441. *The Library, look-
ing north east. It adjoins
the Saloon on the west.*

442. *The Dining Room
in the east side looking
north.*

443. *The ceiling of the Dining Room, attributed to Joseph Rose. The colouring of the walls and ceiling is shades of pale turquoise blue.*

444. *(below, left) A door, in three shades of mahogany.*

445. *(below, right) The Dining Room chimneypiece, with one of the sepia 'reliefs' by T. de Bruyn.*

446. *Ceiling of the Octagon Bedroom.*

447. (*above, left*) *A Bedroom chimneypiece.*

448. (*left*) *Entablature of a typical Bedroom doorway.*

449. *The White Bedroom; the bed of* c. 1810.

repeated the cornice pattern (Figs. 444, 448). Most of the medallions were painted by Theodore de Bruyn, a Swiss, who had worked under Stuart in Greenwich Hospital Chapel. His account (1790) itemises 'nine pictures in chiaroscuro; a sacrifice to Ceres (above the fireplace) 2 ft. 6″ by 2 ft. 9″, 25 gns'. Painted in sepia, they reproduce sculptured relief with deceptive effect. Two further panels, probably those between the windows, were added in 1809 by Thomas Taylor, whose bill for £125 included cleaning and varnishing the others and repainting the room. Taylor exhibited landscapes and ruin-pieces at the R.A. 1792–1811. The mahogany chairs with crimson leather seats were made by Gillows, whose stamp occurs on one of the arm chairs. The adjoining billiard room has now been made the kitchen for the Georgian house.

The impeccable standard of craftsmanship extends to the bedrooms, each with a carved wood chimneypiece of distinct design. Intended for guests, since the family lived in the Jacobean wing, they are of generous scale; two pairs of bed and dressing rooms, served by lateral cross-vaulted passages, fill each side. A similar though shorter passage leads from the head of the stairs past four small closets (Fig. 438) to the principal, Octagon, room over the saloon, of which the ceiling has painted medallions (Fig. 446). The bed in the White Room (Fig. 449) is a Horton inheritance and was probably made for the Countess (d. 1817) of the 3rd Earl of Aberdeen, so is contemporary with most of Farnley's furnishings.

Though Turner did not depict these great light rooms put

450. *The west side and the view over Wharfedale.*

451. *Staircase of the Old Hall.*

to their hospitable use, as he did at Petworth, there are references elsewhere that do. Sidney Smith, J. C. Croker, Charles Waterton the naturalist, were guests whose likenesses are preserved in a series of caricatures by Walter Fawkes II. 'A more agreeable host than Mr Fawkes I have never seen', wrote Hobhouse, recalling a party in 1823 which included the painter; 'an unique place, where a great genius has been loved, and his best work is treasured like a monument in a shrine', Ruskin observed long afterwards.

The Old Hall indeed became a shrine, but of the Fawkes's Cromwellian hero, whose home, Menston, was near Farnley. Turner's exquisitely detailed miniatures, contained in the folio *Fairfaxiana* that is preserved in the house, record the old rooms as at this time. One shows the Oak Hall, the kernel of the 'museum', with Fairfax's wheeled chair (now in York Museum), and another the great painted cupboard devoted to Civil War relics (Figs. 452, 453). The rooms were much remodelled in the next generation to contain further period

fittings, many of great interest, and the panels of the drawing room wainscot were painted *c.* 1825 with hunting subjects, admirably sketched on the oak, by George Walker (1781–1856), author of *Costume of Yorkshire* and a friend of Waterton. At the same time the outside received the added features, some of which are seen in Fig. 430, but not in Fig. 432. Only the Staircase, probably dating *c.* 1700, and abutting on the landing of Carr's Staircase, remained unaltered. Interesting for the study of antiquarianism as are the further changes carried out by the quickly succeeding generations of the family in the 19th century, they are outside this volume's scope[1]—except in so far as they maintained the romantic dualism characteristic of Farnley. On the death in 1943 of the Rev. W. H. Fawkes, last of the Hawksworth line, he was succeeded by his sister's son, Major Le G. G. W. Horton who had assumed the additional name of Fawkes in 1937.

[1] They are traced by Mr Gordon Nares in *Country Life*, May 20th, 1954, on whose description of Farnley this account is based.

452. *J. M. W. Turner's watercolour of the Oak Hall.*
General Fairfax's wheeled chair in the foreground.

453. *A watercolour by Turner from 'Fairfaxiana'.*
The great 'press' open to show Civil War relics.

454. *The entrance (east) front, by Soane.*

CHILLINGTON HALL, STAFFORDSHIRE

Reconstruction for **Thomas Giffard**
Architect (**Smith, 1724**). **Soane, 1786–9**
(Landscape **Brown, Paine,** *c.* **1778**)
Owner **Mr T. A. W. Giffard**

Chillington has belonged to Giffards for 770 years. The great park, with the houses of Whiteladies, Blackladies, and Boscobel, lies in the ancient Forest of Brewood ('Brood') that divided Staffordshire from Shropshire. In so great a

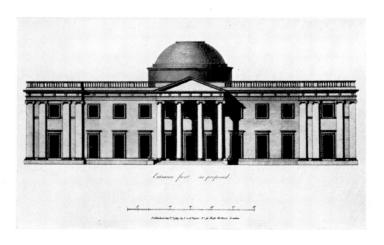

455. *Soane's first proposal for the east front.*

domain with so long a history,[1] the existing house is an almost modern appendage. Its immediate predecessor, still standing in 1761, had been built *c.* 1547 by Sir John Giffard who, having held a succession of offices in Henry VIII's household and acquired large estates both by marriage and after the Dissolution of the Monasteries, died in 1556 aged 90. A quadrangle entered through a gate house, it stood on the present site and in 1585 was surveyed as a possible residence for Mary, Queen of Scots. Sir Amyas Paulet reported that 'the howse is furnished with many fayre lodginges, so as this Queen may be very well placed, with a great chamber, gallery, cabinet, and lodginge for her gentlewomen'. But it was deemed hardly of sufficient strength for so weighty a charge; the windows lay open upon fields or upon a garden with a wall of no great height; and but one tun of beer could be brewed at a time. Eventually Chartley Castle was selected.

For different reasons the old house was again judged unsuitable as a refuge after the Battle of Worcester for Charles II, whom Peter Giffard the Cavalier accordingly concealed first at Whiteladies, a former religious house, and then at Boscobel, owned by others of the family. The King's Letters Patent for the perpetual pensions to his protectors there, who were Giffard's servants, is still preserved at Chillington. About 1768 Brown and Paine, having completed their joint embellishments of Weston Park adjacent, were

[1] For an admirable condensed account, see the articles by Mr Arthur Oswald in *Country Life*, Feb. 13, 20 and 27, 1948.

456. *The oak avenue glimpsed through the portico.*   457. *The south front as built by Peter Giffard, 1724.*

summoned to do likewise by Thomas Giffard. An immense mere was formed about a mile away in the park, around which were erected sundry edifices pertaining rather to landscape than to domestic architecture; and at the time of his early death in 1776 Thomas Giffard was considering designs by Adam for a new mansion, possibly on a site nearer the lake. His son resumed this project immediately on coming of age in 1785 but put it in the hands of John Soane, then only eleven years his senior. Like Adam, Soane seems to have tried to persuade his client to build an entirely new house: rectangular with a central hall surmounted by a dome (Fig. 455). In the event the Tudor hall range, which faced E. to forecourt and gatehouse, was replaced, but Soane had to alter his design, somewhat awkwardly, to retain the existing southern front (Fig. 457). This had been built at right angles to the old hall by Peter, father of Thomas Giffard I, who, coming of the Blackladies branch of the family, had succeeded to Chillington in 1718 on the failure of the senior line. It is dated 1724 on its lead down-pipes and is an excellent example of Early Georgian provincial workmanship in pale red facing bricks with stone dressings. The architect is not recorded, but the stylistic evidence points strongly to the Smiths of Warwick (cf. *E.C.H., Early Georgian*) and very probably to William. The Smiths were born at Tettenhall, five miles from Chillington, and William, associated with many of Francis's undertakings, continued living there.

To the N., a square block between the back of this range and the hall contains the Staircase (Fig. 461). Its walls are decorated with baroque panels framing medallions of stucco bas-reliefs; the ceiling had similar plasterwork (removed twenty-five years ago); and that of the principal ground floor room retains a large emblematic figure in ornate framing: all characteristic though rather mediocre work of the Italians employed by Gibbs and the Smiths. The oak staircase itself is a good example of the 'fully fashioned' kind, with the Giffard crest carved in scrolled brackets supporting each

step. About 1850 the large staircase window was filled with armorial glass designed, it is said, by Francis Giffard, brother of the then owner. The same quality of carpentry was applied to the wainscotting of the lofty first floor rooms with large raised and fielded panels. The doors have their original brass hinges and lock-plates, no doubt the products of the region's growing industry. The chief bedroom (Fig. 463) retains a rare example of a W.C., fitted in an adjoining recess or closet (Fig. 462). In its existing form with enriched mahogany panels to sides and seat and carved paterae on the lintel, this is probably due to Soane.

It is uncertain what directed the younger Thomas Giffard in 1785 to give the little known but ambitious Soane his biggest firm commission. Possibly his father's connection with Brown led through Holland (then fully occupied by the

458. *Soane's (?) Ionic Temple by the lake.*

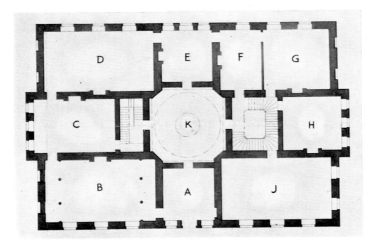

459. *Plan as first proposed by Soane. A. Vestibule. B. Library.
C. Eating room. D. Saloon. E. Ante-room. F. Lady's dressing
room. G. Bed Ch. H. Gentlemen's dressing room. J. Chapel.
K. Saloon. (From the original in Sir John Soane's Museum.)*

Prince and at Althorp) to the latter recommending his former
assistant, who was then building small country houses in
East Anglia. A pavilion by the lake, probably built in 1786
(Fig. 458), is attributable to Soane, who also published a
variant for Chillington of his Gold Medal design for a
triumphal bridge, which may suggest that the contact originated through landscape architecture. However it was, a
drawing at the Soane Museum for the rebuilding of the
house is endorsed 'sent to be executed. June, 1786'. Soane's
proposed façade (Fig. 455), correctly but drearily neo-
classical, is typical of his uncertainty at this period; nor did
its revision 'to be executed' stir his invention any more at
first. The flanking sections were given attics, their pilasters

and the dome omitted, but otherwise the design retained its conventional character (Fig. 454). A drawing shows
that the walls were to be faced with cement, which would
have intensified the oppressiveness. But this was not applied,
so that the pale red brick, never meant to be exposed, gives
some warmth and texture, relating the new front, though
crudely, to the Georgian side, and setting off the pale brown
Tunstall stone of the portico. The actual junction with Smith's
front (Fig. 457) is incredibly clumsy.

A plan in the Soane Museum for the first proposal shows a
square entrance hall flanked by a long library and chapel, and
beneath the central dome a square saloon with canted
corners. As revised to fit on to the Smith wing, and in order
to preserve the walls of the Tudor great hall, Soane fitted
into this his Saloon, which at one time it was proposed
to make the chapel. He also redesigned the three east
rooms erected in front of the old hall, and added a balancing
northern range. This was to contain a library on an interesting tripartite and vaulted plan recalling Dance's ballroom at Cranbury (Fig. 1). Between the new front rooms
and the saloon a transverse corridor with domed compartments links up the rest of the plan. The published variant for
the saloon (Fig. 466) shows arched extensions at both ends
and the whole conceived much in the style of Holland. In
execution both the general plan and the treatment of the
'Great Room' as he termed it were further modified, the
latter in a way that reveals Soane at last discovering himself.

For the final verson (Fig. 464) he evolved a prototype
of that 'Soanic' style which he was to develop in the remodelling of the Bank of England. He received the appointment of architect to the Bank in 1788, when engaged on
Chillington, and although the exact date of the executed design for the Saloon is not known, it is unlikely to be much
after 1788 (when the unexecuted design was published) and

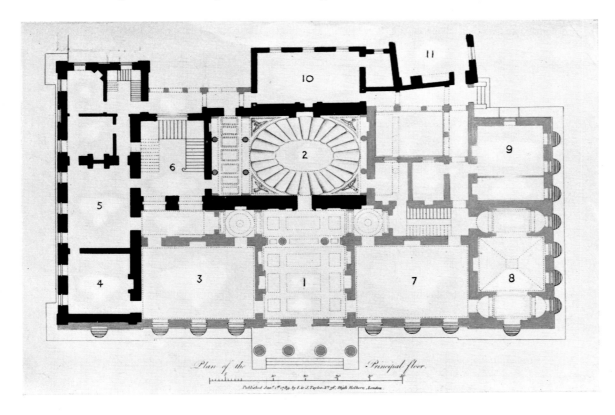

460. *Soane's second
plan; parts only ex-
ecuted. Earlier walls
shown black. The
North is to the right.
1. Vestibule. 2. Saloon.
(Great Hall). 3. With-
drawing room. 4.
Breakfast room. 5. Bil-
liard Room. (in the
1724 wing). 6. Stair-
case (1724). 7. Eating
room. 8. Library. 9.
Housekeeper. 10. Ser-
vants' Hall. 11. Kit-
chen.
(Reproduced, with Fig.
455 and 466, from
Soane's Plans etc.,
published 1788.)*

462. *Closet adjoining the Red Bedroom.*

461. *The main staircase, c. 1724.*

463. *The Red Bedroom in the south wing. On the left can be seen the original lock, and bolt actuated from the bed.*

P

464. The Saloon formed by Soane in the Tudor Great Hall. With the 'medieval' chimney-piece displaying the arms of Sir John Giffard, 1547.

465. The Entrance Hall, looking through to the Saloon.

certainly before 1792 when his first characteristic work at the Bank began. The conditions here were indeed much the same —to provide a clearly lit space within solid or existing walls— and evoked the same recourse to elementary forms: the shallow dome on pronounced pendentives, clerestory lighting, and segmental arches. These are the simple elements, first assembled by Dance in the Guildhall Council Room in 1777, from which Soane was to evolve the Consols Office and its successors. By comparing the result with the previous design (Fig. 466) we can see how the prototype emerged. The latter's screens of columns and incidentally the northern of the two extensions have disappeared; the coffered dome has become an ellipse (Fig. 467) carried on pendentives and coved upwards to a smaller oval clerestory; Roman detail has become Greek, corner pilasters taking the place of Corinthian columns, though the segmental vault of the remaining compartment retains the coffered panels of the earlier design between bands of scrolling acanthus. The pendentives have a curious diaper ornament containing the Gifford crests set in roundels, which, though apparently departing from Soane's intention, are probably his work.

The 'medieval' fireplace reputedly incorporates heraldic carvings originally over the door of the Tudor hall. An inscription reads 'The armys of Syr John Gyffarde Knight The yere of oure lorde MVᶜXLVII (1547) And the fyrste yere of Kyng Edwarde the Syxte. I.G.' The character and freshness of the carvings suggest, however, that they were careful copies.[1] Though it is unlikely that Soane was concerned with the chimneypiece, its presence, together with the pendentives ornament, in his saloon illustrates the 'romantic' element which underlay his work here and was never wholly absent from the neo-classical movement, colouring all Soane's attempts to develop a modern architecture from a synthesis of classical and northern elements.

[1] The standard depicted on the lintel was granted to Sir John in 1523 to commemorate his feat in shooting through the head with an arrow a tame panther which had escaped and was attacking a mother and child—at a spot known as Giffards Cross.

467. *The ceiling of Saloon,* c. 1788. *A prototype for the Bank of England.*

The limitation and simplifying of Thomas Giffard's ambitions for Chillington are said to have been due to the influence of his wife, Lady Charlotte Courtenay, whom he married in 1788. Indeed the other main rooms appear not to have been decorated till their son succeeded in 1827. The library and drawing room are of that date, the latter with a handsome colour scheme of green, pink and gold. In the dining room hang portraits by Pompeo Battoni of both Thomas Giffards, the father painted in 1766 and the son in 1784. In the bedroom above it, prepared by the latter for his bride, a stately domed bed and the window curtains are hung with a lovely flowered chintz, and their impaled arms are painted in the shields attached to the pelmets and bed canopy. The bedposts are of the usual late 18th century form but painted with little sprays of flowers between twists of ribbons; the architectural framework of the dome in the bed canopy is similarly painted, the bed tassels being green.

Thomas Giffard the younger had a large family, of whom one of the younger daughters became the second wife of the notorious Jack Mytton,[1] some of whose more spectacular sporting exploits are said to have taken place at Chillington. The present owner, a great grandson, is the twenty-seventh in succession from the first Peter Giffard living at Chillington in 1178.

[1] Of Halston Park, Salop, see *Appendix*: R. Mylne.

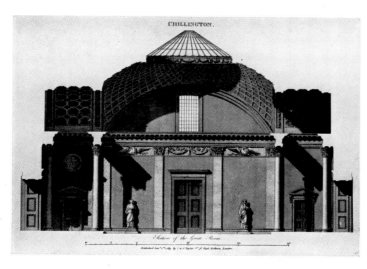

466. *Section of the Saloon (intermediate design).*

COURTEENHALL, NORTHAMPTONSHIRE

Built for **Sir William Wake, 9th Baronet, 1791–3**

Architect **Samuel Saxon**

Landscape **H. Repton**

Owner **Captain Hereward Wake**

The interaction of the three principal trends of our period are represented at Courteenhall with a completeness that gives this relatively modest house exemplary importance. We can see how neo-classical ideals of form and design were combined with the stabilizing influence transmitted by Sir William Chambers, and the type of problem that was raised by consorting them with the 'visual' values which, set forth in the theory of the Picturesque during this decade, were to predominate in the next generation. At Courteenhall, moreover, the opportunity that came so seldom to more eminent architects was given to a little-known pupil of Chambers to design a complete new house on a virgin site: what Repton, who was called on to choose and model it, termed a 'Creation'.

The sketches with which he illustrated his report, or 'Red Book', draw attention however to the fact that the site was only relatively new. The park, five miles S. of Northampton, contained an Elizabethan house built by Richard Ouseley and altered in the 17th century, which Sir William Jones in 1672 bequeathed to his great nephew Samuel, a younger son of Sir W. Wake, 3rd Baronet. This family, which has possessed it ever since, was of Norman descent, settled at Bourne, Lincs., in the 12th century and holding lands that had certainly belonged to Hereward 'the last of the English', from whom they also maintain descent in the female line.

By 1750 Courteenhall and the Wake baronetcy had come together, and the magnificent stable quadrangle (Fig. 469) been built on the ridge above the old house, which it exceeded in size. Perhaps inspired by that at Althorp, its front is broken by two towers flanking a central pediment above its entrance arch. Repton was puzzled how to subordinate so large an adjunct to any new mansion less than a palace. His empirical solution, revealed by moving the flap in his drawing (Figs. 469, 470) was to set the house at an angle to it on the ridge and loosely connected to the stables by trees

468. The garden front facing south east, and the present formal lay-out.

469. *The old house in the hollow, with the stable block above. From Repton's 'Red Book' for Courteenhall.*

470. *The new house on the hill. Repton's proposal for the same view.*

471. *The great stable block on the hill, built about* 1750.

which also partly screened them. He claims to have advised
on the style of the new building, rejecting a symmetrical
composition with balancing wings because the site did not
admit of it but 'absolutely required the kind of house with
three fronts which has been adopted'. Indeed, so far from
attempting to relate the three-storey rectangular block to
its surroundings by 'supporting masses', the principle of
composition which the Picturesque school was already ad-
vocating and Repton himself was soon to adopt, he was at
pains to surround it with 'dressed lawn' only, in the Brown
tradition. Nevertheless, the architect had to extend a wing
for the offices as inconspicuously as possible on the S.W.
side, and an appropriate formal layout (succeeding a Victorian parterre) was appended by General Sir Hereward and
Lady Wake a generation ago.

The architect, 'my ingenious friend Mr Saxon', had already worked with Repton on another of his 'Creations'—
Buckminster, Lincs., for Sir G. Manners; from which we
may infer that Repton introduced him to Wake and, possibly,
that at this time he had Saxon collaborating with him as,
after 1796, Nash did. At the same date Saxon was architect
for the Old Infirmary at Northampton. Born 1757 (the date
of his death is unknown) Samuel Saxon had been trained at
the Royal Academy (1776) and in Chambers's office (1778–
91) to a scholarly reticence which is just saved from bathos
in his elevations by a fine sense of proportion and detail—
qualities in which his internal work excels. In the two main
fronts the segmental arching of the ground storey, economi-
cally furnished with an inset order and sharp profiles, con-
trives to be effective—with the help of the slight colour contrast between the grey Weldon stone dressings and the
creamy local limestone ashlar.

472. *The front door.*

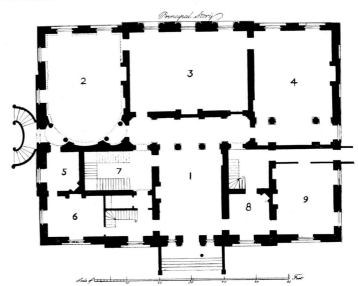

473. *Plan. From 'Vitruvius Britannicus', vol. VI. 1. Hall.
2. Library. 3. Drawing Room. 4. Dining Room. 5. Dressing
room. 6. Study. 7. Pincipal staircase. 8. Anteroom. 9. Billiard
room. The North point is to the left bottom corner.*

The compact plan is much more dramatic, making ingenious use of the circular forms favoured by the new
classicism. Secondary rooms are grouped in the N.W. front
flanking the high and relatively narrow Hall (Fig. 474). Its
inner end, beyond a screen of columns, is a passage extended
to open into the three principal rooms that fill the S.E. front,
and to the main and back stairs. A top-lit corridor bisects
both the first and upper floors on the same traverse (Fig. 476).

The Hall resembles Soane's at Chillington in its arrangement, but the frieze of swags and *paterae* is a Chambers motif.
In the extensions there are in each end three doorways recessed beneath semicircular arches. The Drawing Room, in
the centre of the S.E. front, for some unknown reason never
received its decoration, which was only carried out in the
1920s by Sir Hereward Wake. The photograph shows two of
the notable 17th century portraits that hang in the room comprising three of the series by Mytens, formerly at Raynham,
of 'Lord Vere's Captains': Sir William Lovelace and Sir
Henry Peyton (Fig. 475) and Sir John Congreve.

The Dining Room, with a neo-Corinthian order at
the service end, and painted Wedgwood blue and white
(Fig. 477), shows no Adam influence, being in Chambers's
dignified Roman spirit. The stucco frieze, at once firm and
pretty, has vine swags linking exquisite plaques in relief of
playing children (Fig. 478). Incidentally the bronzes seen
flanking the side-tables are casts of Alfred Stevens's models
for his Wellington Memorial groups. There is also a marble
medallion portrait of James, Duke of York, probably by
William Stanton *c.* 1672, who supplied the monument of Sir
Samuel Jones in Courteenhall church.

Whilst the lucid integration of Saxon's plan can be termed
neo-classical, particularly his handling of the inner passage
within the hall, the emphasis in the decoration, so far, has
been on correctness. In the Library (Fig. 479), he applied the
new mode with charming skill, both to its shaping and adorn-
ing. In the rounded inner end curved doors are contained in

474. *The Entrance Hall, looking inwards to the passage.*

475. *Mytens portraits in the Drawing Room.*

two segmental *exedrae*, the eastern of them with two—the garden door and that to a 'dressing room'. In these alcoves the fluted columns have capitals derived from the Tower of the Winds as given by Stuart and Revett, and their vaults the fan motif which Saxon also employed in the ceiling and, much as Wyatt was using it at Heveningham, in the Dining Room. All the detail of the Library is of much refinement, in what passed then for the Greek rather than Roman idiom. Particularly delicate is the honeysuckle motif in the frieze, below which are eight panels containing female figures emblematic of the Virtues. The recessed shelving of mahogany veneer and the marble fireplace are integral with the wall design which, if compared with Holland's library at Berrington, for example (Fig. 381), illustrates perfectly the development of the neo-classical mode during the decade 1781–91.

The main staircase, top-lit, has walls marbled yellow and a simple iron balustrade of a Chambers pattern. In the upper corridor (Fig. 476) no attempt is made to give the rather awkward space classical character in the Palladian sense, but by means of the arches, some of them containing the doors to the bedrooms, and by the oval of the skylight, the whole is rendered a neo-classical unity.

Since the house was completed no changes of importance have been made, beyond the decoration of the drawing room alluded to, so that Courteenhall is a remarkably perfect and rather unusual example of a medium-sized Georgian country house of the last decade of the century. West of the house, too, is the schoolhouse built by Sir Samuel Jones; a most charming example of the local mason's work of Wren's age.

476. *The first floor corridor.*

477. *The Dining Room, in the 'Roman' manner of Sir W. Chambers. The colouring is Wedgwood blue and white.*

478. *In the Dining Room. The entablature and a neo-Corinthian capital.*

479. The Library. The rounded inner end and 'exedrae'.

480. In the Library: 'exedra' with twin doors.

481. The Library chimneypiece.

482. *The east front, with the wings added* c. 1800, *and the portico of* 1840 *reproducing Campbell's unexecuted design.*

STOURHEAD, WILTSHIRE

Additions for **Sir Richard Colt Hoare, 2nd Baronet, 1796–1800**

Architects (**C. Campbell, 1721**), **W. Reveley (?), 1796**

Furniture **Chippendale the younger**

Owner **The National Trust**

The most beautiful of Georgian landscape gardens, created at Stourton between 1740 and 1772 by Henry Hoare with Flitcroft as his architect, are outside the scope of this volume. They also lie apart from the house built for his father in 1721–25 by N. Ireson of Wincanton from C. Campbell's design. This was a plain rectangular block to which the portico was added in 1840 by Charles Parker to the original design, and was gutted by fire in 1902. Although the contents were saved, and Sir Aston and Mr Dorian Webb carefully reproduced the internal features, Stourhead cannot therefore be regarded as an authentic example of its period. But the wings, added by Sir Richard Colt Hoare, the historian of Wiltshire, between 1796–1800, were untouched and are among the most complete examples of masculine taste at the end of the century.

Recent research[1] has established that Henry Hoare the elder, second son of Sir Richard, the founder of Hoare's Bank, acquired the Stourton property in 1720 from Sir

[1] Notably by Mr Rupert Gunnis, in the private account ledgers at Hoare's Bank.

483. *The south side, and the south wing containing the Library.*

484. *The entrance Hall, as reconstructed after 1902. The equestrian portrait is of Henry Hoare who laid out the gardens, by M. Dahl and Wootton, 1722.*

John Meres of Kirkby Bellars, Leics., whose father had bought it from the 13th Lord Stourton in 1714. Mr Hoare, whose wife was daughter to William Benson of Wilbury, Wren's supplanter as Surveyor General and early patron of Campbell (*E.C.H.*, *Early Georgian*, p. 16), immediately procured for 4 guineas 'Mr Campbell's book' (*Vitruvius Britannicus*, Vol. I), and Nathaniel Ireson, the contractor and supervisor, began to receive quarterly payments of £100–£200. The new house is first referred to as Stourhead in 1723, and an insurance policy taken out in 1724 shows that the building was complete before Henry Hoare died in 1725. But the interior was not finished, for (Sir) Robert Taylor continued to be paid for chimneypieces (£40); Thomas Johnson for ironwork; and Roger Morris, who had received £10 in 1726, was paid £31 in 1734, possibly as architect after Campbell's death. Ten guineas was paid to the latter in 1728 'for 3 copper plates'—those of Stourhead published in *Vitruvius Britannicus*, Vol. III in 1725. 'The balance of the Building account' during 1727–29 reached £5,314 15 0, Ireson receiving £450; and the balance of the Furniture account was £1,148 13 10.

Little more was spent during Mrs Hoare's lifetime, but when the younger Henry succeeded her in 1741, various charges are entered for importing works of art from Italy:

1740, Customs charges on 2 cases of pictures from Mr (Consul) Smith of Venice, £11 7 0; 1742, do· on ten cases of cabinets from Leghorn, £37 1 6; 1758, Sir Horace Mann's bill from Florence £571 7 0; 1762, Thos. Jenkins of Rome, 2 pictures, £67 15 0. The contemporary artists employed were Jonathan Richardson 'for Mr Hoare's picture' £21 (1722); M. Dahl 15 gns and John Wootton £57 15 0 for the equestrian portrait of the younger Hoare (1726); Richard Wilson 'for a landscape of Avernus' £30 (1760). The only furniture makers mentioned are Thomas Woster, partner with Coxhead, £11 (1723), and Jo. North, upholsterer, £150 (1745). Mr Kirkman supplied a harpsichord for £57 (1764) and Charles Green an organ for £65 (1770). But throughout the rooms there are many notable pieces of the Kent and early Chippendale periods, and a range of paintings that represents the taste of the creator of the Stourhead landscape, who died in 1785 aged eighty.

His nephew and successor, Sir Richard Hoare, 1st Baronet (1786), survived him only two years, when the estate passed to his son. Sir Richard Colt Hoare, who inherited his second name from his great-aunt, an heiress and the wife of Henry Hoare II, himself married a daughter of Lord Lyttleton of Hagley. She died very young before he succeeded to Stourhead, and Sir Richard never married again. He consoled

485, 486. *The Picture Gallery in the north wing. It preserves, in its original green painted walls, and furniture by the younger Chippendale, the tastes of a Georgian connoisseur.*

himself first with picturesque travel, in which he was no mean artist, and after the outbreak of war, in British archaeology, particularly that of Wiltshire, of which science his industry and acumen were to constitute him one of the founders.

The wings, which he added *c.* 1796 to N. and S. of the house, observed the scholarly restraint of Campbell's centre—still without the portico. As built they were more austere than they are now, the cresting balustrade having been added after the fire in 1902. Their architect is not known, but Mr Lees-Milne has cogently suggested that, if 'the spirit of that severe classicist, Sir William Chambers, may be detected in their sure and simple lines, then perhaps they are the work of his pupil Willey Reveley, who a few years previously was engaged upon the entrance lodge.'

The wings, identical in elevation, are handled very differently within, though each contains a single large room expressing the interests of the cultivated widower, and shared by many who built at this time. That to the N. is the Picture Gallery (Fig. 485), an oblong room with two tiers of windows in its E. side. These have their original ebonised and gilt pelmets and in the upper tier their red curtains contrasting with green painted walls. The pictures are a characteristic

medley reflecting the taste formed on Reynolds's *Discourses* and on the 'picturesque' aesthetic of such of Sir Richard's contemporaries as Uvedale Price and Payne Knight (cf. Downton Castle, p. 148). Large canvases by Carlo Maratti, Ludovico Cardi and Raphael Mengs hang on the fireplace wall (Fig. 486), and there are a notable Nicolas Poussin ('Hercules between Virtue and Vice'), a Madonna by Trevisani, Panninis and Zuccharellis. Poussin's 'Rape of the Sabines', now in New York, was also here till 1883 and is represented by copies of two groups from it by Samuel Woodforde, a local protégé of Sir Richard's. The two large pictures between the windows, 'Distress by Land' and 'Shipwrecked Mariner' are by the admired Henry Thompson, R.A.

Much of the furniture, as in the Library, was supplied by the younger Chippendale, of whose work Stourhead, with Harewood, is the *locus classicus.*[1] After his death in 1822, George Smith spoke of him as 'possessing a very great degree of taste with great ability as a draughtsman and designer' (between 1784–1801 he exhibited pictures at the Royal Academy). Between 1795–1820 he was paid several thousand pounds for paper hanging and upholstery as well as for furniture at Stourhead, where his expenses show that he

[1] See also Luscombe Castle, *E.C.H., Late Georgian.*

487. *Sir Richard Colt Hoare's Library in the south wing. Sage green walls, green and yellow Wilton carpet, mahogany Chippendale furniture.*

488. *The Library, looking north.*

personally supervised the work. Standing on the old green and pink Turkey carpet in this room the 'twelve sattin wood Arm chairs with broad panelled tops, Ebony bands and carved Paturns with Cross Barrs, Caned seats turned legs and on brass socket casters', made in 1802, cost £5 14 0 each. With the '2 Unique large Rose wood and sofa tables' their admirable design is only lightly influenced by the antiquarian bias of the Regency years. On the other hand the '3 sarcophagus's for the recesses of (the) windows . . . carved and painted white and part bronzed, a Medusa's head in the centre', are so Antique that for many years they graced the Pantheon by the lake. The round satinwood rent table was also probably made by Chippendale, though for another branch of the Hoare family at Wavendon.

The Library, a room of infinite charm (Fig. 487), is designed as a composition of squares and segmental curves, and illustrates an admirable synthesis of neo-classicism with native feeling. In idea it is a Roman room, with its segmental barrel ceiling to the mosaic patterned floor—reproduced in Wilton carpeting of yellow interlacing designs upon squares of orchard green; whilst the furniture is of Roman massiveness adapted to mahogany and comfort. Each wall centres on a rectangular recess between smaller segmental recesses, filled with shelving except in the end. There, doors are surmounted by ovals (containing busts of Dryden and Pope by Rysbrack, from the earlier library). In the W. side one of the lateral recesses admits a window among the books; and in the middle is the Early Georgian chimneypiece.[1] The lunettes formed by the ceiling are filled respectively by canvas panels

painted by Woodforde with scenes from Raphael's 'Parnassus' and, above the three long S. windows, with a Gospel scene in painted glass of two thicknesses by Francis Eginton (*d.* 1805). The furniture, all by Chippendale, is among the earliest designed in the Egyptian taste following Denon's *Voyage . . . en Egypte* (1802); but the appropriate antiquarian element is combined with solid grace in a way that Thomas Hope's later experiments missed. There is an entry in the Stourhead accounts for 1802 of 'a set of 8 mahogany chairs with circular backs . . . elbows carved Egyptian heads and fluted term feet,' of which several are seen in Fig. 487. The great library table, of 1805, has similar heads and legs supporting its curved ends, though elsewhere in it are heads of Western philosophers, and the design is otherwise traditional.

Well indeed might this room, rather than its predecessor, have inspired Gibbon to write the *Decline and Fall of the Roman Empire*: an event which he records did take place during his visit to Stourhead as a boy of fourteen in 1751, when he found in the library 'a common book, the "Continuation of Echard's Roman History".' This library is the actual scene of Sir Richard Colt Hoare's compilation of a no less laborious classic, the *History of Modern Wiltshire*, which he left unfinished at his death in 1838. Stourhead was bequeathed with its contents to the National Trust by the late Sir Henry Hoare in 1946. Besides its intrinsic interest and beauty it exemplifies, with Boreham House, Essex, Luscombe Castle, Devon, and Hoare's Bank, Fleet Street, the taste of a family of Georgian bankers.

Barn Elms, rebuilt by a Hoare at that time. Moved subsequently to Wavendon, it was brought here 50 years ago with several chimneypieces in other rooms.

---

[1] Of carved wood surmounted by a plaster relief depicting the money changers ejected from the Temple, it was at Ranelagh House,

ICKWORTH, SUFFOLK

Begun by **the 4th Earl of Bristol, Bishop of Derry, 1796**
Architect **Francis Sandys**
Sculptors **Flaxman, Carabelli**
Owner **The Marquess of Bristol**

'The Enlightenment' emanating from the French Encyclo-paedists, the neo-classical theory of architecture, natural science, and the impulses of romanticism together went to shaping both the fantastic genius of Frederick Hervey, Bishop of Derry and 4th Earl of Bristol, and the conception of Ickworth—which he never saw erected nor even its first stone laid. As a country residence the structure appears as preposterous as its begetter, regarded as an Anglican prelate; yet it has continued inhabited for 150 years, and he for a time played the role of bishop at least well enough to impress John Wesley. Actually Ickworth was conceived to be primarily a museum and art gallery, a temple of the rationally enlightened individualism that should reclaim an evil world. In that idealistic process the observance of social or merely

'superstitious' conventions positively impeded the complete cultivation of an aristocratic deist's Self. And, seen in this light, an extreme reasonableness underlay the inordinate eccentricities of the Earl Bishop. The same logic can be detected in the megalomania both of Ickworth itself and of that cult of a colossal geometry which was simultaneously alluring French revolutionary architects. It is indeed fortunate that there should survive among English country houses such a monument to the folly of theory, in this case neo-classicism, when unchecked by synthesis with common traditional sense.

The Hervey family had become possessed of Ickworth, near Bury St Edmunds, in the 15th century, but they abandoned the old manor house in 1642, thereafter living principally in the town of Bury. In 1700 John Hervey adapted for residence one of the farm houses in Ickworth parish, the 1,900 acres of which had not then all been thrown into the park. Created Lord Hervey (1703) and Earl of Bristol (1714), he contemplated for fifty years the erection of a mansion, and built large walled gardens with piers and an

490. *The Rotunda from the garden (south).*

491. Downhill on the coast of Antrim, built by the Bishop of Derry, c. 1775.

orangery of fine rubbed brick beside a canal (in which he narrowly escaped drowning in 1717). In the next year, according to his diary, 'Sir John Vanbrugh came to Ickworth and sett out ye scituation of my new house, leaving a plan with me for the same'. But nothing was done, and the plan has never come to light. Thus 'the Lodge' as the temporary house was called, continued to be the family residence throughout the 18th century.

Lord Hervey, eldest of the Earl's seventeen children, was the well known Royal Chamberlain and memorialist of the court of George II, marrying the equally celebrated maid of honour, Molly Lepel. He predeceased his father, but three of

492. Mussenden Temple, Downhill, 1780.

his sons succeeded to the Earldom, of whom Frederick, born in 1730, was the third. Impecunious and without prospects he was reading for the Bar when in 1752 he married a Davers of neighbouring Rushbrook (who ultimately transmitted the inheritance of that beautiful moated house to her son); then in 1754 he transferred from the Law to the Church, as was not unusual for younger sons. An honorary chaplaincy to George III was the only preferment he had obtained (in 1765) before his eldest brother the 2nd Earl, as non-resident Viceroy of Ireland, obtained for him the Bishopric of Cloyne, with reversion to the more desired see of Derry. To this he was translated in 1768. Possessed now of an income of £7,000 a year, he gave immediate rein to his enthusiasms: building, at his palace and much needed bridges; diocesan reforms; and Irish nationalism. Sharing, as Tipping phrased it, with the French philosophers their pleasant theories of universal love and happiness, he assisted Catholics and Presbyterians as freely as members of his own Church, acquiring thereby considerable sectional popularity. He could also resume the pleasures of travel and of the society of his old friend Sir William Hamilton at Naples, whose interests he shared, among them classical antiquities and natural science, notably geology. (Cf. R. P. Knight, Downton; Lord Berwick, Attingham.)

In Ireland, whither he returned in 1772, clever management had increased his bishopric's yield to £20,000 a year and he acquired an estate of 70,000 acres, based on the bleak Atlantic coastline of his See. There, in 1776, his friend Arthur Young saw the shell of Downhill (Fig. 491), the vast mansion, recently demolished, which he was erecting from his own designs on the cliff edge. In view of his later undertakings, it is worth briefly describing this, the first of them. Downhill consisted of a relatively narrow S. front with two very long wings extending back from it, all three elevations having Corinthian pilasters and facetted bays formerly surmounted by domes. At the cliff edge the wings terminated in vast basalt bastions containing courts. For the decoration of the interior he acquired exquisite chimneypieces, many from Italy, and Italian *stuccadors*, among them Placido Colombani.[1]

[1] Decorator of Mount Clare, Richmond, 1780, for Sir G. Dick. For an account of Downhill see E. R. R. Green, *Country Life*, Jan. 6, 1950.

493. *The model of Ickworth.*

494. *Design by Francis Sandys for the north front of Ickworth*

495. *Ballyscullion. Begun by the Earl Bishop in 1787. The prototype of Ickworth.*

496. *Ickworth, the north front from the east wing.*

497. *The north portico.*   498. *Profile of the Rotunda; the west wing beyond.*

He was in Italy again in 1777–78, collecting pictures and sculpture for Downhill, 'which I flatter myself will be a Tusculanium', he wrote. He then met Soane in Rome and found, no doubt, that they had much in common. The latter, lured by 'magnificent promises', cut short his hard-won travels to follow the Bishop but, after remaining at Downhill for six weeks 'without any prospect of professional employment', returned dejectedly to England.

Meanwhile the 2nd Earl of Bristol had been succeeded by his brother Augustus John, of some distinction as a naval officer and of more as husband of Miss Chudleigh, the bigamous Duchess of Kingston. He also died childless in 1779, when his successor, the Bishop, erected a domed temple at Downhill to his memory. Another, intended for a library, was built on the cliff edge itself (Fig. 492) dedicated to his cousin Mrs Frideswide Mussenden.[1] Since coronets alternate with mitres in their enrichment, both buildings must be subsequent to his inheriting the Earldom and a further £20,000 a year. Though Downhill was now at length habitable, the Earl spent Christmas of 1780 with his wife at Ickworth.

There followed his self-appointed leadership of the Irish

[1] The frieze bears an inscription from Lucretius which can be translated: 'Safe on land it is pleasant to survey the sore labours of one battered by the furious waves of a great storm.'

Volunteer movement, with triumphal progresses through Dublin, and further months in Italy (1785–86). On returning to Ireland he set about building another palace, on the picturesque shores of Lough Beg, to be called Ballyscullion. Since it was the prototype of Ickworth, though smaller, it is of value to learn that he derived the germ of its idea from Belle Isle in Windermere (Fig. 25), built by John Plaw, 1775. The Bishop wrote to his daughter, Lady Erne, March 8, 1787: 'The House itself is perfectly circular in imitation of one I saw upon an island in the Westmorland Lakes—it consists of an Oval Lobby and Drawing Room 36 by 18 ft., a Library on the south 63 by 22 ft. and a Dining Room of the same size with the Drawing Room. . . . The Staircase in the centre of the house is oval, and like a double screw includes the Back stairs like Ld. Bessborough's at Roehampton (Manresa Lodge, by Chambers) and that of Marshal Saxe at Chambord.' To Plaw's domed rotunda, containing the domestic quarters, were added quadrant corridors connecting to wings and serving as galleries for his collections. An engraving (Fig. 495), in the *Statistical Survey of Co. Londonderry*, 1802, shows stable courts attached to the wings, as seems also to have been intended at Ickworth. Though it was roofed in 1788, and the Bishop was still interested in it during what proved to be his last visit to Ireland in 1791, Ballyscullion was never finished, and was dismantled in 1813; for he had decided to transfer his treasures, and the design, to Ickworth.

During a short stay there in 1792 he probably selected the site. This needed to be large and level and was found a long way northwards of the old manor house site near the church, in relation to which the 1st Earl had formed the gardens. Then the Earl Bishop set off on his travels again, never to return.

He left in charge two brothers, Francis Sandys, architect,[1] and the Rev Joseph Sandys, undoubtedly Irishmen and probably already responsible for Ballyscullion. In 1794 he wrote from Siena that he hoped to return in the autumn to lay the foundation stone; but in the winter he was in Rome, where this time he met and consulted C. H. Tatham. The latter wrote to Holland, who had sent him to Rome, that, regarding Ickworth, 'the plan is very singular, the House being an oval according to his desire (and) extending nearly 500 ft.' In fact it stretches 600 ft. But the length of the galleries was still not settled in 1798; and in March, 1796, the facing material was still under consideration. The Earl Bishop wrote from Naples to his daughter, Lady Elizabeth Foster, a letter valuable for its evidence of contemporary opinion on two debatable materials:

'You beg me on your knees that Ickworth may be built of white stone bricks ... What! Child, build my house of a brick that looks like a sick, pale, *jaundiced* red brick, that would be red brick if it could, and to which I am certain our posterity would give a little rouge as essential to its health. ... I shall follow dear impeccable old Palladio's rule, and as nothing ought to be without a covering in our raw damp climate, I shall cover the house, pillars and pilasters,

[1] For other works by Francis Sandys, all after 1795 and including Assembly Rooms, Bury St Edmunds, see Appendix and Colvin, op.cit.

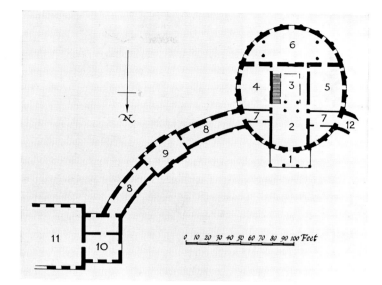

499. *Sketch plan of part of ground floor.* 1. *Portico.* 2. *Entry Hall.* 3. *Staircase hall.* 4. *Drawing Room.* 5. *Dining Room.* 6. *Library.* 7, 7. *Passages to wing corridors.* 8, 8. *East wing corridor.* 9. *Smoking room.* 10. *Entrance Hall to East wing.* 11. *East wing (now the residence).* 12. *Beginning of west wing corridor.*

with Palladio's stucco, which has now lasted 270 years. It has succeeded perfectly well with me at Downhill on that Temple of the Winds .... It has resisted the frosts and rains of Vicenza—*c'est tout dire*—and deceives the most acute eye till within a foot.'

Tatham, as Holland's pupil, who was Brown's, would no doubt have been in favour of white brick; but the Bishop, rightly we may feel, anticipated Nash in preferring stucco for neo-classical architecture, though Ickworth was never painted.

500. *In the east wing corridor.*

501. *The Drawing Room.*

In the absence of definite evidence for the actual date of commencement, we may assume that building of the rotunda followed the visit by Sandys to the Bishop in Rome, of which, in company with Flaxman, he told Farrington (July, 1796), saying that he was 'beginning to build a Palace at Ickworth'. The model (Fig. 493) had presumably been approved, incorporating slight differences from the drawing (Fig. 494) such as a pedimented for a flat portico.

Ballyscullion and Ickworth both departed from the Bishop's model—Belle Isle—in the body being an oval, and for the same reasons of internal planning. For it was the rotunda that was to contain the whole living accommodation; so to increase space in its E. and W. segments for drawing and dining rooms the circular plan was elongated to an oval. The quadrant corridors and the wings provided the art galleries. The model shows each wing consisting in a vestibule opening into a gallery 100 ft. long and occupying the full height. The planning exactly followed that of Ballyscullion except in being bigger, viz.:

	Ballyscullion	*Ickworth*
Total length in feet	350	600
Central Oval	84 by 74	120 by 106
Library	63 by 22	78 by 30

The Library (Fig. 502) fills the whole S. segment of the oval, which in the N. quarter is cut at the corresponding point by the corridors. Dining Room and Drawing Room fill the sides. Between them the centre is occupied by the rectangular Staircase and Hall, which extend from the cross-wall of the library to the portico—a depth at Ickworth of 75 ft. Beneath the dome the staircase was to have ascended in a horseshoe form round a drum containing the back stairs; its gradient would have been steep owing to the great height given to the ground floor rooms: 30 ft. This had been decided empirically on considerations of hygiene, the Bishop observing that 'my Lungs always played more freely, my spirits spontaneously rose much higher, in lofty rooms than in low ones where the atmosphere is too much tainted with . . . our own bodies'.

'I flatter myself that my architectural ideas are Pure and Noble', he wrote in July, 1796, to his old fellow-traveller Professor Symonds of Cambridge, introducing his chaplain—'no bad critic and a connoisseur'. 'I wish to make it quite classical', he continued, 'to unite magnificence with convenience and simplicity with dignity—no redundancy—no superfluity—no one unnecessary room, but the necessary ones to be noble and convenient, to have few pictures but

502. *The Library looking west.*

503. Entrance hall and staircase.

choice ones, and my galleries to exhibit an historical progress of the art of Painting both in Germany and Italy, and that divided into its characteristical schools—Venice, Bologna, Florence etc.' He reveals himself, in fact, as a very notable fore-runner both of the *kunsthistorische* and the millionaire-collector. Whilst he gave pride of place to Raphael and the later Renaissance painters, he recognized at least the historical value of the Primitives, then wholly ignored, acquiring works of 'Cimabué, Giotto, Guido da Siena and all the old pedantry of painting that seemed to show the progress of art at its resurrection.' 'Large mosaick pavements, sumptuous chimneypieces for my new house, marbles without end, first rate Titians and Raphaels, dear Guidos and three old Caraccis' are also referred to.

It was for displaying these that the Sandys brothers differed as to the length of the galleries: 'One deems that 115 ft. will drown my mansion and eclipse its splendour, the other computes that less will not leave sufficient Room in the square of each office yard for Larders, Laundries, etc.'—indicating that these adjuncts were intended to adjoin the wing pavilions as at Ballyscullion. But following the French occupation of Rome, the whole collection was confiscated, and at the end of 1798 the Earl Bishop himself was imprisoned in Milan for nine months. Freed in 1799, he yet made no attempt to return, leasing and enlarging a house in Florence and continuing to buy works of art from im-

poverished Romans. The roads of Italy were so familiar with his equipage that innumerable Hotels Bristol to this day commemorate his princely passage; and on that to Albano this builder of palaces died in 1803—of gout in the stomach, in the outhouse of a cottage to which a peasant would not admit a heretic prelate.

'Pure and noble' the chaste geometry of Ickworth's elemental forms and their high aesthetic purpose could claim to be according to neo-classical ideals. And as such their harmonies of rectangles, segments and cylinders might strike the eye, could they be effectively seen in relationship from any one point. That they cannot is partly due to the failure to synthesize this classical logic with the visual factor—the picturesque—either in their planning or in the planting of the landscape. Although an expert, Mr Griffin, received '£150 on contract for new plantations' in 1801, his scheme—or later tampering with it—obscures the scale and obstructs the significant aspects of the extraordinary pile.

But even within the neo-classical canon the brothers Sandys must be held to have failed to realize the architectural possibilities of the imaginative conception (compare, e.g. Ledoux's arcaded circular Barrière de la Villette). The ordering is monotonous, the immense opportunities for forcible contrast are missed, the scale small and prosaic. Only when the rotunda is examined closely does the small-scale relief in the friezes impart some animation (Fig. 498). They were

504. *Room in west wing corridor decorated* c. 1850.

modelled in terra cotta after Flaxman's designs from the Iliad and Odyssey, by the brothers Carabelli, to whom payments were being made between 1800–03. When the Bishop died the lower tier and part of the upper were complete, but the wings, which were to be similarly enriched, had not risen above 3 or 4 ft., and the whole work was stopped, what the Italians had not finished being replaced with Coade stone reliefs.

On the Earl Bishop's death all his remaining collections together with the Irish properties were left to his cousin the Rev. Henry Bruce, who had all along managed the latter. The 5th Earl, the Bishop's second son, inherited the settled estates only, and would have demolished Ickworth, could he have sold the materials. But receiving the Marquisate in 1826, and his finances improving, he decided on partial completion to a reversed plan. The rotunda was a mere shell, with a wooden staircase to the roof and its decoration not begun. He completed the wings for domestic occupation, the eastern becoming a self-contained family house, and broadened the central section of each corridor to provide a large room. The great rooms in the rotunda were decorated, probably from Sandys's original designs; but, with the W. wing, were used only during periods of entertainment. The room in the W. corridor was decorated about 1850 (Fig. 504) in the Pompeian style as then practised by J. F. Crace, of which we have seen Georgian examples at Heveningham and elsewhere. The hall (Fig. 503) with its columned inner end, where scagliola pillars carry a deep entablature whence

springs the ceiling's segmental vault, will be as the Bishop designed and his son completed it. But the top-lit space beyond was remodelled by the late Marquess. Here there was in 1813 only 'a kind of open wooden staircase'. The Bishop's scheme, as the model shows, used the centre of this for his main stair, opening it out from the hall by a broad column-supported aperture, above which was a great semicircle of glazing resembling a fan-light. The 5th Earl inserted a solid dividing wall which gave a sense of gloom and steepness to the staircase that he also introduced. In 1907, with the advice of the late Arthur Blomfield, the wall was removed up to the entablature, and matching columns inserted. The present staircase commences in the E. side and ascends to a gallery across the back of the space, whence other flights rise to the upper floor of the central portion of the rotunda. On the top floor a room the size of the hall, known as the Museum, contains numerous models in plaster or cork of Roman monuments which the Bishop caused to be made. The great Library, Drawing Room and Dining Room contain a number of the very notable Hervey family portraits by Hogarth, Zoffany and Gainsborough. Angelica Kauffmann's portrait of the Earl Bishop presides in the Hall where, in the well of the Staircase, also stands the only survivor of the sculpture—Flaxman's great group of 'The Fury of Athamas,' commissioned at Rome in 1790 for 600 guineas.

'I cannot conclude,' wrote the sculptor in a letter to Sir W. Hamilton, 'without telling you that the liberality of Lord Bristol has reanimated the fainting body of Art in Rome: for his generosity to me I must be silent, for I have not words to express its value.' Had events fulfilled the neo-classical ideal, and Ickworth been filled with the art-treasures collected for it, we would have shared this judgement of a man much ahead of his time.

505. *The 4th Earl of Bristol. Bust by C. Huetson* (National Portrait Gallery).

APPENDIX

ARCHITECTS OF COUNTRY HOUSES IN ENGLAND AND WALES 1760-1800

This list, for the most part, is condensed from *Country Life* records and Mr H. M. Colvin's *Dictionary of English Architects, 1660–1840*. Extraneous buildings are included in certain cases for their significance in the context. I am indebted to Mr Christopher Gotch for references from his unpublished list of works by Robert Mylne in Shropshire; to Miss D. Stroud, Mr A. S. Oswald, and Mr A. S. Garton and Mr D. R. Sherborn of the Ministry of Housing and Local Government, for help with checking sundry references.

ABBREVIATIONS

★ *House described in this volume*
‡ *Noticed or described in Introduction to this volume*
† *Noticed or described in 'English Country Houses, Early Georgian'*
A. *Designed alterations*
B. *Designed additions*
C. *Complete Architect's Design*
D. *Designed decoration*
F. *Furniture designs supplied*

M. *Modified or altered another architect's design*
P. *Partly remodelled an existing building*
Q. *Repaired or restored an existing building*
R. *Remodelled an existing building*
S. *Subsidiary buildings (garden, stables, offices, etc.)*

n. *House altered or rebuilt subsequently*
g. *House demolished*
r. *House damaged or ruinous*

ADAM, Robert (1728–92)‡. Hatchlands, 1758–61, D.★. Shardeloes, Bucks., 1759–61, B.D. Harewood, 1754–71, M.D.★. Croome Ct., Worcs., 1760 D.S.†. Bowood, Wilts., 1761–64, M.D.F.S.‡. Compton Verney, Warwicks., 1761–65, M.B.D.S.‡. Mersham-le-Hatch, 1762–65, C.F.★. Syon House, 1762–70, R.S.D.F.★. Moor Park, Mddx., 1763–64, B.F.†. Audley End, Suffolk, 1763–65, D. Kedleston, 1760, D.F., 1761–65, M.B.S.★. Kimbolton Castle, Hunts., c. 1765, S. Strawberry Hill, Mddx., 1766, D.†. Nostell Priory, Yorks., 1766–70, B.D.F.†. Ugbrooke, Devon, 1766–67, D. West

506. *Milton Manor House, Berkshire. The Library. Stephen Wright, c. 1765.*

Wycombe Pk., Bucks., 1767–68, B.S.†. Kenwood, Mddx., B.D.F. Newby, Yorks., 1767–80, B.D.F.*. Saltram, Devon., 1768, D.F.*. Luton Hoo, Beds., 1768–75, C.n. Mamhead, Devon, c. 1770, P.g. Alnwick Castle, Northumb., D.n. Stowe, Bucks., 1771–79, P. Highcliffe, Hants., 1773, C.g. The Oaks, Epsom, 1774, A. and temporary pavilion. Woolton Hall, Lancs., c. 1775, R. Moccas Ct., Herefs., 1775, C.D. (see Keck, A.). Hitchin Priory, Herts., 1777, B. Wormleybury, Herts., 1777, D. (see Mylne, R.). Weald Hall, Essex, 1778, D.g. For complete list of Works by R. & J. Adam, see Bolton, A. T., op. cit.

ALEXANDER, D. A. (1768–1846). Mote Park, Kent, 1793–1800. Longford Castle, Wilts., 1802–17, A.B. Trematon Ho., Cornwall (attrib.) c. 1808.

ATKINSON, Peter (1725–1805) ‡. Asst. to Carr of York, Hackness Hall, Yorks., 1796, C.n.

ATKINSON, Thomas (–1798) of York. Bishops-thorpe, Yorks., 1763–69, R. Burton Constable, Yorks., c. 1776, D.†. Tixall, Staffs., c. 1770, B.g.

BADGER, Joseph, of Sheffield. Renishaw Hall, Derbs., 1793–1808, P.S.

BALDWIN, Thomas, of Bath (1750–1820). Hafod, Cards., 1786, C.g.

BELL, John, of Durham. Built Axwell Pk., Dur., etc. under James Paine. Nunwick, Northumb., c. 1770, C. (attrib.).

BONOMI, Joseph (1739–1808)‡. Dale Pk., Sussex, 1784, C.n. Townely Hall, Lancs., 1789, B.n. Langley Pk., Kent, 1790, B.n. Eastwell Pk., Kent, 1793–1800, C.n. Blickling, Norf., 1794, S. Longford Hall, Salop., 1794–97, C. Barrells, Warwicks., c. 1795, g. Piercefield, Mon., 1797, B.n. Hatch-lands, 1797, A.*. Lambton Hall, Dur., 1798, A. Sandling Pk., Kent, 1799, C.g.

BORRA, J. B. Stowe, Bucks., c. 1763, A.S.

BRETTINGHAM, Matthew II (1725–1803)‡. Charlton Ho., Wilts., 1772–76, A.B.

BRETTINGHAM, Robert Furze (1750?–1806). Beech-wood, Herts., c. 1800, A?. Longleat, Wilts., c. 1790, A. Audley End, Essex, 1792, S.

BRIDGES, James (fl. 1757–63). The Royal Fort, Bristol, c. 1760. C.†.

BROWN, Lancelot (1716–83)‡. Croome Ct., Worcs., †. Burghley Ho., Stamford, 1756–83, Q.D.S. Castle Ashby, Northants., 1761, Q.S. Corsham Ct., Wilts., c. 1760†, P.D. (see Keene). Ugbrooke, Devon, c. 1761, P. (see Adam). Redgrave Hall, Suffolk, 1765, P.g. Tong Cas., Salop., 1765, C.s.g. Broadlands, Hants., 1766, R.‡ (see Holland). Fisherwick, Staffs., 1766, R.g. Claremont (see Holland),*. Benham Pl., Berks., 1772, C. Cadland, Hants., 1775, C.g. Cardiff Castle, Mon., 1777, R.n. Himley Hall, Worcs., 1775, A. Nuneham Courtenay, Oxon., 1778, B.

BYFIELD, George (c. 1756–1813). Craycombe. Exh. R.A., 1791 (Fig. 507; but see Mitchell, R.). Spetchley Pk., Worcs., A.

CARR, John, of York (1723–1807)‡. Kirby Hall, Ouse-burn; under Burlington and Morris c. 1750. Arncliffe Hall,

Yorks. (N.R.), 1753, C. Grand stand, York racecourse, 1754. Lytham, Lancs., 1757, C.g. Heath Hall, Wakefield, c. 1760, C. Burton Constable (E.R.) c. 1762, C. Harewood Ho., 1759–71, C.*. Tabley, Ches., 1761–67, C.*. Thoresby, Notts., 168, A.g. Welbeck Ab., Notts., 1764, A.n. Cannon Hall (W.R.) 1765, 1778, 1804, B. Kirkleatham Hall (N.R.), c. 1765. C.g. Castle Howard, 1771–82, S. Kilnwick Ho. (E.R.) 1769, A.g. Panton Hall, Lincs., 1775, C.g. Norton Hall, Lincs., 1776, C. Colwick, Notts., 1776, A. Basildon Pk., Berks., 1776, C. Denton Pk. (W.R.) 1778, ‡C.D. Thornes Ho. (W.R.) 1779–81, C.g. Wentworth Woodhouse (W.R.), c. 1780, B.S.†. Grimston Garth (E.R.) 1781–86, ‡.C. Farnley Hall (W.R.) 1780–90, B.D.*. Undated or attributed: Wigganthorpe (N.R.). Aston (W.R.). Byram Hall, g. Gledstone, C.M.g. Ripley Castle, c. 1780, A.D.

CARTER, John (1748–1817). Midford Castle, Bath, c. 1775, C. Oatlands, Surrey, 1800, A.

CHAMBERS, Sir Wm. (1723–96)‡. Wilton Ho., Wilts., 1759, S. Kew Gardens, Surrey, 1759–62, S. Goodwood Ho., Sussex, 1757–63, A.S.‡. Castle Hill (Duntish Ct.), Dorset, c. 1760, C. Styche, Market Drayton, Salop., c. 1760–64, C. Coleby, Lincs., 1762, S. Walcot, Salop., c. 1764, C.n. Peper Harow, Surrey, 1765–75, C.*. The Hoo, Herts., c. 1764, S. Manresa Ho., Roehampton, Surrey, 1767, C. Ampthill Pk., Beds., 1769–71, A. Blenheim Pal., Oxon., 1769–74, S.D. Stanmore Pk., Mddx., 1770, g. Milton Abbas, Dorset, 1770–74, Q.S. Woburn Ab., Beds., 1770, S. Wick Ho., Richmond, Surrey, 1771, C.n. Milton, Northants, 1771, A.D. Castle Howard, Yorks., S.

COCKERELL, Samuel Pepys (c. 1754–1827). Daylesford Ho., Glos., 1790–96, C.D. Middleton, Carmarthens., 1796; Gore Ct., Kent, 1795. Sezincote, Glos., c. 1805, C.

COLOMBANI, Placido (c. 1744–   ). (Downhill, Co. Antrim, c. 1775, D.*). Mount Clare, Roehampton, Surrey, c. 1780, D.

COUCHMAN, Henry (1738–1803). Packington Hall, Warwicks., 1772, A. Arbury, Warwicks, 1776–90, A.D.*.

CRUNDEN, John (1740–c. 1828). Woolcombe, Dorset, c. 1772, C. Busbridge, Surrey, 1775, A.g. Boodles Club, London, 1775, C.D. Portswood Ho., Hants., c. 1780.

DANCE, George (1741–1825) ‡. Cranbury Pk., Hants., c. 1780, A.D.‡. Pitzhanger Man., Mddx., 1770, B. Stratton Pk., Hants., c. 1803, A.n.2. Coleorton, Leics., 1804, C. Ashburn-ham Pl., Sussex, 1813–17, A. Kidbrooke Pk., Sussex, c. 1814, A. Wilderness Pk., Kent, g.

GANDON, James (1743–1823) published with J. Woolfe Vitruvius Britannicus, Vols. IV and V, 1767–71. Warley Pl., Essex, 1777, g. (Dublin, The Four Courts, 1785, etc.)

HOBCROFT, John, carpenter and builder, Mamhead, Devon, 1766 g. Padworth Ho., Berks., 1769, C.D. See Clare-mont*.

HOLLAND, Henry (1745–1800)‡. Hale, Hants., 1770, P. Claremont, Surrey, 1771, C. (with Brown)*. Berrington, Herefs., 1778–84, C.*. Wenvoe Cas., Glam., C.g. Woburn Ab., Beds., 1787, B.D.S. Althorp, Northants., 1787–1800, R.*. Broadlands, Hants., A.D. (see Brown)‡. Oatlands, Surrey,

507. *Craycombe House, Worcestershire. Attributed to George Byfield*, 1791, *or possibly Robert Mitchell.*

1794. Southill, Beds., 1795–1806, R.D.F.S. Wimbledon Park, Ho., 1801, C.g.

IVORY, Thomas (1709–79) and William (son, 1746–c. 1801) of Norwich. Blickling, Norfolk, A.D., 1767–85, ‡.

JOHNSON, John (1732–1814). Bradwell Ho., Essex, 1781–86, B. East Carlton Hall, Northants., 1778. Gnoll Cas., Glam., 1778. Halswell Pk., Som., S.G. Terling Pl., Essex, 1778, C. Sadborow Ho., Dorset, 1773–75, C. Killerton, Devon, c. 1785, n. Kingsthorpe Hall, Leics. Pitsford, Leics. Whatton, Leics., c 1802. Woolverstone Hall, Essex, 1777, C.

KECK, Anthony (1726–97) of Kings Stanley, Glos. Flaxley Ab., Glos., 1780, Q.P. Moccas Ct., Herefs., (executed Adam's designs); Barnsley Pk., Glos., D. Longworth, Herefs., c. 1788. Beveré, Worcs.

KEENE, Henry (1726–76)†‡. Bowood, Wilts., 1755–60, R.‡ (see Adam). Hartwell, Bucks., 1759–61, R.†. Corsham Ct., Wilts., 1759, A.† (see Brown). Arbury, Warwicks., 1762–76, A.D.★. Uppark, Sussex, c. 1770, S.D. (attrib.),★.

LATROBE, Benjamin (1764–1820). Hammerwood Lodge and Ashdown Ho., E. Grinstead, Sussex, c. 1790. C. (The Capitol, Washington, U.S.A.)

LEADBETTER, Stiff (–1766). Shardeloes, Bucks., 1758–66 (see Adam). Nuneham Pk., Oxon., 1764 (see Brown), C.

LEVERTON, Thos. (1743–1824)‡. Woodford Hall,

Essex, 1771, C.g. Boyles, Brentwood, Essex, 1773. Woodhall Pk., Herts., 1777, C.★. Riddlesworth Hall, Norf., 1781. Scampston Ho., Yorks., 1803, A. Herringston, Dorset, Q.

LEWIS, James (c. 1751–1820). Bletchingdon Ho., Oxon., 1782, R. Hawnes, Beds., 1781–97, P. Lavington Ho., Sussex, 1790–94, C.n. Woolmers, Herts., 1802, C. (Bethlehem Hosp., London, 1812–15).

LIGHTFOOT, ——.†. Claydon, Bucks., 1768–71, B.D.†. Crichel, Dorset, c. 1773, B.(attrib.)★.

LUMBY, William, of Lincoln. Doddington, Lincs., 1761–62, A. Burton Ho., Lincs., A. (See Paine).

MITCHELL, Robert, ‡. Cottesbrooke Hall, Northants., c. 1770, B.D.S. Moor Pl., Much Hadham, Herts., 1777–79, C.‡. Silwood Pk., Berks., n. Published *Plans*, etc., 1801. Attributed: Craycombe Ho., Worcs., 1791, (Fig. 508), on close stylistic analogies. But see Byfield, 9.

MYLNE, Robert (1774–1811)‡. (Almacks Club, London, 1764). Northumberland Ho., London, 1765, A.g. Kings Weston, Glos., 1763–72, A.S.D. Tusmore Ho., Oxon., 1766–69, C. ‡. Wormleybury, Herts., 1767–70, C. (See Adam). The Wick, Richmond, Surrey, C. Kidbrooke Pk., E. Grinstead, Sussex, 1805, R. Houses in Shropshire 1764–80: Halston Pk., 1764–69, P. Condover, 1766, A.n. Loton Pk., A.n. Tern Hall (Attingham †) 1769–77, A.n. Woodhouse, 1773, C. Bryngwyn, 1773, n. Brogyntyn, C. (?). Aston, 1780, C. Sundorne Castle, D.g. Onslow Hall, n. Little Berwick Hall, A.B.n.

NASH, John (1752–1835). See *E.C.H., Late Georgian*.

NEWTON, William (1775–90). (Greenwich Hosp. Chapel, with Stuart, J., 1780–90). Durdans, Epsom, Surrey, 1764, n. Theobalds Pk., Herts., 1765. Hungerford Pk., Berks, 1768, n.

NEWTON, William, of Newcastle (1730–98). Howick Hall, Northumb., 1787, C. Backworth Ho., Northumb., 1792. Cas. Eden, Dur. Heaton Hall, Northumb., A.

PAINE, James (c. 1716–89)‡, works prior to 1760, †. Gibside, Dur., 1760–61, A.r., and Mausoleum, C. Kedleston, Derbs., 1757–61,*. Sandbeck Pk., Yorks., c. 1763–67, C. Worksop, Notts., 1763–67, C.g. Thorndon Hall, Essex, 1764–70, C.r. Brocket Hall, Herts., 1765–80, C.D.*. Weston Pk., Staffs., 1765–70, S. Burton Ho., Lincs., 1767, B.A. Hare Hall, Essex, 1768, C. Chillington, Staffs., c. 1770, S.*. Wardour Cas., Wilts., 1770–76, C.*. Shrubland Hall, Suff., 1772, C.n.

PICKFORD, Joseph, of Derby. Etruria Ho., Burslem, Staffs., 1767. Sandon Ho., Staffs., c. 1770.

PLAW, John (c. 1745–1820)‡. Belle Isle, Westmorland, 1774, C.‡. Other designs in his published works. Died, Prince Edward Island, Canada.

REVELEY, Willey (1760–99). Stourhead, Wilts., lodges and B. (attrib.) 1796, *.

REVETT, Nicholas (1720–1804)†‡. Standlynch (Trafalgar) Ho., Wilts., 1760, B.D.*. West Wycombe Pk., Bucks., 1770–80, B.S.†.

ROBINSON, Sir Thomas (c. 1700–77). Works prior to 1760†. Glynde Ch., Sussex, 1765; Claydon, Bucks., 1771–77, B.g.†.

SANDYS, Francis. (Ballyscullion, N. Ireland, 1787, g.) Ickworth, Suff., 1796,*. Finborough Hall, Suff., 1795. Worlingham Hall, Suff., c. 1800. West Dean Ho., Sussex (?), 1809, n.

SAUNDERS, George (c. 1762–1839). Kenwood, Mddx., 1793, B.

SAXON, Samuel (1757–). Courteenhall, Northants., 1791, C.*. Buckminster. Leics., C.g.

SEARLES, Michael (1750–1813)‡. (Paragon, Blackheath, c. 1795.) Clare Ho., E. Malling, Kent, 1793, C.‡.

SOANE, Sir John (1753–1837)‡. The following are his more notable country house commissions before 1800; cf. Colvin op. cit., and Soane Museum records. Malvern Hall, Warwicks. 1783, B. Mulgrave Cas., Yorks. (N.R.), 1784, B.A. Earsham, Norf., 1784, S. Tendring Hall, Suff., 1784–86, C.g. Shottesham Pk., Norf., 1785, C. Letton Hall, Norf., 1785, C. Chillington Hall, Staffs., 1786,*. Wardour Cas., Wilts., Chapel, 1788,*. Ryston Hall, Norf., 1788, R. Bentley Priory, Mddx., 1789–99, R. Wimpole, Cambs., 1791, A.‡. Tyringham, Bucks., 1793–1800, C.n. Sydney Lo., Hants., 1794, C. Cuffnels, Hants., 1795, A.g. Betchworth Cas., Surrey, 1799, S.g. Pitzhanger Man., Ealing, 1800, A. Aynho Pk., Northants., 1800–04, B.D.

STEUART, George, (–1806). Attingham Hall, Salop., 7743, C.*. Lythwood, Salop., c. 1785, C.g. Earl Stoke, Wilts., 1786, C.g.

STUART, James (1713–88). Works prior to 1760, †. Shugborough, Staffs., 1760, B.D.S.*. Nuneham Pk., Oxon., c. 1764, D. and Ch. Wentworth Woodhouse, Yorks., c. 1768, D.†. Blithfield, Staffs., c. 1768, S. Belvedere, Erith, Kent, c. 1775, g. Wimpole, Cambs., c. 1775, S.g. (London, 15, St James's Sq., 1762, C. Montagu [Portman] Ho., c. 1775–82, C.D.g. Greenwich Hosp. Chapel, 1779–88, C.).

TAYLOR, Sir Robert (1714–88)‡. Works prior to 1760, †. Arnos Grove, Mddx., c. 1775, B. Gorhambury, Herts., 1777–90, C.†. Heveningham Hall, Suff., 1728–80, R.C.*. Copfold Hall, Essex, A.g.

WHITE, John (c. 1747–1813). Glevering Hall, Suff., 1792, C.n. Woolbeding, Sussex, 1791, A. Weston Pk., Staffs., A. (Engaged at Attingham, c. 1785, *).

WOOD, John, the younger, of Bath (1728–81). Buckland Ho., Bucks., 1755, C.†. Standlynch (Trafalgar) Wilts., 1766, B.*. Tregenna Cas., Corn., c. 1773.

WRIGHT, Stephen (–1780)†. After 1760: Clumber, Notts., 1767, C.g. Milton Manor, Berks., 1764–72, B.D., (Fig. 506).

WYATT, James (1746–1813)‡. Fawley Ct., Bucks., 1771, D. Heaton, Lancs., 1772, C.*. Heathfield Pk., Kent, 1773, g. Erdigg, Denb., c. 1774, D. Copped Hall, Essex, 1775, A.g. Shardeloes, Bucks., c. 1775, D?. Ragley, Warws., B. Burton Constable, Yorks., c. 1776, D.†. Bryanston, Dorset, 1778, R.g. Blagdon, Northumb., 1778–91, D.S. Badger Hall, Salop., 1779–83, B.g. Sandleford Priory, Berks., 1780, R. Heveningham, Suffolk, before 1782, D.* Pishiobury, Herts., 1782–84. Lee Priory, Kent, 1783–90, R.g. Cobham Hall, Kent, c. 1783, A.D.S. Roundway Park, Devizes, Wilts., c. 1783, A.g. Sudbourne Hall, Suff., c. 1784, R.n. Wynnstay, Denb., 1785, B.g. Stanstead, Sussex, 1786–90, A.r. Brocklesby, Lincs., 1795, Mausoleum. Ammerdown, Som., 1788, C.n. Chiswick Ho., Mddx., 1788, B.g. (Castle Coole, Co. Fermanagh, 1790–97, C.). Frogmore, Berks., 1792, C.S. Henham Hall, Suff., 1793–97, C.g. Plas Newydd, Anglesey, 1795, R.D. Bishop Auckland Cas., Dur., c. 1795, B.S.D. Hinton St George, Som., c. 1796, B. Fonthill Abbey, Wilts., 1796–1807, C.g. Bowden Ho., Wilts., 1796, C. Windsor Cas., Berks., 1796–1800, A.n. Dodington Pk., Glos., 1798–1808, C. Canwell Hall, Staffs., B.D. c. 1798. Stoke Poges Pk., Bucks., 1800. Norris Cas., I. of W., c. 1799. Goodwood Ho., Sussex, 1800, R.‡. Wilton Ho., Wilts., 1800–1810, B.A.

WYATT, Samuel (1737–1807)‡. Baron Hill, Anglesey, 1776, C. Hurstmonceux Pl., Sussex, c. 1777, R. Doddington Hall, Cheshire, 1777–98, C.*. Hooton Hall, Cheshire, 1778, C. Soho Ho., Birmingham, 1789, C.n. Winnington Hall, Chesh., c. 1790, B.C.. Belmont, Kent, 1792, B.C.‡. (London, Trinity Ho., 1793–95, C.n.) Penrhyn Cas., Carns., 1792, C.g. Tixall Ho., Staffs., c. 1800, D.g. Tatton Pk., Cheshire, 1805, C. Kinmel Pk., Denbs., g.

For further dated works by or attributed to the Wyatts, see *E.C.H., Late Georgian*. Among undated and attributed works prior to 1800 are: Nacton Ho., Suff., R. Powderham Cas., Devon, B. Sheffield Pk., Sussex, R. Thirkleby Pk., Yorks., g. West Dean Pk., Sussex, n. Worstead Hall, Norf.

INDEX

The figures in italics refer to illustrations

Adair, John, 81

Adam, Architecture of Robert and James, A. T. Bolton, 62

Adam, James, 11

Adam, John, 11, 27

Adam, Robert, 9–28, 59, 106, 108, 120, 223; arch. at Hatchlands, 49–54; at Harewood, 61–9; at Kedleston, 70–8; at Syon, 86–97; at Mersham, 98–104; at Saltram, 125–34; at Newby Hall, 141–7; works, 247, 248; *see Works*

Adam, Robert, architectural characteristics of, 12, 13, 15, 54, 62, 76–7, 86, 144

Adam, William, 11

Age of Adam, The, Lees Milne, 145

Alcott, John, decorator, 45; at Shugborough, 85

Alexander, D. A., arch; works, 248

Alken, J., carver, at Peper Harow, 111, 113

All Hallows, London Wall, 17, 123, 124

Althorp, Northants., 22, 28, 203–213, 228

Analytical Inquiry into the Principles of Taste, Richard Payne Knight, 148

Anderson, J. MacV., 213

Anson, Admiral Lord, 79, 85; bust of, *83*

Anson, Thomas, 79, 80, 85, 192

Arbury Hall, Warwick., 11, 41–8

Archaeology, Antiquarianism, influence of, 10, 11, 80, 145, 214, 227, 245

Architectural Review, 27

Architecture in Britain, John Summerson, 10, 11

Armitage, Benjamin, 54

Arundell of Wardour, Lords, *see* Wardour

Asgill House, Richmond, 11

Athens, Antiquities of, Stuart and Revett, 10

Atkinson, J., 216

Atkinson, Peter, arch., 17, 248; works, 248

Atkinson, Thomas, arch., works, 248

Atkinson, William, arch., 55, 59

Attingham, Shrops., 24, 26, 28, 195–202, 240

Ayot St Lawrence Church, 116

Baalbec, Ruins of, 10

Babel, P., 28

Backhuysen, paintings by at Farnley, 216

Bacon, John, 27

Badger, Joseph, arch., works, 248

Bagot, Lord, 18

Baldwin, Thomas, arch., works, 248

Ballyscullion, Ireland, 26, *241*, 242–4

Bank of England, 16, 25, 224, 227

Baron Hill, Anglesey, 20

Barons Court, Co. Tyrone, 196, 197

Baroque architecture, 9, 22

Barry, Sir C., arch. at Harewood, 61, 62, 68, 69

Bartoli, scagliola at Kedleston, 70, 77

Baths, 135, 145

Battoni, Pompeo, paintings at Upark, 37; at Wardour, 123, 124

Bedford Square, No. 1, London, 18

Beighton, H., 41, 42

Bell, John, arch., works, 248

Belle Isle, Westmorland, 10, *24*, 26, 242, 244

Belmont, Kent, 20, *24*; tablet at, *26*, 28

Bernasconi, decorations at Shugborough, 85

Berrington Hall, Herefs., 22, 135, 140, 184–94, 231

Bertram, Matthew, carver, at Tabley, 55, 58, 59

Berwick, 1st Lord, 195

Blackett, Sir E., 141

Blackfriars Bridge, 17

Blickling Hall, Norfolk, 11

Bolton, A. T., 11, 50, 62, 69, 87

Bonomi, Joseph, 18, 158, 179; arch. at Harewood, 49, 50, 51, 54; works, 248

Boringdon, Lord, 125

Borra, J. B., arch., 12, 77; works, 248

Boscawen, Admiral and Mrs. Edward, 49, 52

'Bossi' work, *95*, 97, 179

Boucher tapestries, 144, *147*

Boulton, Matthew, 28, 134; ormolu by at Syon, *92*, 97

Bowood, Wilts., *11*, 13

Brackett, Oliver, 69

Bramante, 15

Brass, balustrading, 120; locks, 222

Brettingham, Matthew, arch., at Kedleston, 70, 71. Matthew, the younger, arch., 17; works, 248

Brettingham, Robert Furze, arch., works, 248

Brick, White, 22, 28, 177, 222, 243; *see* Tiles

Bridges, James, arch., works, 248

Bridgwater, D., 27

Brighton Pavilion, 27, 28

Bristol, 4th Earl of, Bishop of Derry, 27, 28, 239–46; bust of, *246*

Broadlands, Hants., *21*, 22, 212

Brocket Hall, Herts., 11, 105–10

Brocklesby, mausoleum at, 18

Bromwich, decorators, 104

Brooks, James, and Sons, glaziers, 45

Brooks's Clubhouse, London, 22

Brown, Lancelot ('Capability'), 11, 21, 22, 23, 27, 28, 50, 69, 79, 106; arch. at Claremont, 135–40; landscape at Heveningham, 165; at Berrington, 184, 185; at Chillington, 222, 223; works, 248

Bruyn, Theodore de, painter, at Farnley, 214, 219, 220

Buckminster, Lincs., 230

Burghley, Northants., 11

Burke, Edmund, 10, 25

Burlington, Richard Boyle, 3rd Earl of, 11, 13, 16, 17, 56

Byfield, George, arch., 249; works, 248

Byrne, Sir Peter, 55

Cameron, Charles, 17

Campbell, C., arch. at Stourhead, 234, 235

Carabelli, sculptor, at Ickworth, 239

Cardi, Ludovico, painting by at Stourhead, 236

Carlton House, London, 22, 136, 184, 186, 212, 213

Carpets, 28, 97, 104, 114, 134, 179, 190, 198, 238

Carr, John, of York, 17, 24, 75; arch. at Tabley, 55–60; at Harewood, 61–3, 69; at Newby, 141, 142; at Farnley, 214, 215, 217; works, 248

Carracci, A., paintings by at Farnley, 216

Carron ironworks, 9, 27, 77, 100

Carter, Benjamin, 127

Carter, John, arch., 149; works, 248

Carter, Thomas, carver, 127; at Mersham, 98, 99; at Farnley, 214

Casino, Marino, 111

Cast Iron in Architecture, History of, J. Gloag and D. Bridgwater, 27; *see* Iron

Castle Coole, Fermanagh, 21, 197

Ceilings, Book of, George Richardson, 158

Cement, Higgins's, 27. 'Roman', 27; *see* Stucco

Chambers, Sir William, 10, 12, 15, 17, 18, 22, 23, 24, 25, 26, 61, 62, 135, 228, 230, 232, 236; arch. at Peper Harow, 111–14; works, 248

Charles II, equestrian statue of, 141, *142*

Charlton Park, Wilts., 17

Chillington Hall, Staffs., 25, 222–7

Chinese Buildings, Designs for, Chambers, 12

Chinese Export Art in the Eighteenth Century, M. Jourdain and R. S. Jenyns, 28

Chinese taste, the, 97; *see* Wall-paper

Chippendale, Thomas, 28, 182, 183; furniture and decorations at Uppark, 38; at Harewood, 61, 62, *64*, *68*, 69; at Shugborough, 83, *85*; at Mersham, 98–104

Chippendale, the younger, 69; furniture at Stourhead, 234–8, *237*

Chippendale, Haig and Co., 104

Christmas, G., arch., 86

Cipriani, G. B., chiaroscura panels at Syon, 89, *91*; decorations at Trafalgar, 115–18

Clare House, Kent, *24*, 26

Claremont, Surrey, 22, 135–40, 186, 190

Clarke, Dr. E. D., 200

Classical style, the, 22, 23

Claude, 23, 149; painting at Shugborough, 85

Clay, Birmingham firm of, 77

Clay, Henry, 28

Claydon House, Bucks., 155, 158

Clérisseau, C. L., 12

Clive, Lady Mary, 135

Clive, Robert, Lord, 135–40

Coade, George, 27

Coade stone, 12, 22, 26, 27, 28, 85, 163, 167

Cobham, Kent, mausoleum at, 18

Cockerell, C. R., arch., 111, 113

Cockerell, Samuel Pepys, arch., works, 248

Cole, Thomas, builder, 98, 100

Collins, William, reliefs at Kedleston, 70, 75, 77, 78

Colombani, Placido, arch., 240; works, 248

Colvin, H. M., 11, 18, 243

Compton Verney, Warwick., 9, 13

Corsham Court, Wilts., 11, 68, 136

Cottesbrooke, Northants., 26

Cottingham, L. N., 27

Couchman, Henry, arch. at Arbury, 41, 44, 45; works, 248

Courteenhall, Northants., 24, 228–33
Cozens, J. R., 149
Crace, J. F., 246
Cranbury Park, Hants., *8*, 17, 24, 25, 224
Crawford, William, 104
Craycombe House, Worcs., *249*
Crichel, Dorset, 22, 153–9
Croft Cas., Herefs., 148
Croome Court, Worcs., 68, 78
Crunden, John, arch., works, 248
Cuffnells, New Forest, 28
Culzean Cas., Ayr, 149
Curzon, Sir Nathaniel, 70, 76

Dahl, M., painting by at Stourhead, 235
Dale, Anthony, 18
Dall, Nicholas Thomas, 62; paintings and decorations at Shugborough, *79*, 81–3
Dallaway, James, 29
Dance, George, arch., 8, 15–18, 24, 25; paintings at Uppark, 37; works, 248
Dance, George, the younger, 123, 124
Darbys, the, smelters, 26
Dashwood, Sir Francis, 154
Dawkins, Henry, 115–18
Dehl's Mastic, 27
Deighton, Edward, 28
Della Magnificenza, Piranesi, 80
Denon, *Voyage en Egypte*, 238
Denton Hall, Yorks., *17*, 217
Derry, Bishop of, 26–8, 239–46; bust of, *246*
Deval, John, and Son, 212
Deval, John, the younger, 199
Devis, Arthur, paintings at Uppark, 30, *32*, *39*; at Arbury, 43, *45*
Dibdin, 213
Dictionary of British Architects, H. Colvin, 11, 18
Dictionary of British Sculptors, R. Gunnis, 27, 141, 152
Dilettanti, Society of, 79, 85, 118
Director, Chippendale, 83, 85
Dissertation on Oriental Gardening, 135
Dobson, painting at Tabley, 60
Doddington Hall, Cheshire, 160–4
Dodington Park, Glos., 18, 20, 22
Dolci, C., paintings at Farnley, 216
Dolls' house, Sarah Lethieullier's at Uppark, *39*, *40*
Dorset, History and Antiquities of the County of, Hutchins, *154*
Dover House, Whitehall, 30
Downhill, Co. Derry, *240*, 242, 243
Downton Castle, Herefs., 11, 24, 45, 148–52
Doyle, W., 39

Earl Stoke, Wilts., 196, 197
Earth, rammed, 22
Eckhart, A., 28
Eckhart, F., 28
Egerton, Sir Thomas, 20
Eginton, F., 238
Egyptian taste, 238
Empiricism, in Georgian architecture, 9, 24, 87, 148, 154
English Interior Decoration, M. Jourdain, 28
Essai sur L'Architecture, Abbé Laugier, 10
Essay on Taste, Hume, 10
Etruria Hall, 152
Etruscan rooms, *169*, 174, 179, *181*
Evans, William, 114

Facing materials, 27
Farington Diary, 1801, 18
Farnley Hall, Yorks., 17, 24, 214–21
Fawkes, Walter, 214, 215
Fetherstonhaugh, Sir Harry, 29, 35, 37–9
Fetherstonhaugh, Sir Matthew, 29, 30, 37
Fiennes, Celia, quoted, 29
Fisher, J., carving at Farnley, 214, 217
Flaxman, John, 152, 244, sculpture at Ickworth, 239, 246
Flitcroft, Henry, 80, 85
Fonthill Abbey, Wilts., 22, 26
Frenchman in England, A, J. Marchand, ed., 167

Gainsborough, Thomas, paintings at Ickworth, 246
Gandon, James, arch., works, 248
Garrard, G., reliefs at Uppark, 36, 39
Gately Hall, Norf., 127
Gawthorpe Hall, Yorks., 61
Gibbon, Edward, 10, 238
Gibbons, Grinling, 42
Gibbs, James, 25, 106
Giffard, Thomas, 222, 223
Gilbert, John, decorations at Mersham, 98, 100
Gillow, Robert and Richard, furniture at Farnley, 220
Giordano, Luca, paintings at Uppark, 37
Girtin, Thomas, paintings at Farnley, 216
Gloag, J., 27
Glover, Moses, 86
Gobelins tapestries, *14*, 144
Gooding, William, brick maker, 28, 210
Goodwood, Sussex, 12, *23*, 26
Gorhambury, Herts., *16*, 17
Gotch, C. G., 17
Gothick architecture, 22, 25; at Arbury, 41–8; at Downton, 148–52
Graeco-Roman decoration, 22
Greek architecture, revival of, 10, 22, 25
Green, Charles, organ-builder, 235
Green, Samuel, 202
Greenwich Hospital, the chapel, 84
Griffin, landscape gardener, 245
Griffiths, Moses, drawing of Shugborough, *80*
Grimston Garth, Yorks., 17
Guercino, paintings at Farnley, 216
Guido, paintings at Farnley, 216
Guildhall, London, 24, 25
Gunnis, Rupert, 27, 141, 152, 234
Gwynne, J., 27

Hackaert, Philipp, paintings at Attingham, 200
Hackness Hall, Yorks., 17
Hagley Hall, Worcs., 79, 97
Haig, Thomas, 68, 101
Hale, Robson, and Co., 212
Hall, Joseph, of Derby, mason, at Kedleston, 70, 75, 76
Hallett, William, 37
Hamelin's Mastic, 27
Hamilton, Lady, 38, 60
Hamilton, S. B., 27
Hamilton, Sir W., 38, 240
Hamilton, W., paintings at Kedleston, 77
Hancock, J. G., wall-paper manufacturer, 28
Hanwell, W., plasterwork at Arbury, 41, 45, 47

Harewood, Lord, 61, 69
Harewood House, Yorks., 17, 61–9, 111
Harley, Rt. Hon. Thomas, 184
Harleyford, Bucks., 11, 50
Harrington House, Glos., 28
Harris, Lord, of Seringapatam, 26
Harrison, Thomas, of Chester, 60
Hartwell Church, Bucks., 44
Harwood, wall-paper manufacturer, 28
Hatchlands, Surrey, 49–54, 68
Haworth, William and Henry, 27
Hayward, Richard, 44; decorations at Peper Harow, 111, 113
Hearn, T., watercolours at Downton, 152
Heaton Hall, Lancs., 18, *19*, *20*, *21*, 22, 26, 27, 159, 163, 164
Hengrave Hall, Suffolk, 106
Hervey, Frederick, 239
Heveningham Hall, Suffolk, 17, 22, 158, 159, 165–76
Higham, G., plasterwork at Arbury, 41, 44
Hill, Noel, 195
Hiorn, Francis, arch. at Arbury, 41, 43
Hitchcox, W., mason at Arbury, 41, 43
Hoare, Sir Richard Colt, 234–8
Hobcroft, John, carpenter and builder, 190; at Claremont, 135, 136; works, 248
Hogarth, William, paintings at Ickworth, 246
Holkham Hall, Norfolk, 13, 59, 76, 145
Holland, Henry, D. Stroud, 28
Holland, Henry, 16, 21, 22, 25–8, 39, 231; arch. at Claremont, 135–40; at Berrington, 184–94; at Althorp, 203–13; works, 248
Holt, Richard, 27
Home House, London, 176
Hope, Thomas, 238
Hopetoun, Edinburgh, 50, 54
Hopper, Humphrey, craftsman, at Farnley, 214, 217
Hoppner, paintings at Tabley, 60; at Farnley, 217
Hoskins of St Martins Lane, 100
Huetson, C., bust by, *246*
Hume, D., 10
Hurstmonceux Place, Sussex, 20, 26
Hutchins, John, 154
Hutchinson, Mr., marbling at Harewood, 69

Ickworth, Suffolk, 10, 26, 27, 239–46
Inveraray Castle, Argyll, 17
Ireson, Nathaniel, 235
Iron, cast, 12, 22, 26, 27, 77, 100, 202; *see* Carron
Ivory, Thomas, 11; works, 249
Ivory, William, 11

Jackson, Jean Baptiste, 28
Jacobean style, 17
Jansen, G., 86
Jenkins, Thomas, 145, 235
Jenyns, R. S., 28
Jewell, *Tourist's Companion*, 69
Johnson, John, arch., works, 249
Johnson, Thomas, 235
Jones, Inigo, 15, 86; medallion of, *116*
Jourdain, Margaret, 28

Kauffmann, Angelica, paintings at Syon, 86, *92*, 97; at Attingham, 199; at Ickworth, 246

Keck, Anthony, arch., works, 249
Kedleston, Derbys., 12, 13, 15, 27, 28, 70–8, 106, 145, 158
Keene, Henry, 11, 13, 18; arch. at Uppark, 29, 37; at Arbury, 41, 44, 45; works, 249
Kent, William, 16, furniture of, *238*
Kessels, H. S., 27
Kew Gardens, 83
King, Benjamin, carver, at Arbury, 41, 43
King, H., 216
Kings Weston, Glos., 17 (Mylne), 249
Kip, engravings at Uppark, 29, 30, *31*
Kirby Hall, Yorks., 11, 56
Knatchbull, Sir Edward, 98
Knatchbull, Dr. Wyndham, 98, 102
Knight, Richard Payne, 11, 13, 23, 24, 25, 45, 148, 152, 200, 240
Kyre Park, Worcs., 43

Lamb, Sir Matthew, 105–7
Landscape, The, Payne Knight, 23
Larking, John, 26
Lascelles, Edwin, Lord Harewood, 61, 62, 69
Latrobe, Benjamin, arch., works, 249
Laugier, Abbé, 10, 25, 26
Lead, cast, 174
Leadbetter, Stiff, arch., works, 249
Ledoux, C. N., arch., 197, 245
Lee Priory, Kent, 22
Lees-Milne, J., 12, 86, 236
Leicester, Sir John, 59, 60
Leicester, Sir Peter, 55
Lely, paintings at Althorp, 205
Lethieullier family, paintings of by A. Devis, *39*
Leverton, Thomas, 18, 159; arch. at Woodhall Park, 177–83; works, 249
Lewis, James, arch., works, 249
Liardet's Composition stucco, 12, 27
Lightfoot, arch., 155, 158; works, 249
Linnel, John, furniture at Kedleston, 78
'Lithodipyra, Terra-Cotta or Artificial Stone', 27
London and Westminster Improved, J. Gwynne, 27
Loudon, J. C., 214
Loutherbourg, de, paintings by, 124, 216
Lovell, Lord, 119
Lumby, William, arch., works, 249
Luny, Thomas, paintings at Berrington, 194
Lutyens, Sir Edwin, 12, *Life of,* C. Hussey, 12
Lythwood Hall, Salop., 196

Malton, T., engraving of Heveningham, *166*
Manners, Sir G., 230
Manresa College, Roehampton, 12, 135, 242
Mansion House, London, 17
Maratti, Carlo, painting at Stourhead, 236
Marden Hill, Herts., 25
Marlborough, bust of, *114*
Martin, Edward, plasterer, at Arbury, 41, 42
Mastic, Hamelin's or Dehl's, 27
Materials, facing, 27
Materials, prefabricated, 26–8
McClelland, Nancy, 28
Melbourne, 1st Lord, 105, 106. 2nd Lord, 110
Melbourne House, Whitehall, 30
Mengs, Raphael, painting at Stourhead, 236
Mereworth Castle, Kent, 80

Mersham-le-Hatch, Kent, 21, 37, 98–104
Midleton, Viscounts, 111
Miller, S., arch. at Arbury, 41, 43, 45, 46
Milton Abbey, Dorset, 12, 111
Milton Manor House, Berks., 11, *247*
Mitchell, Robert, arch., 24, 26; works, 249
Montagu House, London, 18
Moor, R., plasterer, at Arbury, 41, 43, 44
Moore, Thomas, 28, 104, 134, 179; carpet at Syon, 86, 92, 97
Moor Park, Herts., 24, 26, 78, 144
Morris, Robert, arch. and designer, 56
Morris, Roger, arch., 116, 203, 235
Morris, Thomas, mason, at Arbury, 44
Mortimer, John, 106, 109, 110
Mount Clare, Richmond, 135, 240
'Movement' in architecture, 13, 15, 23, 75, 142
Mylne, Robert, arch., 16, 17; works, 249
Mytens, Daniel, paintings at Courteenhall, 230, *231*

Napier, Sir William, 153
Nares, Gordon, 41, 221
Nash, John, 24, 27, 230, 250; arch. at Attingham, 195–202
Natural Philosophy, influence of, 10, 200, 240
Neilson, 14
Nelson relics at Trafalgar House, 118
Neo-classicism, 9, 10, 16–18, 22, 25, 26, 77, 79, 93, 111, 145, 148, 163, 175, 186, 196, 199, 215
'Neo-Palladian' architecture, 17
Newby Hall, Yorks., 13, 141–7
Newdigate, Sir Roger, 11, 41–4, *45*
Newgate Prison, 17
Newton, William, arch., works, 250
Newton, William, of Newcastle, arch., works, 250
Nielson tapestries, 144, *147*
Nollekens, Joseph, 85
Northampton, Old Infirmary, 230
Northumberland, 1st Duke of, 86
Northumberland House, Charing Cross, 89, *95*
Nostell Priory, Yorks., 62, 70, 106

Oaks, The, Surrey, 18
Oates, James, mason, at Tabley, 56
Oliver, T., stuccoist, at Tabley, 55, 58, 59
Ormolu, 12, 28, 78, 97, 134, 152, *203*
Osterley Park, Middx., *frontis, 13, 14,* 15, 142, 144
Oswald, Arthur, 222

Padworth House, Berks., 136
Paine, James, 11, 16, 22, 27, 29, 30, 50, 59; arch. at Kedleston, 70–8; at Brocket, 105–10; at Wardour, 119, 120, 124; at Chillington, 222; works, 250
Palladio and Palladianism, 10, 11, 16, 17, 22, 80, 116, 119, 133, 134, 154, 205, 208, 214, 243
Palmerston, Lord, 110
Pannini, G., paintings at Shugborough, 85; at Stourhead, 236
Pantheon, Rome, and derivates, 18, 26, 152
Pantheon, The, Oxford Street, 18
Papier-maché, 12, 28, 77
Paragon, Blackheath, 26
Parker, John, 125–7, 133

Parker, R., 28; decorations at Woodhall Park, 177, 181, 182
Parker's 'Roman Cement', 27
Pearce, William, stuccoist, at Claremont, 135; at Berrington, 190
Pencarrow, Cornwall, 133
Pennant, Thomas, quoted, 83
Peper Harow, Surrey, 12, 111–14
Pergolesi, M. A., 97
Pernotin, T. H., panels by, *212*, 213
Peto, Harold, 155
Pickford, Joseph, carver, 59; arch., 250
Picturesque, Essay on the, Uvedale Price, 23
Picturesque, Theory of the, 22, 23, 26, 54, 69, 228, 230
Pincot, Daniel, 27
Piranesi, G. B., 10, 13, 15, 17, 25, 54, 80, 87
Pisé de terre, 22
Plaw, John, arch., 24, 26; works, 250
Portman House, London, 158
Poussin, Gaspar, paintings at Shugborough, 85, at Downton, 152
Poussin, Nicolas, painting at Stourhead, 236
Prefabricated materials, 26–8
Price, Sir Uvedale, 13, 23, 24, 25
Pritchard, T. F., 27
Pugin, A. C., sketch of Attingham, *201,* 202
Pugin, A. W. N., 24, 112, 114
Pyne, W. H., 22

Quarenghi, decorations at Wardour, 119, 124

Ramsbury Manor, Wilts., 29
Ranelagh House, Barn Elms, 238
Raphael's *grotteschi,* 97, 179
Rathbone, Mr., 58
Rawstorne, Thomas, smith, at Claremont, 135, 136
Rebecca, Biagio, 19, 22, 77, 190, 192; decorations at Harewood, 61, 65, 68; at Crichel, 153, 158, 159; at Doddington, 160, 162, 163; at Heveningham, 165, 170, 175, 176
Rembrandt, paintings at Downton, 152
Reni, Guido, 123, 124; paintings at Shugborough, 85
Repton, Humphrey, 23, 24, 25, 54; arch. at Uppark, 29, 30, 38, 39; landscape at Attingham, 195, 202; at Courteenhall, 228–30
Repton, J. A., 38
Reveley, Willey, arch. at Stourhead, 234, 236; works, 250
Revett, Nicolas, 10, 12, 17, 79; arch. at Trafalgar, 115–17; works, 250
Reynolds, Sir Joshua, 13; paintings at Uppark, 35; at Harewood, 65, 68; at Shugborough, 85; at Syon, 97; at Brocket, 110; at Saltram, *128,* 133; at Crichel, 158; at Althorp, 210; at Farnley, 216
Richardson, George, 77, 158
Richardson, Jonathan, 235
Ripley, Thomas, 27
Robinson, Sir Thomas, arch., works, 250
Robson, Hale and Co., wall-paper manufacturer, 28, 212
Rococo, 9–11, 15, 35, 79, 105–10, 116, 127, 136, 125–34, 153
Rococo gothick, 11, 17, 41, 241
Rococo Palladian, 56, 106

Rodney, Adm. Lord, 184, 194
Roe, Roger, joiner, at Arbury, 44
Roman style, 97
Romanticism, influence of, 10, 80, 148
Romney, paintings at Arbury, 45, 47; sketches at Tabley, 60
Rosa, Salvator, 23; paintings at Downton, 152
Rose, Joseph, stuccoist, 15, 142; at Harewood, 61, 65, 68; at Kedleston, 70, 77; at Shugborough, 79, 85; at Syon, 86, 89, 90; at Mersham, 98, 99; at Farnley, 214, 217, 219
Rossi, chimneypieces at Shugborough, 85
Rotunda, Leicester Square, 26
Roubiliac, L. F., busts by at Shugborough, 83, 85
Royal Academy of Arts, 15
Royal Crescent, Brighton, 28
Royal Pavilion, Brighton, 22
Royal Residences, Pyne, 22
Ruins of Palmyra, Wood, 10, 137
Rumbold, Sir Thomas, 177
Rural Architecture, John Plaw, 26
Ruysdael, paintings at Downton, 152
Rysbrack, Michael, sculptor, 54, 238

St Chad's Church, Shrewsbury, 26, 196
St James's Square, No. 15, London, 79
St Martin-in-the-Fields, London, 106
St Peter's, Rome, 13, 18
Sta. Sophia, Constantinople, 18
Saltram, Devon, 28, 125–34
Sandys, Francis, arch. at Ickworth, 239–46; works, 250
Saunders, George, arch., 250
Saxon, Samuel, 24; arch. at Courteenhall, 228, 230; works, 250
Scheemakers, Peeter, sculptor, 80
Scott, Samuel, naval paintings at Shugborough, 85
Sealy, John, 27
Searles, Michael, arch., 24, 26; works, 250
Seats, Neale, 18
Shardeloes, Bucks., *13*, 54, 89
Shillito, D., carver, at Tabley, 55, 58
Shottesham, Norfolk, 25
Shugborough, Staffs., 20, 26, 62, 79–85
Sidney Lodge, Hamble, 28
Sketches and Hints on Landscape Gardening, Humphrey Repton, 23
Sledmere, Yorks., 15
Sloane Place, London, 28
Smith, —, furniture at Shugborough, 85
Smith, Charles, decorator, 97
Smith, William, arch. at Chillington, 222–4
Smithson, Robert, 119
Soane, Sir John, 12, 15, 16, 22–8, 135, 137, 186, 230; arch. at Chillington, 222–7; arch. at Wardour, 119, 124; works, 250
Society of Arts, 15, 28
Soho Works, Birmingham, 9, 27, 28
Somerset House, London, 12, 27, 111
Southill Park, Beds., 22, 39
Spang, Michael, sculptor, 54; at Kedleston, 70, 74, 77, 78
Spencer, 2nd Earl, 203
Spitalfields silk, 97, 106
Stafford General Infirmary, 18
Standlynch House (Trafalgar), Wilts., 115–118

Stansted, Hants., 29
Stanton, William, sculptor, 229
Steuart, George, 25, 26, 28; arch. at Attingham, 195–202; works, 250
Stevens, Alfred, sculptor, 230
Stoke Bruerne, Northants., 70
Stoke Edith, Herefs., 29
Stone, artificial, 22, 27. *See also* Coade stone
Stourhead, Wilts., 234–8
Stowe House, Bucks., 12, 77
Stratfield Saye House, Hants., 12
Strawberry Hill, Middx., 11, 28, 43, 45
Stroud, Dorothy, quoted, 28, 135, 185
Stuart, James ('Athenian'), 10, 11, 17, 28, 50, 62, 158, 231; arch. at Shugborough, 79–85; works, 250
Stucco 243; *see* Cement
Sturt, Humphry, 153, 159
Styche, Shrops., 135
Sublime and Beautiful, Enquiry on the, Burke, 10
Sublime and Beautiful, The, 15–22
Summerson, John, quoted, 10, 11, 12, 15, 18, 27, 86, 111, 119
Sunderland, 2nd Earl of, 203–5
Swallowfield, Berks., 29
Sykes, Sir Christopher, 15
Synthesis, instances of: Adam's, 12–15, 70, 97, 142; Holland's, 210; Soane's, 227
Synthesis, theory of Stylistic, 9, 13, 22–3, 214
Syon House, Middx., 15, 18, 27, 28, 62, 77, 86–97, 106, 120

Tabley House, Cheshire, 17, 55–60, 75
Talman, William, 17; arch. at Uppark, 29, 30, 38
Tankerville, Earl of, 29, 30, 38
Tatham, C. H., 22, 243
Taylor, Sir Robert, 11, 16, 17, 50, 235; arch. at Heveningham, 165–76; at Althorp, 203; works, 250
Thomas Chippendale, Oliver Brackett, 69
Thompson, Henry, painting at Stourhead, 236
Thorndon, Essex, 119
Tiles, 'Mathematical' or rebate, 22, 27, 28, 210
Titian, 23
Toryism, influence of, 15, 41, 55, 184
Torrington Diaries (July, 1793), 195
Tourist's Companion (1819), Jewell, 69
Trafalgar House, Wilts., 115–18
Treatise on Civil Architecture, Chambers, 12
Treatise on Country Residences, J. C. Loudon, 214
Trevisani, painting at Stourhead, 236
Trewithen, Cornwall, 133
Trinity House, London, 84
Tsarskoe Seloe, 17
Turner, J. M. W., paintings at Tabley, *59*, 60; at Downton, 152; at Farnley, *214*, 216, *217, 221*
Tusmore, Oxon., *16*, 17

Underwood, Messrs., 85
University Coll., Oxford, 43, 44
Uppark, Sussex, 11, 29–40

Vanbrugh, Sir John, influence of on Georgian architecture, 9, 13, 17, 21, 23, 24, 135, 240

Vanbrugh, Sir John, The Imagination of, Laurence Whistler, 135
Vandervelde, painting at Shugborough, 85
Vandyck, Sir Anthony, paintings at Downton, 152; at Althorp, 205, 210; at Farnley, 216
Vanneck, Sir Gerrard, 165; Sir Joshua, 165, 167
Views, Watts, 167
Viscentini, Antonio, 18
Visits to Country Houses, Walpole Society, 137
Visual approach to Design, 11, 186; *see* Picturesque, Theory of the)
Vitruvius Britannicus, 56, 61, 62, *63, 71, 118*, 136, *178, 230*, 235

Wake, Sir William, 228, 229
Walcot, Shrops., 135
Walker, George, paintings at Farnley, 221
Wall-paper, 28, 37, 101, 104, 182–3, 212, 213, 236; Chinese, 114, 134, *259–61*
Wall-papers, Historic, Nancy McClelland, 28
Walpole, Horace, 11, 28, 43, 77, 78, 86, 101, 212
Wanstead House, Essex, 197
Wardour Castle, Wilts., 119–24
Wark, David, 27
Warner, R., quoted, 69
Water closets, 135, 192, 222
Webb, Sir Aston, 236
Webb, of Tamworth, painter, 85
Weddell, William, 141, 142, 144, 145
Wedgwood, 134, 191
Wellington, 1st Duke of, 39
Wells, H. G., 39
Westall, W., painting at Downton, 152
Westmacott, Richard, sculptor, 85
Westminster, Palace of, 24
West Sussex, History of, Dallaway, 29
West Wycombe Park, Bucks., 154
Wheatley, Francis, decoration by, 109
Whig taste, 84, 195
Whistler, Laurence, 135
White, John, arch., works, 250
Wick, The, Richmond Hill, 17
Wilkes, John, box lock by, *48*
Wilson, Richard, painting at Claremont, 137; at Stourhead, 235
Wilson, Sir William, 41, 42
Wilton, 1st Earl of, 20
Wilton, Joseph, sculptor, at Peper Harow, 111–14
Wimbledon Park, 213
Wimpole, Cambs., *23*, 25
Winnington Hall, Cheshire, 20
Wise, W., painted ceiling at Arbury, 41, 43
Woburn, Beds., *21*, 22, 39
Wolterton Hall, Norfolk, 58
Wood, Henry, mason-carver, at Claremont, 135–7
Wood, John, the younger, arch. at Trafalgar, 115–18; works, 250
Wood, Robert, 10, 12
Woodhall Park, Herts., 37, 101, 177–83
Woods, R., landscape at Brocket, 106
Wootton, John, paintings at Uppark, 29, *31*; at Althorp, *207*, 208; at Stourhead, 235
Works of Robert and James Adam, The, 13, 86

Worksop, Notts., *16*, 70, 106
Woster, Thomas, furniture at Stourhead, 235
Wren, Sir Christopher, 9, 13, 23; arch. at Arbury, 41, 42
Wren Society, 42
Wright, Stephen, arch., 11, 247; works, 250
Wyatt, James, 10 *et seq.*, 159, 197; decora-tions designed at Heveningham, 165–76; works, 250
Wyatt, James, Anthony Dale, 18
Wyatt, Samuel, 18; arch. at Shugborough, 79–85; at Doddington, 160, 163, 164; works, 250
Wyatt family, 18; style, characteristics of, 18–22, 26, 163–4, 173–6

Young, Arthur, 240

Zoffany, paintings at Ickworth, 246
Zuccharelli, paintings at Kedleston, *77*; at Stourhead, 236
Zucchi, 100; paintings at Harewood, 61, 62, *66*, 68; at Kedleston, *77*; at Saltram, *132*, 133; at Newby, 144